A Sims

Helps to Bible study

with practical notes on the books of scripture

A Sims

Helps to Bible study
with practical notes on the books of scripture

ISBN/EAN: 9783743382077

Manufactured in Europe, USA, Canada, Australia, Japa

Cover: Foto ©Lupo / pixelio.de

Manufactured and distributed by brebook publishing software (www.brebook.com)

A Sims

Helps to Bible study

HELPS TO BIBLE STUDY

With Practical Notes on the Books of Scripture;

OR,

HOW TO READ, SEARCH AND STUDY THE WORD OF GOD SO AS
TO SECURE AN EVER-INCREASING INTEREST IN THE SAME,
A STRONGER FAITH, DEEPER SPIRITUALITY
AND GREATER USEFULNESS.

BY

REV. A. SIMS.

"These were more noble than those at Thessalonica, in that they received the word with all readiness of mind, and searched the Scriptures daily, whether these things were so."—Acts 17:11.

"Search the Scriptures."—John 5:39.

SECOND EDITION. REVISED AND ENLARGED.

PRICE $1.00.

OTTERVILLE, ONT.
REV. A. SIMS, PUBLISHER.

Entered according to Act of the Parliament of Canada, in the year one thousand eight hundred and ninety, by the REV. A. SIMS, Otterville, Ont., at the office of the Minister of Agriculture.

INTRODUCTION.

WHEN we first commenced the work, of which this book is the result, we had no intention of ever publishing it in book form. Realizing our need of a more intimate acquaintance with the Holy Scriptures, we began making a thorough study of each book of the Bible. We found this study so profitable for both mind and heart, that we could not refrain from making the fruits of it known to others. Some friends strongly importuned us to publish, in some permanent form, the notes we had made. We have yielded to their request, hoping that this book will be the means of stirring up Christians generally to more diligence in searching the blessed Word of God.

In addition to original matter, we have added the very best thoughts of the most able writers on helps to the study of the Bible. We have aimed, as far as possible, to make the book useful to all classes.

THE AUTHOR.

CONTENTS.

CHAPTER I.

DIFFERENT METHODS OF BIBLE STUDY 9
  1. Study one book at a time 9
  2. Study the Bible topically 11
  3. Make marginal notes and key words 12
     Signs to be used in Bible marking 16
  4. Study the Bible biographically 18
  5. Study the Bible consecutively 18
  6. Study the Bible chronologically 22
     Plan for reading the Bible in the order of its events in two years 24
  7. Study the Bible analytically 36
  8. Study the Bible systematically 38
  9. Study the Bible inferentially.................... 38
  10. Take a single passage and dwell upon it........ 39
     Additional suggestions 40
     How to prepare Bible readings.................... 41
     Seven-eighths of the Bible misunderstood......... 43

CHAPTER II.

RULES OF INTERPRETATION 48

CHAPTER III.

INTERPRETATION OF BIBLE TYPES, SYMBOLS, PARABLES AND ALLEGORIES 56
  1. Symbolism of number and form................... 63
  2. Symbolism of color............................. 68
  3. Symbolism of mineral substances 70
  4. Symbolism of vegetable substances 71
  5. Symbolism of animals and birds................. 74
  6. Symbolism of buildings and structures 76

CONTENTS.

INTERPRETATION OF BIBLE TYPES, ETC. (*Continued*).   PAGE
   7. Symbolism of persons 78
   8. Symbolism of customs and manners 78
   9. Miscellaneous symbols 79
   Interpretation of prophecy 81
   Interpretation of the precepts of Scripture 82

CHAPTER IV.

HELPS TO THE INTERPRETATION OF SCRIPTURE 83
   1. Geography 83
   2. Natural history 85
   3. Chronology 86
   4. Ancient profane history 87
   5. Ecclesiastical history 89
   6. Manners and customs of the Jews 90
   Various other manners and customs 94
   The difficulties and seeming contradictions of the Bible... 100

CHAPTER V.

THE EXAMPLES OF SCRIPTURE 103

CHAPTER VI.

ANALYSIS OF THE BOOKS OF THE BIBLE 111
   Genesis 111
   Job 115
   Exodus 119
   Leviticus 122
   Numbers 124
   Deuteronomy 128
   Joshua 131
   Judges 134
   Ruth 137
   1 Samuel 140
   2 Samuel 143
   Psalms 145
   The two books of Kings 148
   The two books of Chronicles 152
   Solomon's Song 156

CONTENTS. vii

ANALYSIS OF THE BOOKS OF THE BIBLE (*Continued*). PAGE
Proverbs 158
Ecclesiastes 165
Jonah 167
Joel 170
Amos 172
Hosea 173
Isaiah 176
Prophets near to or during the captivity—
   Micah 178
   Nahum 180
   Zephaniah 181
   Jeremiah 183
   Lamentations of Jeremiah 185
   Habakkuk 186
   Obadiah 187
   Ezekiel 190
   Daniel 193
   Ezra 197
Prophets after the captivity—
   Haggai 200
   Zechariah 201
   Esther 203
   Nehemiah 205
   Malachi 207
Historical summary 210
Preservation of the Old Testament 211
The Apocrypha 211
Books of the New Testament—
   Matthew 212
   1 Thessalonians 218
   2 Thessalonians 220
   Galatians 222
   1 Corinthians 224
   2 Corinthians 227
   Romans 230
   James 232
   Ephesians 235

ANALYSIS OF THE BOOKS OF THE BIBLE (*Continued*). PAGE
Colossians 237
Philemon 239
Philippians 241
Hebrews 243
Luke 246
Acts 252
1 Peter 256
2 Peter 257
Mark 259
1 Timothy 263
Titus 264
2 Timothy 266
Jude 268
1 John 269
2 John 272
3 John 273
Revelation 275
John 280

CHAPTER VII.

MISCELLANEOUS HELPS 285
A model Bible-school 285
The seven Bibles of the world 287
The life-giving Word 288
Great chapters of the Bible 290
Paul's missionary journeys 291
Harmony of the Gospels 299
Bible questions and answers 311
Description of Scripture characters, with key 340

HELPS TO BIBLE STUDY.

CHAPTER I.

DIFFERENT METHODS OF BIBLE STUDY.

1. Study one book at a time. Endeavor to get its scope and general bearing. This plan will be found very profitable. Use such questions as follows:—1. Who is the author; when, where, and for whom did he write? 2. Under what circumstances was this book written? 3. What is the character of its contents—law, poetry, history, philosophy, or prophecy? 4. What is the general aim of the writer, or key-note of the book? 5. What errors are here refuted? 6. What are the practical lessons and doctrines taught? 7. What promises or prophecies are here fulfilled? 8. What biographies does it contain? 9. What connection has this book with other parts of the Scriptures? 10. What is the chronology of the events recorded? 11. For what class of people is this book most suitable?

In studying any portion of the Scriptures, an important question to ask is: Who is it that is here speaking? A judge in court once remarked: "We have the highest authority for saying, 'Skin for skin : yea, all that a man hath will he give for his life.'" The papers next day called attention to the fact that these were the words of the devil, and added, "Now we know who the judge considers as of the highest authority."

Take Genesis; it is the seed-plant of the whole Bible. It tells us of life, death, resurrection—it involves all the rest of the Bible. This book has been truly called the Gospel according to Moses.

Take one word that runs through a book—say the book of Revelation. Did God not wish us to understand this book would he have given it to us? Some say it is so dark and mysterious common readers cannot understand it. Let us only keep digging away at it, and it will unfold itself by-and-by. Some one says it is the only book in the Bible that tells about the devil being chained; and as the devil knows that, he goes up and down Christendom, and says, "It is no use your reading the Revelation, you cannot understand the book, it is too hard for you." The fact is, he does not want you to understand about his own defeat. Look at the blessings it contains (chap. 22 : 14; 16 : 15; 20 : 7).

"The following verse contains the elements of all the great doctrines of salvation subsequently revealed: 'I will put enmity between thee and the woman, and between thy seed and her seed. It shall bruise thy head, and thou shalt bruise his heel.'

"1. The promised Redeemer and Restorer of the race is to be *man*, since he is to be the seed of the woman.

"2. He is to be more than man, and greater than Satan, for he is to be the conqueror of man's conqueror. He must therefore be *divine*.

"3. Man's redemption shall involve a *new nature*, for it shall be at enmity with the Satan nature to which man has now become subject.

"4. This new nature is to be a *regeneration by divine power*, for the declaration is, 'I (Jehovah) *will put enmity,*' etc.

"5. This redemption is to be accompanied by *vicarious suffering*, since the Redeemer is to suffer the excruciating torture of the bruising of his heel in the work of recovery.

"6. This redemption is to involve the ultimate triumph of the woman's seed, and therefore involves a triumph over death, and a resurrection and restoration of humanity to its original estate—the union of a spiritual nature with a physical in complete blessedness, as before the fall."—*Dr. Stuart Robinson.*

2. *Study the Bible Topically.* "Take the word 'Love' and spend a month in searching what the Bible says about love, from Genesis to Revelation. Thus you will learn to love everybody, whether they love you or not. In the same way take 'Holiness,' 'Faith,' 'Assurance,' 'Heaven,' and so on. Take up one word in a book, such as the '*believes*' in St. John. Every chapter but two speaks of believing. Look up the nineteen personal interviews with Christ. Take the *conversions* of the Bible; the seven '*blesseds*' and '*overcomes*' of Revelation. See what 1 John 3 says about '*assurance*' or '*we know.*' In that one chapter there are six assurances. That whole epistle is written on assurance. Take up the five '*precious*' things of Peter; the '*verilys*' of John; the '*seven walks*' of Ephesians; the four '*much mores*' of Rom. 4; the two '*receiveds*' of John 1; the seven '*hearts*' in Prov. 23; and especially an eighth, the '*lookings*,' the '*lookings back*,' the '*beholds*,' the '*I ams*,' and '*I wills*' of the Bible."—*D. L. Moody.*

Look up in Ephesians the seven "works of the Spirit," seven "objects in prayer," seven "things not to talk about," four "gifts given," five "nows," twelve "according to's," six "things about love," eighteen "be's," ten "haths," fifteen "of Gods," eleven "of Christs," seven "walks," three "things to know," past, present and future, fourteen "in Christs," seven "children," seven "views of peace," five "weres," seven "ares," three "things about the unsaved."

The "I wills," the "I ams," and the "shall nots" of St. John; the "betters," "let us's" of Hebrews; the seventy "fear nots" in the Bible, the twenty-three hundred promises.

Look up the eight hundred and forty-five quotations in the New Testament taken from the Old. See how they light the book up.

Trace such words and phrases as these, through the Bible: "able," "arise," "abundantly," "beware," "be of good cheer," "believeth," "daily," "except," "finally," "fools," "follow me," "if any man," "justification," "come," "grace," "faith," "love," "love of God," "now," "mysteries," "delivered," "new," "one thing," "peace," "paths," "seek," "this man," "we know," "trust," "abide," "confess," "great things," "surely," "the blood," "willing," "victory," "fail," "fail not," "receive," "comfort," "blessed," "light," "sowing," "take heed," "wherefore," "evermore," "gave," "persecuted," "ye are," "power," "shepherd," "disciples," "must," "how," "salvation," "repent," "beloved," "righteousness," "reconciled," "free," "take," "whosoever," "whatsoever," "hope," "wisdom," "example," "preach," "communication."

3. Make marginal notes and key-words. Note anything striking or of special service to you. When a preacher gives out a text just take and mark it, and as he goes on preaching, just put a few words in the margin—key-words that shall bring back the whole sermon again. D. L. Moody says: "Every man ought to take down some of the preacher's words and ideas, and go into some lane or alley and preach them out again to others. We ought to have four ears, two for ourselves and two for other people. Then, if you are in a new place, and have nothing else to say, jump up and remark, 'I heard some one say so and so,' and they will always be glad to hear you, if you give them heavenly food. The world is perishing for want of it. My Bible is worth more to me than all the Bibles in this place, and I will tell you why; because I have so many passages marked in it; and if I am called upon to speak at any time, I am ready. I have got these little words in the margin, and they are a sermon to me. Whether I speak about faith, hope, charity, assurance, or any subject whatever, it all comes back to me; and however unexpectedly I am called upon to preach, I am always ready. So, whenever you hear—or read—a good thing just put it down, because if it is good for you it will be good for somebody else; and we should pass the coin of heaven round just as we do the current coin of the realm. This plan of Bible marking, with the insertion of side notes, marginal references, etc., converts the margins of one's Bible into a note-book ready to hand at any moment."

" *You ought*," says Rev. Joseph Cook, "*to mark a Bible every five years so thoroughly that you cannot use it any more.* If, every five years, you can mark a Bible thoroughly, and memorize what is marked, it will be your best diary . . . full of the records of the deepest inmost in your souls, to be intelligible to yourself, and to no one else."

Rev. W. F. Crafts says of his Bible: "A thousand precious things are stored up in it. With it in my hand I am never at a loss for a sermon or word of instruction and help. The best thoughts of many Bible students are tucked away on half blank pages. The outline of scores of sermons, the indicated analysis of many books, the testimony and comments of saints upon certain passages. The help of this is—that you fix things in your mind and heart which you would not otherwise have done. On opening your Bible your mind is at once stirred with a thought or a memory. Indeed, every one's Bible should carry the student's own spiritual history in notes—not necessarily intelligible to any one else."

The Bible and the Sunday School gives the following instructive example: "We will suppose that your theme for study is the first chapter of John. Your Bible lies open before you. You believe that no prophecy is of private interpretation. You therefore begin by asking the Spirit of God to open to you the truth contained for you in this chapter. Then you read it over, at first rapidly; you aim to get a bird's-eye view of it as a whole; you see that its theme is the character, office, and work of Christ. Your question, then, is this: What does this chapter teach me of Christ?

"The first thing that strikes you is that a number of names are given to him here. You count them: Light, Only begotten of the Father, Jesus Christ, Only begotten Son, the Lord, the Lamb of God, Son of God, Master, Jesus of Nazareth, the Son of Joseph, King of Israel, Son of Man. Then he is the Teacher, the Son of God, the Saviour (Jesus, Matt. 1 : 16), the Master, the Atoning Sacrifice, the Incarnate One, the true Man and therefore the perfect Example, the future King. You draw a heavy black line under each title; you connect them by a light line. You now have a body of Christology on a page of your Bible. If you have wrought this out for yourself, you have done a good day's work; certainly, if you have taken home to yourself the truth that he is *your* King, *your* Saviour, *your* Sacrifice, *your* Example.

"The next day you return to your study again. You take up a single passage, verses 12 and 13. Who are the sons of God? As many as received him and were born of God. How? You put your references now in requisition. You look them up. You turn to your Bible Text-book under *Regeneration*. You pass by many texts that at another time will strike you, but do not now. The result of your studies is embodied in a note at the foot of the page : They are born *of* the Spirit, John 3 : 15 ; *by* the Word of God, 1 Peter 1 : 2, 3 ; *with* the word of truth, James 1 : 18 ; *in* Christ Jesus, 1 Cor. 4 : 13 ; who is himself the Only begotten Son of God, verse 18. You have here, in four verses of Scripture, the source, the instrument, the accompaniment, and the result of the new birth. You begin again : What is it to receive Christ? The result of your studies is embodied again in certain references which impress you, and which you accordingly underscore, and in certain other references which you discover, and therefore add in the margin.

"But you have not exhausted this subject. You return to it on the morrow. You study the negatives. Not of blood ; nor of the will of the flesh ; nor of man ; but of God. Your Concordance will tell you the meaning of born of blood, if your own thought has not suggested it to you ; the sons of God are not brought out by merely good breeding, good parentage ; Rom. 8 : 3, 4, 8, 9, tell you what is the meaning of *flesh*, viz., man in his natural state ; we are not born into the kingdom by our own resolution ; the will of man is interpreted to you by 1 Cor. 3 : 5-7 ; we are not brought into the kingdom of God by mere human endeavors. There are three theories of moral reform—good blood, strong will, good education—all repudiated ; and in contrast with them the true Scripture view—the new birth by the Spirit of God, as interpreted in your verses below.

"We have scarcely opened our theme; but we have done enough to give those of our readers, who desire to study the Bible and to preserve the result of their study in their Bible, some idea of how to do it."

Mrs. Menzies, in her *Hints on Bible Marking*, says: "In any given verse underline *only* the word or words required to suggest the thought. Connect these *underlines* by the fine line, always at the end, never in the centre of the underline. If a connection is needed with a reference to another page, carry the fine line (which she calls a *railway*) to the margin, and write the reference there. Draw all lines with a ruler, and as lightly as possible, particularly the 'railways,' with a fine pen and India ink, or some good black ink; the latter is better. Make your own marginal references as freely as possible, referring at *each* verse to the other." It should be added that a good Commentary is a great help in such a study, in giving information as to the meaning of the original and other points, provided it is used as a help to study, not as a substitute for it. Mrs. Menzies uses Alford, and refers to it by the following mark ∴. But the reader may easily make his own system of notation to favorite writers, provided he does not have too many. O A circle round any reference letter calls special attention to that reference. X signifies a Foot-note or Head-note. Cf. signifies Compare. Ctr. signifies Contrast. After entering a foot-note, or group, it is well always to write the number of the page it has been entered upon beside each of the verses referred to in such foot-note or group.

Rev. W. F. Crafts uses the following signs: A red cross +

in the midst of any verse by which inquirers have been led to saving faith and souls converted to God. Red having an especial attraction to the eye, the Christian worker is greatly helped by these red crosses in finding quickly the passages that shall aid the inquirer at his side, while the story of some soul that has cast anchor on this very promise is also brought to mind by the same sign. R for beginning of Scripture reading, and E for its end. X for a text. M for Messianic passages in the Old Testament. ⁂ the mark for Christos in the catacombs and elsewhere in the ancient Church, for references in the New Testament to Christ's divinity. △ for passages on the Trinity. □ for passages on the kingdom of God. 7 for the combination of God and man in Christian work. 10 for Christian perfection. 40 for temptation and trial. A circle for references to the eternal future. A small picture of a harp for references to music. P.P. beside proved promises, and a blue underline for promises in general. C beside references to childhood, and W to woman. The date beside a text from which in private meditation or public teaching at that time a spiritual uplift has been received. A heavy black underline for judgments. A red underline for references to the blood and the cross, especially those passages of prophecy that point forward to it, these red passages giving "the shadow of the cross," as the coming event casts its shadow before it, in the heart of the prophets and of Christ. An arrow ⊷――⋙― to indicate God's warnings, suggested by Jonathan's friendly arrows warning David. A line from a word to the margin when a note is to be written in connection with it, or from one word to another with which it is desirable to connect it.

If the Bible student prefers to use the colors red and

blue for a more comprehensive class of subjects than the above, let him refer to the last section of this chapter beginning with "Seven-eighths of the Bible misunderstood," page 43.

To the above may be added a few more.

| A heavy perpendicular stroke to be placed by the sides of verses which contain duty or command. ——— for choice passages. [] This indicates close connections, and is suitable for enclosing parables, miracles, incidents, sermons, etc. If any passage is explained by a portion of some book you have in your library, refer to it by giving title and page.

4. Study the Bible biographically. "Carefully read all the Bible may say in reference to one character, grouping the scenes of which they were the most prominent human figures around their personal histories. David's psalms ought to be read in connection with his biography, as given in the books of Samuel. They throw much light on the events that suggested them."—*Rev. W. F. Crafts.*

"The life of Paul is an admirable theme for a course of biographical study. The autobiographical passages in his epistles should be studied in connection with Luke's history. For example, Phil. 3 : 4-10, with Acts 9 : 1-8."—*Lyman Abbott.*

We recommend the reader to get a Harmony of the Gospels, and read through the life of Christ, as you would read a biography of Fletcher or Whitfield. The life will thus appear to you in new aspects.

5. Study the Bible consecutively. " It is of the highest importance that we should obtain a comprehensive bird's-eye view of each Bible epistle, each history, each biography, by reading it continuously to the end. It is important to read a whole book of the Bible, or a connected set of books, continuously or comprehensively, to get the great general thought that pervades the whole."

Mr. George Muller, of Bristol, says : "Though in my earlier life I was engaged in the ministry of the Word in my own country, I neglected for four years the consecutive reading of the Bible. The consequence was I was a babe in knowledge and in grace. I made no progress, because I neglected God's own appointed means for nourishing the divine life. But it pleased God to lead me to love his word. I was led to see that the Holy Ghost is the only instructor of the soul, and that the Word is the medium by which he teaches. Spending three hours on my knees, I made such progress that I learned more in those three hours than in years before. From that time I became a lover of the Word of God ; and in this way I have been going on ever since. In July, 1829, I began this plan of reading from the beginning of the Old and the New Testaments. Before I had been treating the Bible as a lottery, reading it just where I opened. Of course, after a time, it opened just in the same place, and I got accustomed to read only certain portions. Consequently, I knew nothing even of the letter of much of the Word of God. But under my new plan, little by little, I made more and more progress, and thus it came to this, that, when I was asked where any text was to be found, I could give chapter and verse—became, in fact, a living concordance. A few years after I began this method, I was in a large drawing-room in a nobleman's house. Most there had known the Lord longer than I, but they referred to me, and I could tell where passages they wanted were to be found. This came by habitually reading the Scriptures through. At one time I came to 1 Chronicles. I thought 'The first ten chapters consist almost entirely of names. I have read them recently; I may pass them over now.' But I reflected that it was the Word of God, and I read the whole. At the fourth chapter I came to Jabez's prayer, 'O that thou wouldest bless me indeed,' etc., and God gave me a rich blessing in my soul in reading that God gave him that which he requested. I now read 1 Chronicles with the same delight as the Gospels, the Psalms, or the Epistles.

"I would recommend you not to read always the Old or the New Testament, but alternately, e.g., the Old in the morning, and the New in the evening. One special blessing that will come to the soul is this: God furnishes a variety of food, and this he gives in his whole revelation. This is deeply important. We are thus kept from partial and favorite views, which are poison to the soul. There seem apparent contradictions in the Word, but by patiently and calmly going on reading and meditating, these are removed. I have read through the Bible a hundred times, and I find no stumbling-block at all. This is because I am satisfied with God. The first, the greatest thing in the divine life is to know God—not according to notions of him current in the Church, but as he is revealed in the Word. You will find him such a lovable Being, of infinite wisdom and power; and he exercises these on behalf of his people. How kind, how gracious, how gentle he is! The great point is to become acquainted with him as he is revealed in his Word, not according to men's notions of him. Have we not thought of him as an austere Being? But he that has become acquainted with God says with the Psalmist, 'They that know thy name will put their trust in thee' (Ps. 9).

HELPS TO BIBLE STUDY. 21

"By thus regularly reading, the love of the Scriptures is kept up. When I have read them through, I am as delighted to begin again as I was forty-six years ago. Of course this is by the grace of God, but instrumentally, it is through this habit of consecutive reading."

Mr. Muller gives two illustrations of the value of consecutive reading, one showing the connection between Exodus 3:5 and Joshua 5:15; the other between John 7:53 and 8:1; both of which would probably be unperceived if the Bible were not consecutively read.

Luke 15 and 16 are but portions of one discourse. The five parables should be consecutively read. Books like Psalms and Proverbs, which have no continuous narrative, need not be read in this way. About two pages a day, in an ordinary-sized Bible, will bring you through in a year.

"Too much importance cannot be attached to the matter of reading the Bible by some systematic plan. Probably not one out of a hundred of those who profess religion do this, and perhaps not one out of a thousand. The great bulk of those who read the Bible at all read at random, both as to the time when they read and where they read. And the profound ignorance of the Scriptures among the masses is not to be wondered at, when it is known how little time and attention is given to the reading of the Word, and how carelessly that little is done.

"How much would a student know of mathematics, or astronomy, or chemistry, or any other science, if he should pursue his studies in that science in the same way that the average Christian studies the Bible? He never could learn anything. The Bible is a systematic book, teaching us the science of salvation, and to learn this science we need to study it systematically and thoroughly. We venture the assertion that there are some portions of the Scriptures that some people professing religion for many years have never read. If the Bible is not read by course, who would ever turn to the first book of Chronicles to read from choice? Some may, but the number is small. But when the Bible is read by course the books of Chronicles are read as often as any other, and should be, for some of the most beautiful passages in the Bible are found in these books, scattered among the hard names, like fragrant flowers among the rocks. And then, '*all* Scripture is given by inspiration of God,' Chronicles as well as other portions, 'and is profitable for doctrine, for reproof, for correction, for instruction in righteousness, that the man of God may be perfect, thoroughly furnished unto all good works.'

"Another reason for the systematic study of the Bible is, that without it we shall lose much of the rarest worth. For God's Word is a deep mine; its treasures are found where we do not expect; nuggets of the purest gold are hidden in the deepest depths; gems and sparkling jewels are found where we thought was nothing but sand and gravel—mere *debris*. Now, to get it all, we must explore the whole, and nothing that God has made in nature or written in his Word is beneath our attention. Then let God's Word be read in its entirety, and till it has become familiar."—*Rev. W. F. Crafts.*

The value of consecutive reading may be further seen from the fact that the sense is often injured by the division into chapters and verses (see 1 Peter 1:4, 5; 1 Cor. 2:9, 10, as to verses, and Isa. 8:22; 9:1-7; 10:1-4; Luke 20:45-47; 21:1-4; 2 Cor. 4:18; 5:1, as to chapters).

6. Study the Bible chronologically. "This means in the order of the narrative, without regarding the ordinary arrangement of the books, nor of their several contents. Thus one book must sometimes be inserted in another, and the different parts of the book transposed. It will give a great additional interest to the historical portions of the Sacred Word to have them thus naturally interspersed with the poetical or prophetical writings, while it will also show the progress of revelation. The reader who has not access to a good 'Harmony' can generally find indications of date in the references, or in the inspired inscriptions of some of the chapters, as, for instance, Psa. 51 : 'A Psalm of David when Nathan the prophet came to him.' So with Psalms 52 and 54, Isaiah 6 and 7, and many others."

"The *order* of the prophetic books," says Rev. W. Crafts, "which is the same in the Hebrew as in the English version, is not the chronological order. They rather appear to be arranged according to the size of the books, the greater being placed first, and the minor prophets last. *If these books were read and studied in their historical order, doubtless they would be much better understood.*"

Much of the obscurity which hangs over the prophetic writings may be removed by perusing them in the order of time in which they were probably written.

Chronological reading is advantageous as regards doctrines as well as history, because they mutually throw light one upon the other; indeed, it is only in this way that *the doctrinal books—especially the Psalms and the Prophets—receive light and distinctness, while much is added to the interest and profitableness of history.* Without the historical foundation, even practical exposition is often, as it were, built in the air; many a colorless Psalm and many a prophetic word are made alive—*many dark or seemingly insignificant verses receive at once light and significance, in their most delicate shades of meaning, by the light of a certain history being brought to bear upon them.* History is rendered much richer, fuller, more interesting, more edifying, and more remarkable, if the Word like a golden thread is interwoven with it. It may create an agreeable surprise to find, for instance, that the Psalms have not altogether ceased with David, but appear now and then at a later period, even after the Babylonish captivity, at the rebuilding of the temple and the city.

The following plan—somewhat altered—of reading the Bible in the order of its events, is given by the above-mentioned author:

"The Bible is divided into weekly portions of about 350 verses each, that is 50 verses per day, requiring about five minutes for the reading alone, with as much additional time for meditation and study as can be given. If the verses are read in the morning, they can be carried in thought, and developed during the activities of the day. This plan will complete the Bible in two years. The divisions are not exact for each day, but as nearly so as the inequality of chapters will allow. Sundays have larger assignments than other days."

Plan for Reading the Bible in the Order of its Events in Two Years.

FIRST YEAR.

Jan. 1..Gen. 1, 2.
2..Job 38, 39.
3..Psa. 33 : 6-9; 104.
4..Isa. 40 : 12-31.
   Jer. 10 : 10-16.
5..Gen. 3.
   Rom. 4 : 12-21.
6..Gen. 4.
   John 3 : 10-15.

Jan. 7..Gen. 5, 6, 7, 8.
8..Gen. 9, 10.
9..Gen. 11.
   Job 1.
10..Job 2, 3, 4.
11..Job 5, 6.
12..Job 7, 8.
13..Job 9, 10.
14..Job 11, 12, 13.

HELPS TO BIBLE STUDY. 25

Jan.15...Job 14, 15.
16...Job 16.
17...Job 17, 18.
18. Job 19.
19...Job 20.
20...Job 21.
21...Job 22, 23, 24, 25.
22...Job 26, 27.
23...Job 28, 29.
24...Job 30.
25...Job 31.
26...Job 32, 33.
27...Job 34.
28...Job 35, 36, 37.
29...Job 40.
30...Job 41, 42.
31...Gen. 12, 13.
Feb. 1...Gen. 14.
    Heb. 6 : 13-20 ; 7.
2...Gen. 15, 16.
3...Gen. 17.
4...Gen. 18:1-15, 16-33; 19.
    Luke 17 : 26-37.
    2 Peter 2 : 4-9.
    Jude 1 : 6, 7.
5...Gen. 20, 21.
6 .Gen. 22.
    Heb. 11 : 1-19.
    James 2 : 21-24.
7...Gen. 23.
8...Gen. 24.
9...Gen. 25.
    Heb. 12 : 14-17.
10...Gen. 26.
11...Gen. 27.
12 .Gen. 28, 29.
13...Gen. 30.
14...Gen. 31.
15...Gen. 32, 33.
16...Gen. 34, 35.
17...Gen. 36.
18...Gen. 37, 38, 39.
19...Gen. 40.
20...Gen. 41.
21...Gen. 42.
22...Gen. 43, 44.
23...Gen. 45, 46.
24 ..Gen. 47, 48.

Feb.25...Gen. 49, 50.
    Heb. 11 : 20-22.
26...Gal. 1, 2.
27...Gal. 3.
28...Gal. 4.
Mar. 1...Gal. 5.
2 .Gal. 6.
3...Ex. 1, 2.
4...Ex. 3, 4, 5.
    Psa. 88.
5...Ex. 6, 7.
6...Ex. 8.
7. Ex. 9.
8...Ex. 10, 11.
9...Ex. 12.
10...Ex. 13, 14.
11...Ex. 15, 16, 17.
12...Ex. 18, 19
13...Ex. 20, 21.
14...Ex. 22.
15...Ex. 23, 24.
16...Ex. 25.
17...Ex. 26.
18...Ex. 27, 28.
19...Ex. 29.
20...Ex. 30.
21...Ex. 31, 32.
22...Ex. 33, 34.
23...Ex. 35.
24...Ex. 36.
25...Ex. 37, 38.
26...Ex. 39.
27...Ex. 40.
28...Psa. 90, 105.
29...Heb. 11 : 24-29.
    Lev. 1, 2.
30...Lev. 3, 4.
31...Lev. 5, 6.
Apr. 1...Lev. 7, 8.
2...Lev. 9. 10.
3...Lev. 11, 12.
4...Lev. 13.
5...Lev. 14.
6...Lev. 15.
7...Lev. 16, 17.
8...Lev. 18, 19.
9. Lev. 20, 21.
10 ..Lev. 22, 23.

26 HELPS TO BIBLE STUDY.

Apr.11..Lev. 24.
12..Lev. 25.
13 Lev. 26.
14..Lev. 27.
    Heb. 1, 2.
15..Heb. 3, 4, 5.
16..Heb. 6, 7.
17..Heb. 8, 9.
18..Heb. 10.
19..Heb. 12, 13.
20..Num. 1.
21..Num. 2, 3.
22..Num. 4.
23 .Num. 5.
24..Num. 6.
25..Num. 7.
26..Num. 8.
27..Num. 9, 10.
28..Num. 11, 12, 13.
29..Num. 14.
30..Num. 15.
May 1..Num. 16.
2..Num. 17, 18.
3..Num. 19, 20.
4 .Num. 21.
5..Num. 22, 23.
6..Num. 24, 25.
7..Num. 26.
8..Num. 27, 28.
9..Num. 29, 30.
10..Num. 31.
11..Num. 32.
12. Num. 33, 34.
13..Num. 35, 36.
14..Psa. 119 : 1-56.
15..Psa. 119 : 57-96.
16..Psa. 119 : 97-136.
17..Psa. 119 : 137-176.
18..Psa. 106.
19 .Deut. 1, 2.
20..Deut. 3.
21..Deut. 4.
22..Deut. 5.
23 .Deut. 6, 7.
24..Deut. 8, 9.
25..Deut. 10, 11.
26..Deut. 12, 13, 14.
27..Deut. 15, 16.

May28..Deut. 17, 18.
29..Deut. 19, 20.
30..Deut. 21, 22.
31. Deut. 23, 24.
June 1..Deut. 25, 26.
2..Deut. 27, 28.
3..Deut. 29, 30.
4..Deut. 31.
5..Deut. 32.
6..Deut. 33, 34.
7..Josh 1, 2.
8..Josh 3, 4.
9..Josh. 5, 6, 7.
10 Josh. 8.
11..Josh. 9.
12..Josh. 10.
13 .Josh. 11, 12.
14..Josh. 13, 14.
15..Josh. 15.
16..Josh. 16.
17..Josh. 17, 18.
18..Josh. 19.
19..Josh. 20, 21.
20..Josh. 22, 23.
21..Josh. 24.
22..Eph. 1, 2.
23..Eph. 3, 4, 5, 6.
24..Col. 1.
25..Col. 2.
26..Col. 3.
27..Col. 4.
28..Judges 1, 2.
29..Judges 17, 18.
30..Judges 19, 20.
July 1..Judges 21.
2. Judges 3, 4.
3..Judges 5, 6.
4..Judges 7, 8.
5..Judges 9.
6..Judges 10, 11.
7..Judges 12, 13, 14, 15, 16.
8..Neh. 9.
  ..Heb. 11 : 30-40.
9..Ruth 1, 2.
10 .Ruth 3, 4.
11..1 Sam. 1.
12..1 Sam. 2.
13..1 Sam. 3, 4, 5.

HELPS TO BIBLE STUDY. 27

July 14..1 Sam. 6, 7, 8.
15..1 Sam. 9, 10.
16..1 Sam. 11, 12, 13.
17..1 Sam. 14.
18..1 Sam. 15.
19..1 Sam. 16.
    Psa. 19, 23.
20..1 Sam. 17.
21..1 Sam. 18.
    Psa. 8, 9, 29.
22..1 Sam. 19.
    Psa. 58, 59.
23..1 Sam. 20.
    Psa. 11, 64.
24..1 Sam. 21.
    Psa. 56, 70, 34, 40.
25..1 Sam. 22 : 1, 2.
    1 Chron. 12 : 8-18.
    2 Sam. 23 : 13-17.
    1 Chron. 11, 15, 19.
    Psa. 57.
26..Psa. 13, 141, 142.
27..1 Sam. 22 : 3-19.
    Psa. 52, 17.
28..1 Sam. 23 : 1; 22 : 20-23; 23 : 6, 2-5, 7-12.
    Psa. 31.
29..1 Sam. 23 : 13-23.
    Psa. 54.
    1 Sam. 23 : 24-29.
    Psa. 35, 36.
30..1 Sam. 24.
    Psa. 7, 12, 120.
31..1 Sam. 25.
    Psa. 53.
Aug. 1..1 Sam. 26 ; 27 : 1-7.
    1 Chron. 12 : 1-7.
    Psa. 16, 38, 39.
2..1 Sam. 27 : 8-12 ; 28 ; 29.
3..1 Chron. 12 : 19-22.
    1 Sam. 30.
4..1 Sam. 31.
    1 Chron. 10.
5..2 Sam. 1 ; 2 : 1-7.
    Psa. 27, 101, 95.
6..2 Sam. 2 : 7-32.
7. 2 Sam. 3.

Aug. 8..2 Sam. 4 ; 5 : 1-3 ; 23 : 8-12, 18-39.
9..1 Chron. 11 : 1-3, 10-14, 20 47 ; 12 : 23-40.
10..2 Sam. 5 : 4-10.
    1 Chron. 11 : 4-9.
11..Psa. 108, 110, 122, 131, 132.
12..2 Sam. 5 : 11-25.
    1 Chron. 14.
    Psa. 21, 124.
13..2 Sam. 6.
    Psa. 132.
14..Psa. 24.
15..Psa. 78.
16..2 Sam. 7.
    1 Chron. 17.
{ 17..Psa. 2, 45.
{ 18..Psa. 22, 110, 118.
19..2 Sam. 8.
    1 Chron. 18.
    Psa. 60, 84.
20..Psa. 44, 20.
21..2 Sam. 9, 10.
    1 Chron. 19.
22..2 Sam. 11 ; 12 : 26-31.
    1 Chron. 20 : 1-3
{ 23..Psa. 6, 69.
{ 24..Psa. 103, 32, 139.
25..2 Sam. 12 : 24, 25; 13.
26..2 Sam. 14 : 1-7, 15-17, 8-14, 18-33.
27..2 Sam. 15 ; 16 ; 17 : 1-24.
{ 28..Psa. 4, 3, 5, 144.
{ 29 Psa. 26, 28, 61, 62, 143.
{ 30..Psa. 42, 55, 41, 109, 69, 86, 121.
31..2 Sam. 17 : 25-29 ; 18 : 1-6.
    Psa. 43.
Sep. 1..2 Sam. 18 : 7-33 ; 19.
2..2 Sam. 20.
3..2 Sam. 21.
4..2 Sam. 22.
5..1 Chron. 20 : 4-8.
    2 Sam. 23.
    Psa. 18.

HELPS TO BIBLE STUDY.

Sep. 6..2 Sam. 24.
    1 Chron. 21 : 1-6 ; 27 : 23, 24 ; 21 : 7-30.
    Psa. 30.
7..1 Chron. 22.
    1 Kings 1.
8..1 Chron. 23, 24.
9..1 Chron. 25, 26.
10..1 Chron. 27 : 1-22, 25-34; 28.
11..1 Chron. 29 : 1-25.
    Psa. 72, 67.
12. Psa. 68.
13..Psa. 91, 145, 65.
14..1 Kings 2 : 1-9.
    2 Sam. 23 : 1-7.
    1 Chron. 29 : 26-30.
    1 Kings 2 : 10, 11.
15..1 Kings 2 : 12.
    2 Chron. 1 : 1-12.
    1 Kings 3 : 4-28.
    2 Chron. 1 : 13.
16..1 Kings 2 : 13-38 ; 5.
17..2 Chron. 2.
    1 Kings 2 : 39-46 ; 3 : 1-3 ; 6 : 1-8, 15-36.
18..1 Kings 7 : 13-50.
19..1 Kings 6 : 9-14, 37, 38 ; 7 : 51.
    2 Chron. 3, 4, 5, 1.
20..1 Kings 8 : 1-11, 62-64, 12-61, 65, 66.
21.. 2 Chron. 5 : 2-14 ; 7 : 4-7 ; 6.
22..2 Chron. 7 : 3, 8, 10.
    Psa. 47 : 97.
23..Psa. 98, 99, 100.
24..1 Kings 7 : 1-12 ; 9 : 1-9.
    2 Chron. 7 : 11-22.
    1 Kings 9 : 10-23, 25.
25.. 2 Chron. 8 : 1-10, 12-16.
    1 Kings 9 : 24.
    2 Chron. 8 : 11.
26..⎫
27..⎭ Song of Solomon.
28..1 Kings 4 : 1-28 ; 10 : 26 ; 9 : 26-28 ; 10 : 14-25, 27-29.

Sep. 29. 2 Chron. 9 : 26, 25 ; 1 : 14 ; 8 : 17, 18 ; 9 : 13-21, 24 ; 1 : 15-17 ; 9 : 27, 28.
30..1 Kings 4 : 29-33.
    2 Chron. 9 : 22.
    Prov. 1.
Oct. 1..Prov. 2, 3.
2..Prov. 4, 5.
3..Prov. 6.
4..Prov. 7, 8.
5..Prov. 9, 10.
6..Prov. 11.
7..Prov. 12, 13.
8..Prov. 14.
9..Prov. 15.
10..Prov. 16.
11..Prov. 17, 18, 19.
12..Prov. 20.
13..Prov. 21.
14..Prov. 22.
15..Prov. 23.
16..Prov. 24.
17..Prov. 25.
18..Prov. 26, 27, 28.
19..Prov. 29.
20..Prov. 30.
21..Prov. 31.
22. 1 Kings 4 : 34 ; 10 : 1-13.
    2 Chron. 9 : 23, 1-12.
23..1 Kings 11.
24..Ecc. 1, 2.
25..Ecc. 3, 4, 5.
26..Ecc. 6, 7.
27. Ecc. 8, 9.
28..Ecc. 10, 11.
29..Ecc. 12.
30..2 Chron. 9 : 29-31.
    1 Kings 12 : 1-19.
    2 Chron. 10.
31..1 Kings 12 : 20-33.
    2 Chron. 11.
Nov. 1..1 Kings 13.
    2 Chron. 12.
2..1 Kings 14.
3..1 Kings 15.
4..2 Chron. 13, 14.
5..2 Chron. 15, 16, 17.

HELPS TO BIBLE STUDY.

Nov. 6..1 Kings 16.
7. 1 Kings 17.
8..1 Kings 18, 19.
9..1 Kings 20.
10..1 Kings 21.
11..1 Kings 22.
12..2 Chron. 18, 19.
    Psa. 82.
13..2 Chron. 20.
    Psa. 115.
14..2 Kings 1, 2.
15..2 Kings 3, 4.
16..2 Kings 5.
17..2 Kings 6.
18..2 Kings 7, 8.
19..2 Chron. 21.
20..2 Kings 9.
21..2 Kings 10.
22..2 Kings 11.
    2 Chron. 22, 23.
23..2 Chron. 24.
    2 Kings 12.
24..Jonah 1, 2, 3.
25..Jonah 4.
    2 Kings 13.
26..2 Kings 14.
    2 Chron. 25.
27..2 Kings 15 : 1-4.
28..Hosea, 1, 2, 3.
29..Hosea 4, 5, 6, 7.
30..Hos. 8, 9, 10.
Dec. 1..Hos. 11, 12.
2..Hos. 13, 14.
3..Amos 1, 2.
4..Amos 3, 4.
5..Amos 5, 6.
6..Amos 7, 8, 9.
7..Joel 1. 2.

Dec. 8..Joel 3.
    2 Chron. 26 : 1-22.
9..Isa. 1 : 1 ; 6, 2.
10..Isa. 3. 4.
11..Isa. 5.
12..2 Chron. 26 : 23; 27 : 1-6.
    2 Kings 15 : 5-36.
13..Micah 1, 2.
    2 Kings 15 : 37, 38 ; 16 : 1-5.
    2 Chron. 28 : 1-4.
14..Isa. 7, 8.
15. Isa. 9; 10 : 1-4; 17.
16. 2 Chron. 28 : 5-16, 21, 17-20.
    2 Kings 16 : 6-9.
17..Obadiah.
18..Isa. 1 : 2-31.
19..Isa. 28.
20..2 Chron. 28 : 22-25.
    2 Kings 16 : 10-18.
    Hosea 5, 6.
21..2 Kings 16 : 19, 20.
    2 Chron. 28 : 26, 27.
    Isa. 14 : 28-32.
    2 Kings 17 : 1-3; 18: 1, 2.
    2 Chron. 29.
22..2 Chron 30, 31.
23..2 Kings 18 : 3-6.
    Isa. 15, 16.
24..Micah 3, 4, 5.
25. Micah 6, 7.
26..2 Kings 17 : 4.
    Hosea 7, 8, 9.
27..Hosea 10, 11, 12, 13, 14.
28..2 Kings 17: 6-23; 18: 9-37; 19 : 20.

SECOND YEAR.

Jan. 1..Isa. 23 ; 10 : 5-34.
2..Isa. 11, 12, 13.
3..Isa. 14 : 1-27 ; 24.
4..Isa. 25, 26, 27.
5..Isa. 22 : 1-14 ; 21.
    2 Kings 18 : 13-16.
    2 Chron. 32 : 1-8.

Jan. 5..Isa. 36 : 1 ; 20.
6..Isa. 29, 30.
7..Isa. 31.
    2 Kings 20 : 1-6, 8-11, 7.
    Isa. 38 : 1-6, 22, 7, 8, 21, 9-20.
    2 Chron. 32 : 24.

HELPS TO BIBLE STUDY.

Jan. 8..Isa. 32, 33.
9..Isa. 34, 35.
Nah. 1.
10...Nah. 2, 3.
2 Kings 20 : 12-19.
Isa. 39.
2 Chron. 32 : 25, 26.
11..2 Kings 18 : 17-37 ; 19.
12..Psa. 73, 75, 76.
13..Psa. 86.
Isa. 36 : 2-22.
14..Isa. 37.
2 Chron. 32 : 9-32.
Psa. 46.
15..Isa. 40, 41.
16..Isa. 42, 43.
17. Isa. 44, 45.
18..Isa. 46, 47, 48.
19..Isa. 49, 50.
20..Isa. 51 ; 52 : 1-12.
21..Isa. 52 : 13-15 ; 53.
22..Isa. 54, 55, 56.
23 .Isa. 57, 58.
24..Isa. 59, 60.
25..Isa. 61, 62, 63.
26..Isa. 64, 65, 66.
27..2 Kings 20 : 20 ; 21: 1-16.
2 Chron. 32 : 27-33 ; 33 : 1-10.
28..Isa. 22 : 15-25.
2 Kings 17 : 24-41.
2 Chron. 33 : 11-17.
2 Kings 21 : 17-22.
2 Chron. 33 : 18-23.
29..2 Kings 21 : 23-26 ; 22 : 1, 2.
2 Chron. 33 : 24, 25 ; 24 : 1-7.
Jer. 1 : 2.
2 Kings 22 : 3-20 ; 23 : 1-20.
2 Chron. 34 : 8, 28-33.
30..Zeph. 1, 2, 3.
31..2 Kings 23 : 21-27.
2 Chron. 35 : 1-19.
Jer. 3 : 12-25.
Feb. 1..Jer. 4.
2..Jer. 5.

Feb. 3..Jer. 6.
4..Hab. 1, 2. 3.
5..Jer. 7, 8.
6..Jer. 9, 10.
7..Jer. 11, 12.
8..2 Kings 23 : 29, 30.
2 Chron. 35 : 20-27 ; 36 : 1, 2.
2 Kings 23 : 33-37.
2 Chron. 36 : 3-5.
Jer. 13.
9 .Jer. 14, 15.
10..Jer. 16, 17.
11..Jer. 18, 19.
12..Jer. 20; 22 : 1-23 ; 26.
13..Jer. 46 : 1-12 ; 35.
14..Jer. 25 ; 36 : 1-8 ; 45.
15..2 Kings 24 : 1.
2 Chron. 36 : 6, 7.
Dan 1 : 1-4, 6, 7, 5, 8-17.
Jer. 36 : 9 32.
2 Kings 24 : 1.
16..Dan. 1 : 18-21 ; 2.
17..2 Kings 24 : 5-9.
2 Chron. 36 : 8, 9.
Jer. 22 : 24-30 ; 23.
18..2 Kings 24 : 10-19.
2 Chron. 36 : 10-12.
Jer. 52 : 1, 2 ; 24 ; 29 : 1-14, 16-20, 15, 21-32.
19..Jer. 30, 31.
20..Jer. 27, 28.
21..Jer. 48.
22 Jer. 49.
23..Jer. 50.
24..Jer. 51.
25..Ezek. 1 ; 2 ; 3 : 1-21.
26..Ezek. 3 : 22-27 ; 8, 9.
27..Ezek. 11, 12.
28..Ezek. 13, 14. 15.
Mar. 1..Ezek. 16.
2..Ezek. 17, 18.
3..Ezek. 19, 20.
4..Ezek. 21, 22.
5..Ezek. 23.
6..Jer. 37 : 1, 2.
2 Kings 24 : 20.
2 Chron. 36 : 13.

HELPS TO BIBLE STUDY. 31

Mar. 6..Jer. 52:3.
    2 Chron. 36 : 14-21.
    Ezek 24.
  7..Jer. 34 : 1-10 ; 32.
  8..Jer. 33.
    Ezek. 29 ; 1-16, 26.
    Isa. 23.
  9..Jer. 37:5; 47; 34:11-22;
    37 : 6 ; 21.
10..Jer. 38 ; 39 : 15-18.
11..Ezek. 30 : 20-26 ; 31.
    2 Kings 25 : 2, 4-7.
    Jer. 52 : 5-7 ; 39 : 2-7,
    11-14.
12..2 Kings 25 : 8-21.
    Jer. 52 : 12 30; 39 : 8-10.
    Psa. 74, 79, 83, 94.
13..Lam. 1, 2.
14..Lam. 3.
15..Lam. 4, 5.
16..2 Kings 25 : 22-24.
    Jer. 40.
    2 Kings 25 : 25, 26.
    Jer. 41 ; 42 ; 43 : 1-7.
17..Jer. 43 : 8-13; 46 : 13-28;
    44.
18..Jer. 52 : 28-30.
    Ezek. 33 : 22-33.
    Psalms 10, 49, 50, 67, 77,
    80, 89, 92, 93, 123, 130,
    137.
19..Ezek. 25, 27, 28, 32.
20..Ezek. 33 : 1-20 ; 34.
21..Ezek. 37, 38.
22..Ezek. 39.
23..Ezek. 40.
24..Ezek. 41, 42.
25..Ezek. 43, 44.
26..Ezek. 45, 46.
27..Ezek. 47, 48.
28..Ezek. 29:17-21; 30:1-19.
    Dan. 3.
29..Dan. 4.
30..2 Kings 25 : 27-30.
    Jer. 52 : 31-34.
    Dan. 7, 5.
31..Dan. 8, 9.
    Psa. 102.

Apr. 1..Dan. 6.
    2 Chron. 36, 22, 23.
    Ezra 1 : 1-4.
    Psa. 126, 85.
  2..Ezra 1 : 5-11 ; 2 ; 3 : 1-7.
    Psa. 87, 107, 111, 112,
    113, 114, 115, 117,
    125, 128, 134.
  3..Ezra 3 : 8-13.
    Psa. 84, 66.
  4..Ezra 4 : 1-5, 24.
    Psa. 129.
  5..Dan. 10, 11.
  6..Dan. 12.
  7..Ezra 5 : 1.
    Hag. 1 : 1-11.
    Ezra 5 : 2.
    Hag. 1 : 12-15; 2 : 1-9.
    Zech. 1 : 1-16,
    Hag. 2 : 10-23.
    Zech. 1 : 7-21.
  8..Zech 2, 3, 4, 5, 6.
    Ezra 5 : 3-17 ; 6 : 1-22.
  9..Psa. 81, 146.
10..Psa. 147, 148.
11..Psa. 149, 150.
12..Ezra 4 : 6-23.
    Esther 1.
    Ezra 7.
13..Esther 2 : 1-20.
    Ezra 8, 9.
    Zech. 9, 10.
14..Zech. 11, 12.
15..Zech. 13, 14.
16..Esther 2 : 21-23; 3.
17..Esther 4, 5.
18..Esther 6, 7.
19..Esther 8.
20..Esther 9, 10.
21..Neh. 1, 2.
22..Neh. 3, 4.
23..Neh. 5, 6, 7.
24..Neh. 8, 9.
25..Neh. 10, 11.
26..Neh. 12 : 1-9.
27..Neh. 13 : 1-3.
    Psa. 1.
28..Psa. 119 : 1-64.

Apr.29..Psa. 119 : 65-120.
  30..Psa. 119 : 121-176.
May 1..Mal. 1, 2, 3 : 1-15.
  2..Neh. 13 : 4-31.
     Mal. 3 : 16-18; 4.
  3..1 Chron. 1, 2.
  4..1 Chron. 3, 4.
  5..1 Chron. 5, 6.
  6..1 Chron. 7, 8.
  7..1 Chron. 9.
     Neh. 12 : 10-26.
  8..Luke 1 : 1-4.
     John 1 : 1-18.
  9..Luke 1 : 5-25.
 10..Luke 1 : 26-38.
 11 Luke 1 : 39-56.
 12..Luke 1 : 57-79.
 13 Matt. 1 : 18-25, 1-17.
     Luke 3 : 23-38.
 14..Luke 2 : 8-20.
     Matt. 1 : 25.
     Luke 2 : 21.
 15..Luke 2 : 22-38.
 16..Matt. 2 : 1-23.
     Luke 2 : 39.
 17..Luke 2 : 40-52.
 18..Matt. 3 : 1-12.
     Mark 1 : 1-8.
 19 John 1 : 8; 3 : 1-17.
 20..Matt. 3 : 13-17.
     Mark 1 : 9-11.
     Luke 3 : 21-23.
 21..Matt. 4 : 1-11.
     Mark 1 : 12, 13.
 22..Luke 4 : 1-13.
 23..John 1 : 19-34.
 24..John 1 : 35-51.
 25 John 2 : 1-12.
 26. John 2 : 13-25.
 27..John 3 : 1-21.
 28..John 3 : 22-36.
 29..Matt. 4 : 12; 14 : 3-5.
     Mark 1 : 14; 6 : 17-20.
     Luke 3 : 18; 4 : 14; 3 : 19, 20.
 30..John 4 : 1-26.
 31..John 4 : 27-42.
June 1..Matt. 4 : 17.

June 1..Mark 1 : 14, 15.
     Luke 4 : 14.
     John 4 : 43-54.
  2..Matt. 4 : 13-16.
     Luke 4 : 15-31.
  3..Matt. 4 : 18-22.
     Mark 1 : 16-20.
     Luke 5 : 1-11.
  4..Mark 1 : 21-28.
     Luke 4 : 31-37.
  5..Matt. 8 : 14-17; 4 : 23-25.
  6..Mark 1 : 29-39.
  7..Luke 4 : 38-44.
  8..Matt. 4 : 2-4.
     Mark 1 : 40-45.
     Luke 5 : 12-16.
  9..Matt. 9 : 2-8.
     Mark 2 : 1-12.
     Luke 15 : 17-26.
     Matt 9 : 9.
     Mark 2 : 13, 14.
     Luke 5 : 27, 28.
 10..John 5 : 1-18.
 11..John 5 : 19-30.
 12..John 5 : 31-47.
 13..Matt. 12 : 1-8.
     Mark 2 : 23-28.
     Luke 6 : 1-5.
 14..Matt. 12 : 9-21.
     Mark 3 : 1-12.
     Luke 6 : 6-11.
 15..Matt. 10 : 2-4.
     Mark 3 : 13-19.
     Luke 6 : 12-19.
 16..Matt. 5 : 1-16.
 17..Matt. 5 : 17-30.
 18..Matt. 5 : 31-48.
 19..Matt. 6 : 1-18.
 20 Matt. 6 : 19-34.
 21..Matt. 7 : 1-14.
 22..Matt. 7 : 15-29.
 23..Luke 6 : 20-49.
 24..Matt. 8 : 1, 5-13.
     Luke 7 : 1-17.
 25..Matt. 11 : 2-19.
     Luke 7 : 18-35.
     Matt. 11 : 20-30.
 26..Luke 7 : 36-50.

HELPS TO BIBLE STUDY. 33

June 27..Matt. 9:35; 12:22-37.
    Mark 6:6; 3:20-30.
    Luke 8:1-3; 11:14-23.
  28..Matt. 12:38-45.
    Luke 11:16, 29-36, 24-26.
  29..Luke 27, 28.
    Matt. 12:46-50.
    Mark 3:31-35.
    Luke 8:19-21.
  30..Luke 11:37-54.
July 1..Luke 12:1-59; 13:1-9.
  2..Matt. 13.
  3..Mark 4:1-34.
  4..Luke 8:4-14.
  5..Matt. 8:18-27.
    Mark 4:35-41.
    Luke 8:22; 9:57-62; 8:22-25.
  6..Matt. 8:23-34.
    Mark 5:1-20.
    Luke 8:26-39.
  7..Matt. 9:1.
    Mark 5:21.
    Luke 8:40.
    Matt. 9:18-26.
    Mark 5:22-43.
    Luke 8:41-56.
  8..Matt. 9:27-34; 13:54-58.
    Mark 6:12, 13.
    Luke 9:6.
  9..Matt. 14:6-12.
    Mark 6:21-29.
    Matt. 14:1, 2.
    Mark 6:14-16.
    Luke 9:7-9.
    Mark 6:30, 31.
    Luke 9:10.
  10..Matt. 14:13-21.
    Mark 6:14-16.
    Luke 9:10-17.
    John 6:1-14.
  11..Matt. 14:22 36.
    Mark 6:45-56.
    John 6:15-21.
  12..John 6:22-71; 7:1.
  13..Matt. 15:1-20.
    Mark 7:1-23.
  14..Matt. 15:21-28.

July 14..Mark 7:24-30.
    Matt. 15:29-31.
    Mark 7:31-37.
  15..Matt. 15:32-39.
    Mark 8:1-10.
    Matt. 16:1-4.
    Mark 8:11, 12.
  16..Matt. 16:4-12.
    Mark 8:13-26.
  17 Matt. 16:13-20.
    Mark 8:27-30.
    Luke 9:22-27.
  18..Matt. 17:1-3.
    Mark 9:2-13.
    Luke 9:28-36.
    John 1:14.
    2 Peter 1:16-18.
    Matt. 17:14-21.
    Mark 9:14-29.
    Luke 9:37-43.
  19..Matt. 17:22, 23.
    Mark 9:30-32.
    Luke 9:43-45.
    Matt. 17:24-27.
    Mark 9:33.
  20 Matt. 18:1-35; 9:46-50.
  21..Matt. 10:1-10.
  22..John 7:2-53; 8:2-11.
  23..John 8:12-59.
  24..John 9:10.
  25..Luke 10:17-37.
  26..Luke 11:1-13; 13:10-35.
  27..Luke 14.
  28..Luke 15.
  29..Luke 16; 17:1-10.
  30..Luke 17:11-19.
  31..Luke 9:51-56; 17:12-19.
Aug. 1..Luke 17:20-37.
  2..Luke 18:1-14; 10:38-42.
    John 10:22-42.
  3..John 11.
  4..John 19:1, 2.
    Mark 10:1-12.
    Matt. 19:13-15.
    Mark 10:13-15.
    Luke 18:15-17.
    Matt. 19:16-30; 20:1-16.

34 HELPS TO BIBLE STUDY.

Aug. 4..Mark 10 : 17-31.
Luke 18 : 16-30.
5..Matt. 20 : 17-19 ; 10 : 31-34.
Luke 18 : 31-34.
Matt. 20 : 20-28.
Mark 10 : 35-45.
6..Matt. 20 : 29-34.
Mark 10 : 46-52.
Luke 18 : 35-43 ; 19 : 1-28.
7..John 11 : 55-57 ; 12 : 1, 9-11.
Matt. 21 : 1-11. 14-17.
Mark 11 : 1-11.
Luke 19 : 29-44.
John 12 : 12, 50.
8..Matt. 21 : 18, 19, 12, 13.
Mark 11 : 12-19.
Luke 19 : 45-48.
Matt. 21 : 23-46 ; 22 : 1-14.
Mark 11 :27-33; 12:1-12.
Luke 20 : 1-19.
9..Matt. 22 : 15-46.
Mark 12 : 12-37.
Luke 20 : 20-44.
10..Matt. 23 : 1-39.
Mark 12 : 38-40.
Luke 20 : 45-47.
Mark 12 : 41-44.
Luke 21 : 1-4.
11..Matt. 24:1-51; 25 : 1-30.
Mark 13 : 1-37.
Luke 21 : 5-36.
Matt. 25 : 31-46 ; 21 : 37, 38.
12..Matt. 26 : 1-16.
Mark 14 : 1-11.
Luke 22 : 1-6.
John 12 : 2-8.
13. Matt. 26 : 17:19.
Mark 14 : 12-16 ; 22 : 7-13.
Matt. 26 : 20.
Mark 14 : 18-21.
Luke 22:14, 24-30, 15-18.
John 13 : 1-20.

Aug.14..Matt. 26 : 21-25.
Mark 14 : 18-21.
Luke 22 : 21-23.
John 13 : 21-35.
15..Matt. 26 : 31-35.
Mark 14 : 27-31.
Luke 22 : 31-38.
John 13 : 36-38.
16..Matt. 26 : 26.
Mark 14 : 22.
Luke 22 : 19.
1 Cor. 11 : 23, 24.
John 14.
Matt 26 : 27-29.
Mark 14 : 23-25.
Luke 22 : 20.
1 Cor. 11 : 25.
17..John 15 : 1-27; 16 : 1-33.
18...John 17 : 1-26.
Matt. 26 : 30, 36-46.
Mark 14 : 26.
Psa. 113-118, inclusive.
Mark 14 : 32-42.
Luke 22 : 39-46.
John 18 : 1.
19..Matt. 26 : 47-56.
Mark 14 : 43-52.
Luke 22 : 47-53.
John 18 : 2-12.
20..Matt. 26 : 57, 58, 69-75.
Mark 14 : 53, 54, 66-72.
Luke 22 : 54-62.
John 18 : 13-18, 24, 27.
Matt. 26 : 57, 59-68.
Mark 14 : 53, 55-65.
Luke 22 : 66-71, 63-65.
John 18 : 19-23, 28.
21..Matt. 27 : 1, 2, 11-14.
Mark 15 : 1-15.
Luke 23 : 1-5.
John 18 : 28-38.
Luke 23 : 6-12.
Matt. 27 : 15-23.
Mark 15 : 6-14.
Luke 23 : 23-25.
John 18 : 39, 40.
22..Matt. 27 : 26-31.
Mark 15 : 15-20.

HELPS TO BIBLE STUDY. 35

Aug.22..Luke 23 : 23-25.
      John 19 : 1-16.
      Matt. 27 : 3-10.
      Acts 1 : 18, 19.
  23..Matt. 27 : 35-50.
      Mark 15 : 21-23.
      Luke 23 : 26-33.
      John 19 : 17.
  24..Matt. 27 : 35-50.
      Mark 15 : 24-37.
      Luke 23 : 33-46.
      John 19 : 18-30.
  25..Matt. 27 : 51 61.
      Mark 15 : 38-47.
      Luke 23 : 45, 47-56.
      John 19 : 31-42.
      Matt. 27 : 62-66.
  26..Matt. 28 : 2-4 ; 27 : 52, 53.
      Mark 16 : 1.
      Matt. 28 ; 1 : 5-8.
      Mark 16 : 2-8.
      Luke 24 : 1-11.
      John 20 : 1, 2.
  27..Luke 24 : 12.
      John 20 : 3-10.
      Mark 16 : 9 11.
      John 20 : 11-18.
      Matt. 28 : 9-15.
  28..Mark 16 : 12, 13.
      Luke 24 : 13-36.
      1 Cor. 15, part of verse 5.
  29..Mark 16 : 14-18.
      Luke 24 , 36-49.
      John 20 : 19-29.
  30. Matt. 28 : 16.
      John 21 : 1-24.
      Matt. 28 : 16-20.
      1 Cor. 15 : 6, 7.
      Acts 1 : 3-8.
  31..Mark 16 : 19-20.
      Luke 24 : 50-53.
      Acts 1 : 9-12.
      John 20 : 30, 31 ; 21 : 25.
Sep. 1..Acts 1 : 1-3, 12-14 ; 2.
   2..Acts 3, 4 ; 1 : 31.
   3..Acts 4 : 32-37 ; 5.
   4..Acts 6, 7.
   5..Acts 8, 9.

Sep. 6..Acts 10, 11.
   7..Acts 12, 13.
   8..Acts 14, 15.
   9..Acts 16:1-6; 1 Tim. 1, 2, 3.
  10..Gal. 1, 2.
  11..Gal. 3, 4.
  12 .Gal. 5, 6.
  13..Phil. 1, 2.
  14..Phil. 3, 4.
  15..Acts 17 : 1-10.
      1 Thess. 1.
  16..1 Thess. 2, 3.
  17..1 Thess. 4, 5.
  18..2 Thess. 1, 2.
  19..2 Thess. 3, 4.
  20..Acts 17 : 10-34; 18 : 1-18.
      1 Cor. 1.
  21..1 Cor. 2, 3, 4.
  22..1 Cor 5, 6, 7.
  23..1 Cor. 8, 9.
  24 .1 Cor. 10, 11.
  25..1 Cor. 12, 13.
  26..1 Cor. 14.
  27..1 Cor. 15.
  28 .1 Cor. 16.
  29..2 Cor. 1.
  30..2 Cor. 2.
Oct. 1..2 Cor. 3.
   2..2 Cor. 4.
   3..2 Cor. 5.
   4..2 Cor. 6, 7, 8.
   5..2 Cor. 9.
   6..2 Cor. 10.
   7..2 Cor. 11.
   8..2 Cor. 12.
   9..2 Cor. 13.
  10..Acts 18 : 19-28 ; 19 ; 20.
  11..Eph. 1, 2, 3.
  12..Eph. 4, 5, 6.
  13..Acts 21, 22, 23.
  14..Acts 24, 25, 26.
  15..Acts 27 ; 28 : 1-10.
  16..Acts 28 : 11-31.
      Rom. 1.
  17..Rom. 2.
  18..Rom. 3.
  19..Rom. 4.
  20..Rom. 5.

Oct. 21..Rom. 6.	Nov. 26..Jas. 5.
22..Rom. 7.	27..1 Peter 1.
23..Rom. 8.	28..1 Peter 2.
24..Rom. 9.	29..1 Peter 3, 4.
25..Rom. 10.	30..1 Peter 5.
26 Rom 11.	Dec. 1 .2 Peter 1.
27..Rom. 12.	2..2 Peter 2.
28..Rom. 13.	3..2 Peter 3.
29. Rom. 14.	4..1 John 1.
30..Rom. 15.	5..1 John 2.
31..Rom. 16.	6..1 John 3.
Nov. 1..Philemon.	7..1 John 4.
2..Col. 1.	8..1 John 5.
3..Col. 2.	9..2 John.
4..Col. 3.	10..3 John.
5..Col. 4.	11..Jude.
6..Titus 1.	12. Rev. 1.
7..Titus 2.	13..Rev. 2, 3.
8 .Titus 3.	14..Rev. 4, 5.
9..Heb. 1.	15 Rev. 6.
10..Heb. 2.	16..Rev. 7.
11..Heb. 3; 4:1-13.	17..Rev. 8.
12..Heb. 4:14-16; 5.	18..Rev. 9.
13..Heb. 6.	19..Rev. 10.
14..Heb. 7.	20..Rev. 11.
15..Heb. 8.	21..Rev. 12.
16..Heb. 9, 10.	22..Rev. 13.
17..Heb. 11.	23..Rev. 14.
18..Heb. 12.	24..Rev. 15.
19..Heb. 13.	25..Rev. 16.
20..2 Tim. 1, 2.	26..Rev. 17.
21..2 Tim. 3, 4.	27..Rev. 18.
22..Jas. 1.	28..Rev. 19.
23..Jas. 2.	29..Rev. 20.
24..Jas. 3.	30..Rev. 21.
25..Jas. 4.	31..Rev. 22.

7. *Study the Bible analytically.* " Read special portions of Scripture analytically, looking into the deeper meanings, as astronomers search into the depths of the skies. New stars may be found in the most studied chapters."—*Rev. W. F. Crafts.*

" There is more of valuable truth yet to be gleaned from the sacred writings, that has thus far escaped the attention of commentators, than from all other sources of human knowledge combined."—*D. Webster.*

"When you read your Bible, be sure you *hunt for something.* Read the same chapter over and over again till you understand it. We would add—make yourself thoroughly familiar with St. Paul's epistles. They are the key to all the Holy Scriptures."—*Moody.*

After a chapter has been read, analyze it and draw up *your own table of contents.* We are indebted to an English gentleman for this suggestion, and as an illustration of our meaning, give such a table as made by him:

CONTENTS OF CHAPTER I. MARK'S GOSPEL.

(The numbers give the verses.)

Three principal Persons mentioned—
John the Baptist: (4) Preached repentance—(9) Baptized Jesus—(7) Pointed to Christ.
Jesus Christ: (9) Baptized by John—(13) Tempted of Satan—(35) Prayed to God.
Satan: (13) Tempted Jesus—(23, 32) Got possession of men—(25, 34, 39) Cast out by Jesus.

Three Titles given to Jesus—
By Mark: (1) Jesus Christ. By God: (17) My beloved Son. By Satan: (24) Holy One of God.

Three Miracles wrought by Jesus—
(23) On an unclean spirit—(30) Simon's wife's mother—(40) Leper.

Three Contrasts—
(8) Baptism of John—baptism of Jesus. (13) Satan tempts—angels minister. (23, 24) Unclean spirit of devil—Holy One of God.

Four Disciples—
Simon and Andrew, James and John : (16, 17) Called—
(18, 20) Forsake all—(18, 20) Follow Jesus.

A remarkable result of disobedience—
Because the healed leper published his cure (when Jesus told him to " say nothing ")—(verse 44)—Jesus could no more openly enter into the city" (verse 45).

Let any one adopt and carry out such a plan as this, or a similar one, and it will wonderfully increase and intensify Bible knowledge.

8. Study the Bible systematically. " In gathering doctrinal truth from Scripture, bring together all the texts that refer to the same subject, whether they be doctrines, precepts, or promises, impartially compare them, restrict the expressions of one text by those of another, and explain the whole consistently. We must gather our views of Christian doctrine primarily from the New Testament, interpreting its statements consistently with one another, and with the facts and clear revelations of the Old. Explain figurative passages by those that are clear and literal. Notice what things are omitted in one book ; things that are oftenest recommended ; what is common to the two dispensations ; observe the value ascribed in Scripture itself to any truth or precept which it contains. Nothing must be made a matter of faith which is not a matter of revelation.

" Employ and interpret the doctrines of Scripture with special regard to the practical purposes for which the Scripture reveals them. Remember, too, that deductions from Scripture are not necessarily true, unless those deductions are themselves revealed."—*Angus.*

9. Study the Bible inferentially. " It is incredible," says

Bishop Horsley, " to any one who has not made the experiment, what a proficiency may be made in that knowledge which maketh wise unto salvation, by studying the Scriptures with reference to the parallel passages without any other commentary or exposition than that which the different parts of the sacred volume mutually furnish for each other. Let the most illiterate Christian study them in this manner, and let him never cease to pray for the illumination of that Spirit by whom these books were dedicated, and the whole compass of abstruse philosophy and recondite history shall furnish no argument with which the perverse will of man shall be able to shake this learned Christian's faith."

" Lessons may be drawn from the words of Scripture, from the words in their place in the sentence ; from words in connection with the context ; from the scope either of the book, or of the particular passage ; from parallel passages, not merely verbal parallels, but parallelisms of thought."— *Angus*.

10. *Take a single passage and dwell upon it*, using 2 Tim. 3 : 16-17, as a personal glass through which to read each passage, asking what reproof, what instruction is there here for me ? Read and study the passage as if it were written for yourself, always taking the plain and simple meaning of a passage. Ingenious interpretations are usually dangerous. Another plan is : Consider the external *circumstances*, both as to the writer and the subject matter itself ; consider the *scope* of the paragraph or chapter containing the passage ; remark the *structure ;* compare it with its *connection ;* and with marginal *references ;* ponder the *words ;* endeavor to *grasp the idea* of the words ; and make the required *application*. This is a delightful and profitable spiritual exercise."

ADDITIONAL SUGGESTIONS.

1. Learn at least one verse of Scripture each day. Verses from memory will be wonderfully useful in your daily life and work (see Josh. 1 : 8 ; Psa. 119 : 11).

2. Do not be satisfied with simply reading a chapter, but *study the meaning* of at least *one verse every day.*

3. Read and study the Bible *socially.* This is done in Teachers' Meetings, Bible Classes, etc. Each one's views are sure to be somewhat supplemented and stimulated by the views, arguments, and suggestions of others.

4. Set apart at least *fifteen minutes each day for studying it.* This little will be grand in results, and never be regretted.

5. Study how to use the Bible so as to "*walk with God,*" and lead others to Christ.

6. Read the book as if it were *written for yourself.* Always ask God to help you to understand it, and then EXPECT that he will.

7. Carry a Bible or Testament with you.

8. Do not get a Bible too large to be handled comfortably, nor of too small type to be read easily.

9. Read the Bible with a view of *living* rather than merely *learning* it, coming to it not only perfunctorily for lessons and sermons, but also *for loving conversation,* "as a man talketh with his friend."

10. Have Young's Analytical Concordance and a Bible text-book at hand. Also in all cases refer to parallel passages and marginal notes, and take time to think before consulting commentaries.

11. Study the Bible in the freshness of the morning rather than the weary hours of the evening. Open and

read it in the morning before opening any other book or paper.

12. Believe in the Bible as God's revelation to you, and act accordingly.

"Some distinction," says Dr. Anderson, "should be made between the study of the Bible, the reading of the Bible, and meditation upon certain portions of the Bible. Each is essential in its way; the three combined give completeness to searching the Scriptures in order to abiding communion with God. The study of the Bible is needful in order to get a thorough knowledge of the contents of the sacred volume, the meaning of words and phrases, the fulfilment of types, the interpretation of ceremonial observances, prophetic utterances, etc. The reading of the Bible is necessary in order to hear God's voice speaking to us, so that divine communion may be encouraged and perpetuated. The meditation of the Bible is indispensable in order to be fed with the sincere milk of the Word, or the strong meat thereof, that we may grow thereby. Meditation is to the reading and study what digestion and assimilation are to the eating of our daily food. Finally, let the Bible be studied critically and read devotionally; let it be meditated upon reverently and diligently, comparing spiritual things with spiritual, and allowing Scripture to explain itself by Scripture."

HOW TO PREPARE BIBLE READINGS.

By H. W. S.

For your study of the Bible you require four things:

1. A Bible, with references, if possible.
2. A complete *Cruden's* or *Young's* Analytical Concordance.

HELPS TO BIBLE STUDY.

3. A blank-book that can be ruled in columns.

4. An undisturbed desk or table, where you can keep the above three things, with pen and ink, always ready. Having provided these few necessary things, proceed as follows:

1. Commit yourself, in a few words, to the Lord, asking for light and guidance, and expecting to receive them.

2. Choose a subject appropriate to the occasion.

3. Find in the Concordance all the words referring to this subject, and select from among the texts given such as seem to you best to elucidate it; noting them down under their appropriate headings in your blank-book.

4. Read over these selected texts carefully, and make a list of the most striking on a separate piece of paper, putting them in the order that will best develop the lesson. Begin this list with a familiar text, and gradually progress to those not so well known, letting each successive text develop the subject a little more clearly than the last. Close the list, if possible, with some practical instance from Bible history, or some typical illustration.

5. Having thus prepared your list, open your Bible at the first text, and on the margin beside it write the reference to the second text on your list. Turn to this second one, and write beside it the reference to the third. Turn to the third, and write beside it the reference to the fourth. And so on through the whole list.

6. On a blank page at the end of your Bible write down an index of all the subjects you have thus studied, with a reference at each to the first text on your list concerning that subject. If you have no blank leaves at the end of your Bible, gum the edge of a half sheet of note paper and fasten it in.

7. By this plan you will have a complete chain of texts

on any given subject running all through your Bible itself, each verse referring you to the next one you wish to read, without having the trouble of loose slips of paper to embarrass you. Also, having once studied out a subject, you have it all ready for any future use; and by turning to your index list, you can at a moment's notice open your Bible at the foundation text, and can then turn to one text after another through the whole course of your lesson, without hesitation or embarrassment.

SEVEN-EIGHTHS OF THE BIBLE MISUNDERSTOOD.

The following remarks—with a few verbal changes— from the pen of Mr. Edward Hine in his work, *Forty-seven Identifications of the British Nation with the Lost Ten Tribes of Israel*, are well worthy of a serious perusal :—

"Bible students would find it most useful, because greatly facilitating their reading and understanding of Scripture, if they would underline in red ink all parts of the Bible having a direct reference to Israel only, and to underline, in blue ink, those parts referring to Judah alone, and, also, in green ink, those parts that refer directly to the Gentile world, apart from Israel or Judah. By doing this they would arrive at the readiest method of ascertaining the positive fact, that seven-eighths of the entire Bible have reference only to the literal, social and historical affairs of Israel and Judah; that only about one-eighth of the whole Bible has any real bearing upon the Gentiles, and that those parts marked red, as referring to Israel, largely predominate. It follows that not to understand the distinction of Israel from Judah, is positively to misunderstand seven-eighths of the Bible, and yet it is an undeniable fact that 99 per cent. of our people do not recognize any difference as existing between Israel and Judah; and that, when you speak to them about Israel, they immediately think you are referring to the Jews, and they read their Bibles with this same false impression. Nationally, to this day, both Oxford and Cambridge are under this delusion, as well as all the Dissenting colleges of the land; how, then, can we be surprised at the amount of stupid blundering and erroneous statements issuing from our pulpits, or wonder at the fact that our pulpit ministrations do not gain the respect of the masses?

"Is it not a lamentable assertion to make in 1890 that seven-eighths of the Bible are misunderstood? Yet it is, too truly, a fact. By not distinguishing Israel from Judah, we set all the prophetical books at variance with each other; we make one prophet give the direct falsehood to another; we make Isaiah call into question the prophecies of Jeremiah, and Jeremiah impugn the statements of Hosea. We set Joel against Amos, Jeremiah against Zechariah, and make Ezekiel contradict them all. Hundreds of proofs are at hand to substantiate these statements, but a few must suffice. Isaiah, Hosea and Christ declare Israel to be lost (Isa. 7 : 8 ; Hosea 1 : 10 ; 6 : 2 ; Matt. 15 : 24). Jeremiah and Ezekiel declare Judah to be known (Jer. 24 : 9 ; Ezek. 22 : 4). Hosea declares Israel to be as the sand for multitude (Hosea 1 : 10). Jeremiah declares Judah to be few in number (Jer. 15 : 7). Isaiah, David and Micah declare Israel to be the strongest war power upon earth (Isa. 41 : 11 ; Psa. 105 : 24 ; Micah 7 : 16). Whereas Jeremiah declares Judah to be without might (Jer. 19 : 7). God, Samuel, David, Isaiah, and Jeremiah declare Israel to be a monarchy (2 Sam. 7 : 12-13 ; Psa. 89 : 4 ; Isa. 37 : 31 ;

HELPS TO BIBLE STUDY. 45

49 : 23 ; Jer. 33 : 26). Jeremiah states Judah to be without government (17 : 4). Isaiah and Obadiah state Israel to be an island nation with large colonies (Isa. 49 : 1, 8 ; Obadiah 17). Jeremiah and Ezekiel state Judah to be strangers in all countries, without geographical inheritance (Jer. 24 : 9; Ezek. 22 : 16). Isaiah, Hosea, Micah, Habakkuk and Paul declare Israel to be a Christian people (Isa. 44 : 23 ; Hosea 2 : 19; Micah 5 : 7; Hab. 3 : 13 ; Rom. 6 : 14). Whereas Ezekiel, Nahum, Zechariah, Christ and Peter declare Judah to be under the Mosaic law (Ezek. 43 : 18-27; Nahum 1 : 15; Zech. 9 : 11; Mark 7: 9 ; Luke 13 : 35; 1 Peter 2 : 8). Many scores of such illustrations might be given. These statements are, in reality, perfectly harmonious. It is only when we read Scripture in our blindness, under the impression that each statement refers to one and the same people, that it becomes contradictory; then it is that the whole Bible seems one mass of confusion, defying the genius of man to bring forth a shadow of reconciliation, without doing material damage to other parts of the book. Tom Paine fell into the common error of looking at the Jews as the house of Israel, and states boldly in his writings that he was led into infidelity because he saw that the Jews could never verify the promises given to Israel ; he, therefore, gave the Bible up as a myth. The very understanding of the difference between the two houses is the key by which almost the entire Bible becomes intelligible; and we cannot state too strongly, that the man who has not yet seen that the Israel of the Scriptures are totally distinct from the Jewish people, is yet in the very infancy, the mere alphabet of Biblical study, and that, to this day, the meaning of fully seven-eighths of the Bible is completely shut out to his understanding."

On page 2 he says: "The House of Judah is composed of two tribes, *i.e.*, Judah and Levi. These are the Jews of the present day. They have never been lost, it being the desire of the Almighty that they should be known wherever they go by all people. At the time of the separation, and up to the siege of Jerusalem by Titus, the house of Judah contained the tribe of Benjamin. But that tribe separated from Judah before the siege, by virtue of the prophecy commanding them to do so (Jer. 6 : 1), so that Benjamin is not now with the Jews. Indeed it is almost unpardonable to allude to the Jews as embodying Judah and Benjamin, though it is an error commonly made.

"The term Ephraim is synonymous with Israel, and embodies the Ten Tribes as a consolidated people. Manasseh is a thirteenth tribe, decreed by the Almighty to be 'a great people'—*i.e.*, a distinct nationality; nevertheless, Ephraim was to 'be greater than he' (Gen. 48 : 18)—that is, a distinct nationality from Manasseh, so that it testifies of ignorance to include Manasseh as one of the Ten Tribes. Ephraim and Manasseh must be two distinct nations, though of the same stock.

"The Jews are 'of Israel,' therefore purely Israelites, but the people of the Ten Tribes were never Jews. This is an important distinction to bear in mind. Scripture often speaks of Judah under the term of Israelites, especially the prophet Ezekiel; yet when this term is applied to Judah, and it becomes needful to distinguish the Ten Tribes from her, it is done by using the terms 'all Israel,' 'the whole House of Israel,' 'the House of Israel wholly.' These terms are copyright to Israel, and are never applied to Judah."

Again, on pages 65, 66, he says: "The term 'spiritual

Israel' has no foundation in the Scriptures. It may have answered a purpose in the past; but, in these present times, it involves a misapplication of words that has a most mischievous tendency; and though apparently simple, their usage in these days would become really a power to prevent one fully understanding the Scriptures; therefore it is important to notice the mistake. The term 'Israel' throughout the Judges, Kings and Prophets denoted a nation, applied distinctly to a nationality. To this day, whenever Israel is referred to, either in the Old or the New Testaments, the reference is always to Israel—as a nationality—as the positive, legitimate, lineal descendants of Israel of old, even though they may have been lost so long. The prevailing notion of the present day is, that an Israelite means a believer in Christ. This is wrong.

"We fail to find that when Christ was on the earth, he called his followers Israelites. Christ called them 'friends' and 'disciples.' Elsewhere they are called 'heirs of God,' 'faithful,' 'believers,' 'brethren' and 'Christians.' Christ called Nathanael 'an Israelite,' not because he knew him to be a man of God—not because he was prevailing with God in prayer, under the fig tree; but because Christ knew he was not of Judah, but that he belonged to Israel—of that tribe of Benjamin—the one tribe of Israel that was left in the land, on purpose to be a light in the days of Christ; in this sense only, was he 'an Israelite indeed.' Why should we depart from Bible usage, and coin a term inconsistent with the Holy Book?—which we do, when we talk about 'spiritual Israel.' The only purpose it has served is to take us off the right track in searching for lost Israel. It has perpetuated 'the blindness' that was to happen 'to Israel' (Rom. 9:6); for many of us have, by this error, concluded that literal Israel were never to be found—that Christians were a spiritual Israel, substituted in its place. But a greater wrong could not be inflicted upon the Word of God than such a supposition—the Bible being plenteous in emphatic promises that Israel—the Ten Tribes—should be found, and Palestine restored to them."

CHAPTER II.

RULES OF INTERPRETATION.

The great advantage of rules of interpretation is not to discover the meaning of plain passages of Scripture, but to ascertain the meaning of such as are ambiguous or obscure. The following rules are condensed from the larger works of Horne, Angus, Nicholls, and others :—

1. Whether words are used literally or tropically, ascertain the meaning affixed to them by the persons in general by whom the language either is now or formerly was spoken, and especially in the particular connection in which such a meaning is affixed. The meaning of a word used by any writer is the meaning affixed to it by those for whom he immediately wrote.

2. It is sometimes necessary to look beyond the words, and even the sentence, to the immediate context, *i.e.*, what goes before or follows a particular sentence, verse or chapter.

The danger of quoting detached passages of Scripture without regard to their context, or to the light which other parts of God's Word may throw upon their interpretation, is seen in the fact that the devil thus brought forward passages from Scripture in order to lead our Lord to sin; and such perversions of the Word of God, as has been truly said, are among the deepest and most dangerous of his devices.

For instance, "Neither hath this man sinned, nor his parents" (John 9 : 3). "All have sinned and come short of the glory of God" (Rom. 3 : 23), but the context of the former passage shows the meaning to be, that his blindness was not the punishment of any particular sin; and that, therefore, neither he nor his parents had sinned in the way the Jews thought they had.

"My kingdom is not of this world" (John 18 : 36). The charge against our Lord, when tried by the Sanhedrim, was that of blasphemy; but the only charge by which the Jews could interest Pilate, the Roman governor, was a charge of treason—an attempt on the part of our Lord to set up a kingdom in opposition to Cæsar (see Luke 23 : 2). In reply, then, to this charge, repeated by Pilate in his inquiry, "Art thou the King of the Jews?" our Lord says, "My kingdom is not of this world," *i.e.*, I do not come to set up a temporal kingdom, a kingdom which can interfere with Cæsar's power, our Lord's being a spiritual kingdom over the hearts of men.

"Go and prosper" (1 Kings 22 : 15). The context shows that the very reverse of this is meant. See also 2 Kings 10 : 3. "Rise and go" (Num. 22 : 20), as is clearly shown by the context in verses 12 and 32, does not imply God's approbation, but the contrary; as though God had said to Balaam, If, after you know what you ought to do, your heart is still set on acting contrary to it, I give you up to your own heart's lust (Psa. 81 : 12).

2 Sam. 17 : 14. The Lord had determined to defeat the *good* counsel of Ahithopel. It was atrociously wicked

counsel, but the context shows in what respects it might be termed good, as being the best means to accomplish the end which Absalom had in view. In the same sense, as we have before observed, the unjust steward is commended by his lord for having done wisely (Luke 16 : 1-8).

2 Sam. 4 : 11. Ish-bosheth, though in his opposition to David he acted contrary to the revealed will of God, and, therefore, very unrighteously, is termed by David a *righteous* person ; the context explains this : he was righteous as to his murderers, having done them no injury, and having given them no provocation.

"Judge me according to my righteousness" (Psa. 7 : 8), *i.e.*, his innocency in reference to the charge which Cush, the Benjamite, brought against him. In the same sense Dan. 6 : 22 is to be reconciled with 9 : 4.

"Who fell upon two men more righteous than he" (1 Kings 2 : 32)—referring to Abner and Amasa. But they were both wicked men, though relatively better than Joab.

"Thy sisters are more righteous than thou" (Ezek. 16 : 52)—referring to Sodom and Gomorrah. These cities were very depraved ; but the expression is used in order to show the still deeper guilt of Judah.

"To him that worketh not" (Rom. 4 : 5), *i.e.*—as appears from the context—so as to seek justification by it. In every point of view, works are necessary.

1 Cor. 11 : 29. Taken out of its connection, the word here rendered by our translators "damnation," might be understood in too strong a sense, as applying exclusively to the eternal doom of the wicked. But the context—verses 30-32—shows that it refers principally to temporal judgments, as bodily distempers, etc., and it is material to observe that the word "damnation," when the Bible was

translated, meant no more than condemnation ; that is, any sentence of punishment whatever, without a particular reference to the eternal doom to which the impenitently wicked will be consigned at the last day.

"I please men in all things" (1 Cor. 10 : 33); and, "If I yet pleased men, I should not be the servant of Christ" (Gal. 1 : 10). St. Paul *pleased all men*, by accommodating his dealings with them, as far as he could, to their respective circumstances, and condescending to their habits, and feelings, and prejudices ; not seeking his own profit, but the profit of many, that they might be saved ; with this object, to the Jew he became a Jew, etc. Again, he *did not please men*, for he did not seek to gain their favor by any such condescensions as were inconsistent with truth and duty.

"Casting all your care upon him" (1 Pet. 5 : 7), taken apart from its context might be abused, as an encouragement to inaction, and can only be understood when taken in connection with the next verse.

"This is my blood" (Matt. 26 : 28). After consecration, the wine is still called "the fruit of the vine" (verse 29). The passage, therefore, cannot be used as an argument for the popish error of transubstantiation. The same remark applies to 1 Cor. 11 : 24, as compared with 26-28, where the apostle after consecration calls the elements bread. This passage may of itself be considered as decisive against the doctrine of transubstantiation, which thus appears repugnant to the plain words of Scripture.

"This is the true God and eternal life" (1 John 5 : 20). The context shows that this refers to Jesus Christ, and is an unanswerable proof of his divinity.

3. When the words, the connection of the sentence, and the context, fail in removing all ambiguity, or in giving the

full meaning of the writer, it is then necessary that we look at the scope or design of the book itself, or of some large section, in which the words and expressions occur, and this can only be obtained by the repeated and continuous study of the books themselves. Sometimes the scope of a passage and that of the book are different.—*Angus.*

4. Compare Scripture with Scripture in passages containing the same *word* or *phrase* in similar sense, or speaking of the same thing, or having a like thought to justify a comparison.—*Angus.*

The need of comparing Scripture with Scripture is seen in the fact that the immediate connection of a passage is sometimes interrupted.

1. By digression or parenthesis. This is frequent in St. Paul's writings. Thus in Eph. 3 : 1-14, verses 2-13 are a digression ; the immediate connection of verse 1 is not with verse 2, but with verse 14.

2. By the division into verses and chapters. Thus Isaiah 9 : 8 to 10 : 4 is a distinct poem, having no connection with what goes before or follows. Also the subject of Isaiah 53 properly begins chapter 52 : 13 ; and chapter 51 ought to include the first twelve verses of chapter 52. The first three verses of the eighth chapter of Jeremiah ought not to have been separated from those of the preceding chapter. The sixth verse of the third chapter begins a distinct prophecy, which continues to the end of the sixth chapter.

Some critics consider Psalms 42 and 43 to be but one Psalm, and more than thirty manuscripts confirm this opinion. Obviously the first verse of the fourth chapter of the epistle to the Colossians ought to be joined to the third chapter ; and the fourth and fifth chapters of the second epistle to the Corinthians ought to be read together.

HELPS TO BIBLE STUDY. 53

The subject of the seventh chapter of the second book of Kings (the account of the siege of Samaria) is begun at the 24th verse of the sixth chapter; and the importance of attention to this appears from comparing 7 : 1 with the last verse of the sixth chapter. The gracious promise of deliverance was made by Elisha in reply to the impious declaration of Jehoram, "Why should I wait for the Lord any longer?"

The 21st and 22nd chapters of the Acts of the Apostles are closely connected with each other.

The first verse of the seventh chapter of 2 Corinthians should have been included in the sixth chapter, being the conclusion of the argument of the latter part of that chapter.

3. The books of Scripture, though written by different persons, and at different times, are so connected together, as parts of one system, that it is often necessary to bring together passages from various parts, before they can be properly understood. "They made a calf in Horeb" (Psa. 106 : 19), *i.e.*, it appears from Exodus 32, on the very spot where, and at the time when, God was taking them into covenant. "They worshipped the molten image," and that so soon after they had seen the terrible plagues inflicted on the Egyptians for their idolatry, and had in the most solemn manner pledged themselves against it. "But the ships were broken" (1 Kings 22 : 48). In 2 Chron. 20 : 35-37, the reason is stated; and the comparison of the two passages gives a practical illustration of the admonition, "If sinners entice thee, consent thou not;" for if we are partakers of other men's sins, we shall be also of their plagues.

From 2 Kings 9 : 26, it appears that Naboth's sons also were murdered by Jezebel. This is not recorded in 1 Kings 21.

By comparing Isaiah 6 : 1 with John 12 : 41, we find that Isaiah then saw the glory of Christ.

Acts 15 : 39. Why should Barnabas so warmly espouse the cause of Mark? Col. 4 : 10 tells us he was his nephew.

Matthew 11 : 28, compared with John 6 : 35, shows that by coming to Christ is meant believing on him.

"There was not one feeble person among their tribes" (Psa. 105 : 37). A very remarkable fact, but not mentioned in the narrative of their departure in Exodus, 12th chapter.

"Drink ye *all*," "They *all* drank" (Matt. 26 : 27 ; and Mark 14 : 23). That this command of Christ to receive the cup of the Lord extended to the laity, and was not confined to the apostles or priests, is proved by 1 Cor. 11 : 23-28. In six different passages, the eating of the bread and drinking of the cup are mentioned together by the inspired apostle ; and to all Christians indifferently he gives the same charge : " Let a man examine himself, and so let him eat of that bread and drink of that cup " (1 Cor. 11 : 28).

The history of Balaam affords an illustration of the importance of comparing Scripture with Scripture. In order to obtain a complete view of his character, we must turn not only to the narrative in the book of Numbers, but also to the 2nd epistle of St. Peter, where we are informed what motive influenced him ; and again to that of St. Jude, in order to see the deep hold which covetousness had upon him ; while the book of Revelation particularly draws our attention to a very remarkable fact concerning him, that it was at his instigation Balak threw that temptation in the way of the Israelites which caused the destruction of 23,000 of them in one day.

The disregard of this rule of comparing Scripture with Scripture, was one thing that led the Jews to reject Jesus as the Messiah, and even to justify that rejection by an appeal to Scripture. " We have heard out of the law that Christ abideth forever; and how sayest thou, The Son of man must be lifted up?" That Christ was to abide forever, they gathered from those passages of Scripture where his kingdom is represented to be everlasting, as Dan. 7 : 14; Ezek. 37 : 25; Isa. 9 : 7, and from God's promise to David, Psa. 89 : 36, 37. But had they also sufficiently attended to other passages, in which our blessed Lord is represented as a suffering Messiah, they would have had their scruples removed, and would have readily believed what he so frequently foretold concerning himself (see Psa. 22 : 18; 40 : 6; Isa. 53 : 2-12; Dan. 9 : 26).—*Nicholls.*

5. Study the circumstances in which a book was written.

6. Consider the relation of a given paragraph to the whole book.

7. Study the meaning of particular words and phrases.

8. Examine other statements of the same writer on the topic treated in a given passage.

9. Begin with the plainer passages, reserving the more obscure ones until greater skill is acquired.

10. Remember the responsibility that attends the right of private judgment.

CHAPTER III.

INTERPRETATION OF BIBLE TYPES, SYMBOLS, PARABLES, AND ALLEGORIES.

The following chapter is largely compiled from *Helps to the Study of the New Testament*, by Rev. W. F. Crafts; *The Mine Explored*, by Rev. B. E. Nicholls; *Hand-Book to the Bible*, by Dr. Angus, and from other sources.

RULES.

1. Ascertain what is the scope, either by reference to the context, or to parallel passages; and seize the one truth which the type or parable is intended to set forth, distinguishing it from all the other truths which border upon it, and let the parts of the parable which are explained be explained in harmony with this one truth.

2. Even of doctrines consistent with the design of the parable or type, no conclusion must be gathered from any part of either of them, which is inconsistent with the clearer revelations of divine truth.

3. It is important that neither types nor parables be made the first or sole source of Scripture doctrine. Doctrines otherwise proved may be further illustrated or confirmed by them, but we are not to gather doctrine exclusively or primarily from their representations. — *Angus*.

4. Guard against fanciful interpretations. For instance, the parable of the good Samaritan was obviously intended to illustrate the second great commandment of the law, "Thou shalt love thy neighbor as thyself." But it sometimes has been thus perverted: The good Samaritan has

been said to mean our blessed Lord ; the half-dead and wounded traveller, Adam and his sinful race; the priest and Levite, the moral and ceremonial law; the oil and wine, pardon and sanctification ; the two pence, the two ordinances of baptism and the Lord's supper; the inn, the Church ; the landlord, a pious minister of the Gospel, etc.

Such modes of interpretation are a dangerous departure from the simplicity of the Gospel. They have the effect of producing a morbid longing for what is ingenious rather than for what is true. While fancy is amused and self-conceit gratified, the practical instruction really intended is overlooked, and principles of interpretation sanctioned, which not only tend to make Scripture ridiculous in the eyes of the world, but shake the foundation of all truth ; giving the impression that the Scriptures have no definite meaning ; "making of anything," as Hooker says, "what it pleases, and bringing, in the end, all truth to nothing."

5. Never attempt to prove any point of doctrine or duty from single phrases or incidental circumstances.

From the circumstance of the rich man addressing Abraham, to infer the propriety of prayers to glorified saints is altogether unwarrantable. Throughout the whole of this awful parable, which sets before us in so striking a manner the danger of worldliness and of the neglect of duty, the state after death is described by images borrowed from the present life and from the objects of our senses; because by these means only can such subjects be brought down to our understanding. For instance, the expression that Lazarus was in Abraham's bosom refers to the Jewish mode of reclining at feasts. Three or more persons lay on one couch ; and the place of chief honor was that of the guest who lay in such a manner that he might repose his head on the bosom of the master of the feast. It was thus that St. John, at the Last Supper, "was leaning on Jesus' bosom." The mention, therefore, of this fact in the parable of which we are speaking, is intended to imply that Lazarus was received to a place of peculiar honor.

It sometimes happens that a parable contains circumstances which contribute to the general design of a speaker only so far as the drapery in a picture contributes to the general object of the painter. We must be careful, therefore, not to make a doctrinal application of circumstances which were only introduced in order to fill up the body of the narrative, or to give it ornament and variety. For instance, in the parable of the wicked husbandman, it is said, "They will reverence my son." No one for one moment imagines this to imply that God was ignorant of the actual reception which his Son would meet with from the Jews.

Matt. 25 : 1. We cannot infer from the parable of the ten virgins that, because five are represented as wise and five foolish, half of those who make a profession of religion will finally be saved, and half finally perish.

Luke 15 : 4. In the parable of the lost sheep, only one in a hundred went astray; in that of the ten pieces of silver, the proportion lost was one in ten; evidently showing that too much stress is not to be laid on every circumstance of a parable; otherwise the Bible may soon be made to contradict itself.

6. Consider carefully the design of the speaker (1 Kings 22 : 19-23). Micaiah's speech is parabolical; and several of the circumstances which are thrown into it are, in a great measure, ornamental, and designed only to illustrate the narrative. They are not, therefore, to be taken in a literal sense, but in such a manner as other parables are,

where the design of the speaker is chiefly to be considered; which in Micaiah's case was—to show that God justly punishes wicked men, when they obstinately refuse to hear him, permitting them to be deceived by the evil one to their own destruction (2 Thess. 2 : 11, 12).

Our Lord's design in the parable of the ten virgins is declared by him in Matt. 25 : 13 ; and his design in the parable of the lost sheep, the lost piece of money, and the prodigal son, may easily be inferred from the occasion which introduced them (see Luke 15 : 2).

Chrysostom remarks, "We ought not to lay too much stress upon single words and phrases. When we have learned the scope and design of the parable, we need not be anxious about anything but the moral or useful instruction principally intended thereby."

Luke 15 : 11. In the parable of the prodigal son we need not determine who are meant by the hired servants, or seek for any far-fetched spiritual interpretation of the ring, etc. As a part of the parable, the putting on the ring naturally expresses the prodigal's perfect restoration to all the privileges of a son, and so far falls in with the general scope of the parable ; but to pursue it further might be to pervert its meaning.

Luke 16 : 1. In the parable of the unjust steward, if we do not attend to the design of our Lord, we may feel a difficulty in the fact that he did not more pointedly condemn the man's injustice. " Hierom of old thought this parable was very obscure ; and Julian and other apostates, together with some of the heathen philosophers, took occasion from it to reproach the doctrine of Christ, as teaching and commanding acts of unrighteousness ; " whereas, by observing that the single point here is the *means* used for the attainment of the end, the whole difficulty vanishes; for it is evident that, in reference to the means which the unjust steward used, he showed a forethought well calculated to secure his end; and that in this single point of comparison, the children of this world are in their generation wiser than the children of light; that is, they better adapt their means to their end.

7. The sacred writers, and our Lord in his parables, sometimes argue with men on their own principles, rather than on what is true in fact.

Luke 15 : 7. The Pharisees were not really "just men, who needed no repentance," but they thought themselves so. Again, verse 25, the elder brother represents the Pharisees; but it is not true that they had served God, and never transgressed his commandment; or that to them, more than to others, belonged the privileges of God's people; but they thought so; and, upon their own principles, our blessed Lord shows how wrong was their opposition to those publicans and sinners who sought mercy at his hands (see also Luke 19 : 22).

8. It is important to consider the circumstances of those to whom the parable was immediately addressed, and in what sense it is probable that they would have understood it.

Our notion of the Pharisees, for instance, is that of very bad men, because the hypocrisy of their character has been so fully exposed by our Lord; but the notion a Jew had of them was just the contrary; and this must be our clew to the interpretation of the parable of the Pharisee and the publican, the design of which is to show that the only ground of justification before God, even for those whom we may consider the best of men, is the plea of mercy; that if we trust in our righteousness, though, like the Pharisee, we acknowledge it to be the gift of God, we shall go away from his presence unforgiven (Luke 18 : 9).

9. Some of our Lord's parables are prophetic.

That of the mustard seed foretells the spread of the Gospel from very small beginnings; that of the husbandman the malice of the Jews in putting Christ to death, and their consequent destruction; that of the sower is prophetic of the various effects which the Gospel produces upon the hearts of men; that of the tares, and that of the net, show that there will be a mixture of good and bad "in the field till the day of judgment." Our Lord's parables frequently point to the day of judgment; and "no doubt, other prophecies will then be discovered in them which are yet unregarded."

"All Scripture is profitable for conviction, conversion and culture." Bible similes, metaphors, allegories, parables, symbols and *types are, then, "profitable Scripture,"* not chaff, as superficial Christians have often intimated.

They are *abused* by pressing comparisons too far and too literally; by naming as *types*, that is, picture prophecies of the *future*, what are only *symbols*, that is, signs of *present* things; by fanciful rather than Scriptural interpretations; by making what is a good "illustration" into a counterfeit symbol or type; and by neglecting or excluding the Bible's own interpretations.

But these *abuses* should no more turn us aside from the prayerful study of these inspired hieroglyphics of truth than the abuses of other passages by Romanists and slaveholders should drive us from those portions of the Word.

Types and symbols have *uses* as well as abuses. As in other departments of knowledge, so in religion, we must learn the unseen by comparison with the seen, the unknown through the known, "first the natural, then that which is spiritual." It was necessary in the childhood of the church to use the analogies of God's visible world to teach the invisible truths of his Word, but it is no less necessary in reaching the children of to-day with divine light to use these or similar "likes" for advanced Christians as well as for those who are babes in spiritual knowledge. Few, if any, are so fully developed in Christian life that they do not need the symbols and types which Christ, as well as Moses, used in reaching through the eye and ear both cultured men, like Nicodemus, and unlettered hearers, like the woman of Samaria.

The New Testament gospel to-day is most deeply and richly understood by those who come to it by way of Genesis through the interpreting lights of types and symbols. Low views of Christ's atoning work are the natural result of a study of the New Testament gospels without a previous examination of the deep, blood-stained foundations in the Old Testament gospels of Moses and the prophets.

The types and symbols of Scripture have as distinct laws as other forms of language. There are laws for determining whether a passage is figurative or not that are often given about as follows: First, "If a phrase does not make sense when taken literally, it must be taken figuratively; and secondly, if the connection determines that the subject spoken of relates to visible objects and outward facts, then this imagery must be interpreted accordingly; but if the context determines the figurative phrase to refer to spiritual verities and facts, the imagery requires a corresponding spiritual interpretation."

Another law guides us in naming the figurative language.

HELPS TO BIBLE STUDY. 63

When a passage is found to be figurative—a simile, metaphor, allegory, parable, symbol or type—it should not be positively classed as a God-appointed "*symbol*" of present truth, or an inspired "type" of future things, unless it is distinctly called so in Scripture. In case of doubt it should be named an "illustration," thus avoiding controversy and uncertainty.

For the interpretation of Bible types and symbols the study of oriental customs, manners, literature and inscriptions, as found in Palestine, Assyria, Egypt and other eastern countries, gives fixed laws and principles nearly as clear as those which govern the translation of one language into another. The following table is the condensed results of such study, aided by scientific and thorough books, such as Atwater's *Sacred Tabernacle of the Hebrews*, VanLennep's *Bible Lands*, and *Symbolical Language of Scripture*, in Spottiswoodes' *Centenary Bible*.

I. SYMBOLISM OF NUMBER AND FORM.

Three, and also the three-sided figure, the triangle, △, represent Deity. The benediction was therefore anciently given with the thumb and two fingers extended and the others closed. The ascription, "Holy, Holy, Holy," is three times uttered. So deeply was the threefold personality of God impressed on the heart of man at the world's beginning that even heathen nations conceive of a trinity about their numerous idols.

Three seems also to be a symbol of earnestness (Matt. 26 : 44 ; 2 Cor. 12 : 8).

Four represents the kingdom of God on earth. A four-sided figure, either square or oblong, is the *monogram* of God's kingdom. Hence every part of the tabernacle and temple is four-sided—the ground plan, the walls, the roof,* the altars, the tables, the mercy seat, the laver, etc.

Seven, being the sum of "Three" (Deity) and "Four" (God's kingdom on earth), represents the union of the finite and infinite; any transaction or covenant in which both God and man are engaged or intimated. The God-man is symbolized by the seven golden candlesticks. The seventh day, seventh month, seventh year, and the year following seven groups of seven years, were all special times of God's blessings upon man.

On the seventh day of the seventh moon, a holy observance was ordained to the children of Israel, who feasted seven days and remained seven days in the tents. The seventh year was directed to be a Sabbath of rest for all things; and at the end of seven times seven years commenced the grand jubilee; every seventh year the land lay fallow; every seventh year there was a grand release from all debts, and bondmen were set free. From this law, for aught we know, may have originated the custom of binding young men to seven years' apprenticeship, and of punishing incorrigible offenders by transportation for seven, twice seven, or three times seven years.

Every seventh year the law was directed to be read to the people. Jacob served seven years for Rachel, and got Leah, and another seven years, and got Rachel. Noah had seven days' definite warning of the flood, and was commanded to take the fowls of the air into the ark by sevens, and the clean beasts by sevens. The ark touched the ground on the seventh month, and in seven days a dove was sent out, and again in seven days after.

The seven years of plenty and the seven years of famine

---

* Atwater on *The Sacred Tabernacle of the Hebrews*.

were foretold in Pharaoh's dream by the seven fat and the seven lean beasts, and the seven ears of full and the seven ears of blasted corn. Miriam was shut up seven days to be cleansed of her leprosy. The young animals were to remain with the dams seven days, and at the close of the seventh, to be taken away.

By the old law man was commanded to forgive his offending brother seven times; but Jesus, our lawgiver, extended his humility and forbearance to seventy times seven. "If Cain shall be revenged sevenfold, truly Lamech seventy times seven." In the destruction of Jericho, seven priests bore seven trumpets seven days. On the seventh they surrounded the walls seven times, and after the seventh time, the walls fell.

Balaam prepared seven bullocks and seven rams for a sacrifice; seven of Saul's sons were hanged to stay a famine. Laban pursued Jacob seven days' journey. Job's friends sat with him seven days and nights, and offered seven bullocks and seven rams as an atonement for their wickedness. David, in bringing up the ark, offered seven bullocks and seven rams. Elijah sent his servant seven times to look for the cloud; the ark of God remained with the Philistines seven months. Saul was ordered by Samuel to tarry at Gilgal seven days; the elders of Jabesh requested of Nahash, the Ammonite, seven days' respite. The men of Jabesh-Gilead fasted seven days for Saul. The Shunammite's son raised to life by Elisha, sneezed seven times. Hezekiah, in cleansing the temple, offered seven bullocks, and seven rams, and seven he-goats for a sin-offering. The children of Israel, when Hezekiah took away the strange altars, kept the feast of unleavened bread seven days.

Solomon was seven years in building the temple, at the

dedication of which he fasted seven days. In the tabernacle were seven lamps; seven days were appointed for an atonement upon the altar; and the priest's son was ordained to wear his father's garments seven days.

The children of Israel ate unleavened bread seven days. Abraham gave seven ewe lambs to Abimelech as a memorial for a well. Joseph mourned seven days for Jacob. The Rabbins say, God employed the power of answering this number to perfect the greatness of Samuel; his name answering the letters in the Hebrew word which signify seven; whence Hannah, his mother, in her thanks says, "that the barren had brought forth seven."

Solomon mentions seven things that God hates, and that the sluggard is wiser in his own conceit than seven men that can render a reason. The house of wisdom in Proverbs had seven pillars.

The elders of Israel were seventy; the blood was to be sprinkled before the altar seven times; Naaman was to be dipped seven times in the Jordan; Apuleius speaks of dipping the head seven times in the sea of purification. In all solemn rites of purgation, dedication and consecration, the oil or water was seven times sprinkled.

Out of Mary Magdalene were cast seven devils. The apostles chose seven deacons. Enoch, who was translated, was the seventh from Adam, and Jesus Christ the seventy-seventh in a direct line. Within the number are connected all the mysteries of Apocalypse revealed to the seven churches of Asia; there appeared seven golden candlesticks, and seven stars in the hand of him that was in the midst; seven lamps being the seven spirits of God, the book with the seven seals, the Lamb with seven horns and seven eyes, seven angels with seven seats, seven kings, seven thunders, seven thousand men slain, the dragon with seven heads and seven crowns, the beast with seven heads, seven angels bringing seven plagues in vials of wrath.

There are, also, numbered seven heavens, seven planets, seven stars, seven wise men, seven champions of Christendom, seven notes in music, seven primary colors. Perfection is likened to gold seven times purified in the fire. Anciently a child was not named before seven days old, not being counted fully to have life before that periodical day; the teeth sprung out in the seventh month, and are shed (renewed) in the seventh year, when infancy is changed into childhood.

At thrice seven years the faculties are developed, manhood commences, man becomes legally competent to all civil acts; at four times seven a man is in full possession of his strength; at five times seven he is fit for the business of the world; at six times seven he becomes grave and wise, or never; at seven times seven he is in his apogee, and from that day decays; at eight times seven he is in his first climacteric, or year of danger; at ten times seven, or three score years and ten, has, by the royal prophet, been pronounced the natural period of human life.

The seventh thousand years is believed by many to be the Sabbatical thousand, or millennium, and on the seventh day God rested from his labors, after creating the heavens and the earth. It is well to be conversant with "the times and seasons which God hath" revealed to us clearly, or more darkly and indefinitely, for a wise and good purpose; but let us not be wise above what is written. "Search the Scriptures," for in them duty and destiny are revealed.

Ten—used but seldom—represents completeness, as will

be seen by studying passages in the concordance under the word Ten—Ten Commandments, Ten Virgins, etc.

Twelve is the monogram number of God's Israel, first literal, then spiritual, *e.g.*, twelve patriarchs, twelve tribes, twelve spies, twelve apostles, etc., sometimes doubled into twenty-four (Ezek. 10:6-19; Rev. 4 : 4; 7:4-8; Matt. 19 : 28).

Forty was the symbol of probation and trial, and was thus used of Christ's forty days' temptation, and also of similar scenes in the life of Moses and others.

II. SYMBOLISM OF COLOR.

White represents purity and splendor, holiness and glory. Being a royal color during a part of the Bible times, it then represented kingship and priesthood combined, as in the Transfiguration, and also in the picture of the "kings and priests unto God " in heaven as clad in white robes. In the high priest's dress the white linen doubtless represented the glory and holiness of Christ, the great High Priest. Miss Sarah Smiley says : "This linen was not like ours, but the soft, silky, snowy, shining hysus. In Rev. 19 : 8, we find that it signifies the righteousness of saints." The pale, white horse symbolized death.

Blue represented heavenliness. It was the chromatic mark of heaven and of everything pertaining to it. Hence, when the Jews were told to wear as a badge (Num. 15 : 37-41) "a riband of blue " and to use it about the tabernacle, it was the ticket which indicated that their destination was "heaven," and that their thoughts and characters were to be heavenly while "pilgrims and strangers " on earth, seeking their home in heaven. The use of blue by the high priests indicated that Christ was to come down from heaven.

HELPS TO BIBLE STUDY. 69

It is this same association with the blue of the "heavens" that has led to the idea of *fidelity* as connected with a badge of blue. He who wears it as a temperance man, or in any other organization, pledges himself to be as *true* as heaven to his vows and not to *the* laws of heaven, and proclaims his citizenship in "the kingdom of heaven."

Purple, in a part of Bible times, was the symbol of kingliness (Dan. 5 : 7).

Scarlet,* the blood color, represented *life*, since "the life is in the blood." Hence all the references to atonement by "blood" mean atonement by the substitution of one life for another, the laying down of one life instead of another, as was done in all the ancient sacrifices, and last of all the Cross. "The scarlet thread" of Rahab represented the pledge of life which had been given to her, and besides, as the New Testament would indicate, some degree of "faith" in the Lamb of God, whose life should be given for her (Heb. 11 : 31).

Red sometimes pictured war and bloodshed.

Black, affliction.

The symbolism of color has been beautifully brought out in connection with the twelve colors of the heavenly wall, in Rev. 22 : 19, 20, by Mrs. Whitney in *Hitherto*, of which the following list is a compend :

1. Jasper (crimson), passion, suffering.
2. Sapphire (blue), truth, calm.
3. Chalcedony (white), purity.
4. Emerald (green), hope.

---

* In Isaiah 1 : 18, this word is used to represent merely fast colors, the most difficult to remove, and that passage and one in Revelation, about the "scarlet woman," are exceptions to the usage of other parts of the Bible.

5. Sardonyx (mixed color), tenderness and pain and purifying.
6. Sardius (blood red), love, including anguish.
7. Chrysolite (golden green), glory manifest.
8. Beryl (serenest blue), bliss.
9. Topaz (flame), joy of the Lord.
10. Chrysoprase (azure), peace that passeth understanding.
11. Jacinth (purple), } promises of future glory.
12. Amethyst (purple),

See! This crimson that lies at the beginning—it is the color of passion, suffering. Out of the crimson we climb into the blue—that is the truth and calm. Beyond is the white glistening chalcedony, for purity; and next flashes out the green - the hope of glory. Then they mingle and alternate—the tenderness and the pain and the purifying—it is the veined sardonyx stands for that—the life story.

III. SYMBOLISM OF MINERAL SUBSTANCES.

Salt represents preservation, incorruptibleness, unchangeableness. Hence to "eat salt" with a man, or "make a covenant of salt," that is, to eat food with him, was a pledge of unchangeable and enduring friendship.

Gold represents kingliness and power.

Silver, being the metal used in paying the "redemption money," was a symbol of redemption from sin.

Precious stones, of all kinds, represented rank and high privileges (Rev. 21; Mal. 3 : 17).

Brass seems to have represented enduring strength, as connected with Christ's sacrifice of himself. Also, sometimes, the endurance of obduracy.

Rock was the hieroglyphic and simile of strength, shelter (Psa. 18 : 2; Isa. 17 : 10); and of Christ as our strong refuge. A smitten or cleft rock typifies Christ's sufferings.

Brimstone, torture.

Iron, severity (Rev. 2 : 27).

IV. THE SYMBOLISM OF VEGETABLE SUBSTANCES.

Isa. 61 : 3 ; Psa. 1 : 1-3 ; 104 : 16 ; Gen. 49 : 22 ; Isa. 35 : 1, 2, 7 ; 41 ; 19 ; 61 : 11 ; Gal. 5 : 22, 23, are passages in which the prosperity of God's people and his cause are pictured by the general *prosperity of vegetation*. The *growth* of vegetation suggests spiritual growth (Isa. 55 : 10, 11). On the other hand, the weakness and adversity of those who oppose God's truth is pictured in *fading vegetation* (Jer. 8 : 13 ; Isa. 1 : 30 ; 38 : 4 ; Jude 1 : 12).

Branch, offspring (Isa. 11 : 1 ; Jer. 23 : 5 ; Zec. 3 : 8).

Cedar and *Acacia*, being the most enduring kinds of wood, represent continuance, eternity. The cedar also symbolizes strength (Can. 5 : 15 ; Psa. 92 : 12 ; Isa. 60 : 13 ; Hos. 14 : 5, 6) ; and hence also great men (Zec. 11 : 2 ; Isa. 2 : 13 ; Ezek. 17 : 4).

The *Palm* tree, or its branches, represents royalty, and also prosperity (Psa. 92 : 12 ; Rev. 7 : 9). The palm branches waved before Christ on Palm Sunday were a pictured way of saying "God save the King." The palm branches in the hands of the saints in glory mean the same as their white robes and crowns—that they are "kings unto God," and shall "reign with him" (Psa. 92 : 12 ; John 12 : 13).

Apple tree represents plainness, combined with fruitfulness (Can. 2 : 3).

Willow, sorrow (Psa. 137); also prosperity, by their rapid growth (Isa. 44 : 4).

Olive, cultivated, fatness and fruitfulness of Christians (Jud. 9 : 9; Psa. 52 : 8; Jer. 11 : 16; Rom. 11 : 24).

Wild Olive, man by nature (Rom. 11 : 17).

Oil, strength by anointing, and hence, the strength which comes through the Holy Spirit. Perfumed oil, "joy in the Holy Ghost." When the oil was *lighted* it represented the influence, knowledge and holiness that shines forth from the heart in which the Holy Spirit dwells. The wise virgins had oil in their lighted lamps, the Holy Spirit shining forth from their hearts, and so went in to the marriage supper—the joys of heaven. As there was an incessant preparing of the olive oil by the priest, so we must be continually taught of the Spirit.

Almonds, connected with the golden candlesticks, represented *life* as the source of light (John 1:4).

In Ecc. 12:5, the blossoms of the almond tree, which seem to be white, are made to represent the white hair of the aged.

Lily, beauty and prosperity (Hos. 14:5).

Hyssop, a plant having a very powerful aroma, purification (Psa. 51:7).

Shittim wood, probably Christ's lowly humanity.

Myrrh, grief.

Spices and perfumes, graces of Christianity.

Incense, the pleasure of God in receiving our prayers. It pictures also Christ's intercession. The horns of the altar of incense, being touched with blood (representing Christ) and fire (Holy Spirit), showed that prayer should be offered *through the Spirit* and *in the name of Christ*.

Corn and wine, being the two principal products of the

people of Palestine, symbolize all the fruits of a man's labors, physical, mental, and spiritual; and when offered in sacrifice, represent a thankful acknowledgment of God as a Creator and King, and also the dedication to his glory of all fruits of the worshipper's labors.

Bread, livelihood generally (Matt. 6:11); God's truth as brought in life and word by Christ to feed the soul (John 6:58).

Vine, usually the Church of God, sometimes yielding fruit of good works, and sometimes only wild grapes of wickedness (Psa. 80:8-14; Isa. 5:1; John 15:1; Hos. 14:7; Jer. 2:21; Isa. 5:1-7; Matt. 21:33-41). In general it represents luxuriant productiveness.

Pomegranates, a fruit made up of many parts, the law, many yet one.

Reed, weakness (Isa. 36:6.)

Root, usually humiliation (Isa. 53:23). Sometimes, however, origin, source.

Brambles, Briers, Thorns, Thistles, etc., *evil* influences (Judg. 9:7-15; Ezek. 2:6; Matt. 7:16-20; Gal. 5:19-21).

Husks, Chaff, Heath, the worthlessness and doom of evil (Psa. 1:4; Luke 15:16; Jer. 17:5, 6; 23-28; Isa.17:13; Job. 21:18; Matt. 3:12).

Grass is frequently referred to as a symbol of insignificance (Isa. 40:6; Psa. 103:15, 16; Jas. 1:11).

Leaves represent the outward appearance and signs of religion (Psa. 1:3; Rev. 22:2; Luke 3:9; Mark 11:14; Job. 15:30). Faded leaves picture the shortness of life (Isa. 1:30; 64:6; Jer. 8:13).

Ashes were put upon the head as a mark of sorrow. One sat in ashes to manifest grief. " The ashes of an heifer " which had been burned with her blood, represented the cleansing power of blood (Heb. 9 : 13, 14).

The Tree of Life represents the blessedness of piety. *Fruit*, the outward activities of life.

V. SYMBOLISM OF ANIMALS AND BIRDS.

Animals or Birds, used as food, when offered in *sacrifice*, represented food given to God, the altar being God's table, and the sweet savor of worship being received by God's heart as food; while the priest's eating of the sacrifice represented eating with God, and from his table (altar), as a friend restored to his favor by the sacrifice.

A *living animal or bird* represented the living owner. If offered alive, it showed the entire consecration and self-surrender of its owner; if slain, the owner's acknowledgment that he deserved to be executed for his sins, and his acceptance of a substitute to bear the penalty "in his stead." Christ as slain lamb (John 1 : 29 ; Rev. 1 : 18).

The animal substitute (the scapegoat) being sent into the wilderness, represented him that "*taketh away* the sin of the world." A bird or animal being set free, as in the case of one of the two birds in the leper's cleansing, symbolized the freedom of the redeemed person, whom the bird represented.

The *perfection of animals* for sacrifice, according to the requirement, " without blemish and without spot," symbolized not the worshipper, but the great, sinless Substitute, who, having no sin of his own to atone for, could take the place of those who had.

Wringing, plucking, breaking or *bruising* a sacrifice (whether animal or vegetable) represented Christ's sufferings (Isa. 53).

The Dove represented the gentle influences of the Holy Spirit, and *the Lamb* the meek and lowly qualities of Christ; which, when transferred to his followers, made them his flock of lambs (children), sheeplings (youth), and sheep (adults) (see John 21 : 15 ; Isa. 40 : 11).

The *ram skins and badger skins* on the outside of the tabernacle seem to represent the humiliation of Christ, who was " without form or comeliness."

Blood, the most vital part of the physical system, represented life, spiritual life more than physical. *Blood shed* for another, represented life sacrificed as a substitute. *Blood, sprinkled*, indicated new life imparted. Dean Stanley, in an article more fanciful than biblical, explains the meaning of " the blood of Christ," as used in the New Testament, to be " the love of Christ," but one needs only to try this interpretation in the passages where the " blood " occurs, to see that it utterly fails to make good sense, as it fails also to provide any way by which a guilty soul can escape from an awful past by the acceptance of a surety. " It is the blood that maketh the atonement, with the *life*."

The Eagle symbolized power, vision, and motion, in their highest forms.

The Lion indicated supreme *strength*.

The Ox represented *submission*.

When " Man," " Eagle," " Lion," and " Ox " are combined in one symbolic figure, it represents humanity raised to its highest cherubic perfection, its full and perfect life in glory. The " living creatures " in Revelation and Ezekiel represent this cherubic perfection of glorified humanity (Ezek. 1 : 5-25 ; Rev. 4 : 6-8 ; Heb. 9 : 5 ; Ps. 18 : 10).

The critics, who ridiculed the mothers for speaking of their " cherub boys " in heaven, it seems, were not warranted in their criticisms. The latest studies indicate that cherubim are glorified and perfected humanity (Rev. 5 : 8-11; 14 : 1-5; 4 : 6).

The Oxford Teachers' Bible gives the following additional symbolism of animals and insects :

Beast, tyrannical, usurping powers of men (Isa. 11 : 6-8; 2 Pet. 2 : 12 ; Dan. 7 : 3-7; 8 : 3-8; Rev. 13 : 2; 20 : 4).

Bear, foolhardy, ferocious enemy.

Bull, furious foes (Ps. 22 : 12).

Dog, uncleanness and apostasy (2 Pet. 2 : 22 ; Ps. 22 : 16; Isa. 56 : 10, 11 ; Phil. 3 : 2).

Crocodile, Egypt, anti-Christian power.

Goat, Macedonian power, Alexander, the wicked generally.

Horse, agent of war, symbol of worship of the sun (Zech. 1 : 8 ; Rev. 6 : 21).

Leopard, cruel, deceitful foe.

Lion, energy and dominion (Ps. 22 : 13 ; 1 Pet. 5 : 8 ; Rev. 5 : 5).

Locust, destruction, a divine scourge.

Bee, Assyria, a fierce invader.

Swine, impurity and gluttony (Matt. 7 : 6).

Horn, power, might (Ps. 32 : 17 ; Rev. 5 : 6 ; Ps. 92 : 10 ; Luke 1 : 69).

Fox, deception (Luke 13 : 32).

Wolf, a faithless minister (John 10 : 12).

VI. SYMBOLISM OF BUILDINGS AND STRUCTURES.

The Tabernacle symbolized the God-man, beautiful within, but uncomely without ; the God-man, who should bring the divine presence visibly near to men, and become the meeting-place of deity and humanity. John 1 : 14—"The Word became flesh, and *tabernacled among us.*"

The Temple also symbolized Christ embodied permanently on the earth in his Church (John 2 : 21 ; Eph. 2 : 21). *Jerusalem* itself and *Mount Zion,* through their connection with the temple, often represent the Church, both on earth and in heaven (Heb. 12 : 22).

The Temple Altars were God's tables.

The Temple Court represented the life of the unsaved ; separation from God through sin.

The Holy Place was the picture of Christian life, sending up its daily incense of prayer, shedding forth the light of spiritual influence, and feeding upon spiritual bread.

The Holy of Holies represents heaven, the kingdom of God perfected in us there, as it was in Christ.

The Veil represented Christ's flesh (Heb. 10 : 20).

The Mercy Seat pictures Christ also, especially as our Intercessor. Rom. 3 : 25—"propitiation" meaning "mercy seat."

The Ark itself undoubtedly represented Jesus Christ. " Its interior dimensions were so large that twelve ordinary men could be closely packed into it. God never wasted anything. Why was it so large, since it only contained the two tables of testimony, the pot of manna, and the rod that budded? Is it not a type of the great heart of Jesus, in which the law is kept?"

Door, when open, opportunity ; closed, opportunity lost.

Keys, stewardship, authority (Isa. 22 : 22 ; Rev. 1 : 18 ; Luke 11 : 52).

Gates, the seat of power (Ps. 9 : 13 ; Matt. 16 : 18).

VII. SYMBOLISM OF PERSONS.

The High Priest represented Christ as pure (in his white robes after his atonement for himself), pre-eminent, atoning for us, entered into heaven.

Priests were the symbol of all believers made "priests unto God."

Woman is the symbol of the Church (Jer. 6 : 2).

There are seven different aspects in which woman is viewed as a type of those whom Christ redeems. 1. Virgin (Ps. 45 : 14 ; 2 Cor. 11 : 2). 2. Betrothed (Hosea 2 : 19, 20). 3. Wife (Isa. 54 : 5 ; Jer. 3 : 14 ; Rev. 19 : 7 ; 21 : 9). 4. Mother (Gal. 4 : 26). 5. Widow (Isa. 54 : 4; Luke 18 : 3). 6. Desolate and forsaken (Isa. 49 : 21 ; 54 : 1). 7. Married again (Isa. 62 : 4).

Adultery pictured unfaithfulness to God in the Church (Matt. 12 : 39).

Daughter, the population of a city, as if the latter were a mother (Isa. 37 : 22 ; Jer. 8 : 21, 22 ; Ps. 45 : 12 ; 137 : 8).

The Oxford Teachers' Bible gives the following symbolism of the hands :—

Hands, symbolic of action ; *wash* h— freedom from moral guilt or ceremonial pollution ; *right* h— power, place of honor, friendship ; to *lift up* right hand, an oath ; to lift up both, an imprecation ; *imposition* of h— transmission of blessing, authority, spiritual influence, guilt.

Hand of God, chastisement.

Arm, power manifested (Isa. 51 : 9 ; 52 : 10 ; 53 : 1).

VIII. SYMBOLISM OF CUSTOMS AND MANNERS.

Shooting arrows indicates declaration of war and promise of conquest (1 Sam. 20 : 18-22 ; 2 Kings 13 : 15-19).

Eating together was an acted covenant of friendship.

Keys were a badge of authority, carried by persons of distinction and of high office in the regal governments of antiquity. It was a custom of the Jews to accompany and denote the taking of the office by the delivering of a key. "To confer a key" is a phrase equivalent to bestowing a situation of great trust and distinction.

Binding and loosing were terms in frequent use among the Jews, and meant bidding and forbidding, granting and refusing, declaring what was lawful or unlawful.

A *Girdle* put on indicated service, as when Christ girded himself to wash his disciples' feet (Luke 2 : 27 ; John 13 : 4, 5).

Putting anything on the shoulder was the symbol of authority.

Putting on sackcloth betokened sorrow.

IX. MISCELLANEOUS SYMBOLS.

Water symbolized the cleansing power of the Holy Spirit ; sometimes also, its joy, and sometimes the Bible (Hosea 14 : 5 ; Isa. 12 : 3 ; 35 : 7). *The Brazen Sea*, with twelve oxen beneath it ; three of them looking toward the East, three West, three North, and three South, represented the power of the Holy Spirit to cleanse all parts of the world.

A *Cloud*, especially "a bright cloud," when connected with a voice or worship, or miraculous help, represented God the Father ; sometimes means a multitude (Isa. 60 : 8 ; Jer. 4 : 13).

Fire, the cleansing power of the Holy Spirit, and also the holy wrath of God and the trials of affliction.

Light is a symbol of joy, especially joy in the Holy Ghost, and, also, of *truth*, the garment of Deity.

An Anchor is the symbol of hope.
Light, the divine presence, joy.
Babylon, an idolatrous, persecuting enemy.
Balance, justice, fair dealing.
Crown, authority, victory.
Light, joy (Ps. 112 : 4); foreknowledge (Eph. 5 : 8 ; 1 Thess. 5 : 5); outward influence for good (Matt. 5 : 14-16) ; purity (1 John 1 : 5 ; Ps. 37 : 6).
Dew, gentle, divine influence (Hosea 14 : 5 ; Ps. 110 : 3).
Rain, stronger divine influence (Isa. 55 : 10, 11).
Seal, security (Rev. 7 : 2-4).
Leaven, any diffusive, silent influence, bad or good (Matt. 13 : 33 ; 16 : 6 ; 1 Cor. 5 : 6-8).
Dust, human frailty (Job 13 : 12 ; Ps. 103 : 14).
Leprosy, } to God's eye sin is as loathsome as these to
Filthiness, } us.
Blindness, unbelief.
Chain, bondage, affliction (Lam. 3 : 7).
Circumcision, putting away sin (Phil. 3 : 3).
Cross, self-denial for the sake of others (Matt. 16 : 24) ; generally, the Christian religion (1 Cor. 1 : 17, 18 ; Gal. 5 : 11-24 ; 6 : 12-14 ; Phil. 3 : 18).
Day, an appointed time (Isa. 34 : 8 ; 63 : 4); a period (Rom. 13 : 12); a life (Job 14 : 6 ; John 11 : 9).
Cup, our portion in life.
Fire, God's wrath (Ps. 18 : 8 ; Jer. 48 : 45 ; Ezek. 22 : 21, 22); his purifying afflictions (Mal. 3 : 3).
Harvest, the consummation of all things (Matt. 9 : 37 ; John 4 : 35 ; Joel 3 : 13 ; Rev. 14 : 15); also present opportunity (Jer. 8 : 20 ; John 4 : 35).
Death, separation (Col. 3 : 3); separation from God (Rom. 5 : 6); insensibility to spiritual things (Matt. 8 : 22 ; Rev.

HELPS TO BIBLE STUDY. 81

3 : 1) ; second death, a future separation from God (Rev. 2 : 11).

Life, union with God (Col. 3 : 4 ; 1 John 5 : 11, 12).

Chariot, government and protection.

Girdle, when tightened, preparation for activity (Luke 12 : 35 ; 1 Pet. 1 : 13) ; when loosened, repose (Isa. 5 : 2).

Hunger and Thirst, intense desire (Matt. 5 : 6 ; Luke 1 : 53).

Incense, prayer (Ps. 141 : 2 ; Rev. 5 : 8).

It should be borne in mind, that in a type every circumstance is far from being typical ; for instance, the high priest, on the day of atonement, was eminently a type of Christ ; but we cannot infer from the high priest offering for his own sin, that therefore Christ partook of our sinful nature. The contrary is the fact.

INTERPRETATION OF PROPHECY.

The peculiarities of the prophetic Scriptures are, as to *time:*

1. The prophets often speak of things that belong to the remote future as if present to their view.

2. They speak of things future as past.

3. When the precise time of individual events was not revealed, the prophets describe them as continuous.

As to *language:* the whole is often described in figurative and allegorical or symbolic terms. If prophecy had everywhere consisted of literal description it would have defeated its object, and either have prevented the fulfilment, or have taken from the fulfilled prophecy all evidence of a divine original. Rules :

1. Let the student of prophecy ascertain the exact position of the prophet in relation both (1) to his age, and (2) to his predictions.

(1) Each prophet was a messenger to his own times. From the circumstances of his country he borrowed his imagery, and to the moral and physical condition of his country, as existing or as foreseen, he adapted his message.

(2) Ascertain also his standing-point in relation to his own predictions. Let the student also take his place, if possible, by the prophet's side, and look with him on the past and on the future.

2. Familiarize yourself with the language of prophecy— its figures and symbols.

3. It is a golden rule that, as prophecy is not "self-interpretative" (of private interpretation, 2 Pet. 1 : 20, 21), each of the predictions of Scripture must be compared with others on the same topic, and with history, both profane and inspired.

4. Mark the principles of prophetic interpretation sanctioned by the New Testament.

INTERPRETATION OF THE PRECEPTS OF SCRIPTURE.

To comprehend the full extent of the ten commandments, it will be requisite to observe the following rules:

1. When any sin is forbidden in them, the opposite duty is intended to be enjoined; and when any duty is enjoined, the opposite sin is forbidden.

2. When the highest degree of anything evil is prohibited, whatever is faulty in the same kind, though in a lower degree, is prohibited. This is illustrated by our Lord's interpretation of the sixth and seventh commandments (Matt. 5 : 22, 28).

3. Where one instance of virtuous behavior is commanded, every one that hath the same nature, and the

same reason for it, is understood to be commanded also. The command, "Honor thy father," etc., includes the duty of paying respect to all superiors—as magistrates, masters, etc.

4. When we are expected to abstain from any sin, we are expected to avoid, as far as we can, all temptations to it and occasions of it; and when we are expected to practise any virtue, we are expected to use all fit means that may better enable us to practise it.

5. All that we are bound to do ourselves, we are bound, on fitting occasions, to exhort and assist others to do, when it belongs to them; and all that we are bound not to do, we are to tempt nobody else to do, but keep them back from it as we have opportunity.

CHAPTER IV.

HELPS TO THE INTERPRETATION OF SCRIPTURE.

The following helps to the interpretation of Scripture will be found of great value:

1. Geography. Without a knowledge of ancient geography many fulfilled prophecies must be unintelligible. Thus: Balaam's wonderful prophecy of the conquests of Alexander and his successors, and of the Romans over the Assyrians and Jews, and of the destruction of the Macedonian and Roman empires, would be unintelligible to those who knew not that the family of Chittim, or Kittim (the son of Javan), settled in Macedonia and Italy; that Asshur refers to the Assyrians, and Eber to the Jews (Gen.

10 : 4). Sometimes, for a want of a knowledge of geography, the peculiar force and beauty of a passage of Scripture is lost to us. Thus: "Woe to the crown of pride" (Isa. 28 : 1). This city, beautifully situated on the top of a round hill, and surrounded immediately by a rich valley, and a circle of other hills beyond it, suggested the idea of a chaplet or wreath of flowers, worn upon the head on occasions of festivity. Thus the expressions of the proud crown and fading flowers of the drunkards add much to the force of the metaphor.

A knowledge of geography often removes apparent contradictions. In Luke 24 : 50—referring to our Lord's ascension—it is said, "Jesus led his disciples out as far as Bethany," etc.; but in Acts 1 : 2, we read that the disciples returned from Mount Olivet. Olivet was situated between Bethphage and Bethany, and our Lord ascended from that part of the mountain which lay next to Bethany. So that the two accounts are quite consistent.

A knowledge of geography enables us also to appreciate the minute accuracy of the historian. Thus (John 4 : 49) the nobleman, in an agony of mind, says, "Come down ere my child die," etc. The expression of his coming down to Capernaum is singularly illustrated by the present features of the country; for, in fact, the whole route from Cana, according to the position of the place now so called, is a continued descent toward Capernaum. The distance from Cana to Capernaum was about twenty-three miles.

Sometimes a knowledge of geography sheds a lustre on character, and suggests some important moral lessons. "Behold a man of Ethiopia," etc. (Acts 8 : 27), that is, African Ethiopia, lying below Egypt. Geography thus teaches us that this great officer of state had come from a great distance to worship at the temple. Ought trifling excuses, then, to keep us from the house of God?

2. *Natural History.* There are many allusions made in the Scriptures which can only be explained by some knowledge of the natural history of the countries of the East. In Gen. 49 : 14, Jacob compares Issachar to an ass. Now we attach to this the idea of slowness, stupidity and degradation; but, in the East, the idea of bodily strength and vigor is suggested by this resemblance : so that though we should say, a bridle for the horse and a whip for the ass, in the book of Proverbs it is said, " A whip for the horse and a bridle for the ass," the ass of Eastern countries going more freely than the horse. This also enables us better to understand the sublime description given in Job of the wild ass (Job 39 : 5, 8). To express the confidence of his faith in God under very trying circumstances, Habakkuk says, " He will make my feet like hind's feet," etc. (Hab. 3 : 19). The hart, or hind, is remarkably swift-footed, and able to walk with ease and safety on the dangerous cliffs of the steep rocks. See the same metaphor used in Psa. 18 : 33, which was written by David at the conclusion of his wars. It was employed also by Isaiah in a prophecy, of which we see a striking fulfilment in Acts 3 : 8, etc.

Jer. 8 : 7. The prophet, after upbraiding the Jews for their foolish and shameless apostasy, makes a beautiful allusion to that species of birds styled " birds of passage," the stork, the turtle, the crane and the swallow. They, by instinct, return annually at a set time to the country they had left ; whereas by all the reasoning and all the exhortation in the world, obdurate man cannot be prevailed upon to forsake his iniquity and return to God who made him.

1 Kings 17 : 6. A knowledge of the voracious habits of

the ravens strengthens the force of the miracle, their natural appetites having been so restrained that they brought meat to Elijah. Who can question the means which God possesses of providing for his creatures, when he sees the very ravens forget their own hunger, and bring food to Elijah? If our faith be not wanting to God, his care shall never be wanting to us.

3. Chronology. The science of computing and adjusting periods of time is called chronology; and on the application of this science depends, in a great measure, the advantage to be derived from history. The consideration of the time when one event happened, as compared with some other event, may be easily shown to be of great importance in the interpretation of Scripture. For instance, it is an awful aggravation of the guilt of Sodom and Gomorrah, not only that they were the descendants of holy Noah, but that when they had become so utterly wicked, Noah had probably not been dead one hundred years. Chronology teaches this.

1 Sam. 4:8. When from chronology we learn that this remark of the Philistines was made more than three hundred years after those plagues had been inflicted, it shows the deep impression which the miraculous facts of the Jewish history made on the surrounding nations.

2 Kings 23:13. The high places which Solomon built for Ashtaroth, etc., appear to have remained more than three hundred and fifty years. Solomon probably died a penitent; but chronology assists us to show in this instance, that they who introduce corruptions into religion know not how far they will reach, nor how long they will last.

"Honor the king" (1 Pet. 2:17). It adds to the force of this command to learn from chronology that the tyrant Nero was then the emperor of the Roman empire.

HELPS TO BIBLE STUDY. 87

4. Ancient profane history often affords assistance in the study of the Bible. Thus, Gen. 46 : 34, " Every shepherd is an abomination to the Egyptians." We learn from profane history (*i.e.*, from a fragment of Manetho, preserved by Josephus) that the Egyptians, about 2,159 years before the birth of Christ, had been invaded and subdued by a tribe of Cushite shepherds from Arabia, whose yoke they had not long before shaken off. Hence their prejudice against the family of Jacob, because they came from the neighborhood (Palestine) to which these shepherds had been driven. This fact may also serve, perhaps, to explain the accusation brought against the brothers of Joseph that they were spies, as well as the unwillingness of the Egyptians to eat with the Hebrews (Gen. 42 : 9, 31).

Thus the providence of God overruled oppression and prejudice, so as to make it a shield to his Church ; for by the patriarchs following a profession despised by the Egyptians, that evil communication was checked which might have immediately corrupted their manners, and plunged them into idolatry, and profane history assists us to discern this.

Archelaus (as we are informed by Josephus), immediately on succeeding his father Herod, caused the murder of three thousand Jews for having expressed their disapprobation of an act of his father's cruelty. This shows the reason of the fear expressed by Joseph (Matt. 2 : 22).

So again, the best commentary on Deut. 28, and our Lord's prophecy of the destruction of Jerusalem, is Josephus's history of the Jewish wars. Does not our Lord, for instance, say, " Thine enemies shall cast a trench about thee ? " etc. Josephus relates the literal fulfilment of this prophecy, telling us that Titus did thus surround Jerusalem with a trench and rampart of thirty-nine furlongs in length, with thirteen castles or forts, for the purpose of preventing the escape of the inhabitants, and that the utmost distress and misery arose from the famine which ensued. Josephus was a Jew, born at Jerusalem about A. D. 37, and the singular value of his testimony arises from these facts—that he was an eye-witness of the siege of Jerusalem; and that the truth of his account of it is attested by the Emperor Titus, under his own hand; and that he never embraced Christianity. When, therefore, he records anything that confirms the truth of the Gospel, he ought to be considered as a most impartial and independent witness.

"Then had the churches rest" (Acts 9:31). This rest cannot be attributed to the conversion of Saul, as the persecution continued three years after. But profane history enables us to account for it. The rest here mentioned corresponds exactly in time (A. D. 40) with the attempt which the Emperor Caligula made to set up his statue in the Holy of Holies. The consternation into which this threatened profanation of their temple threw the Jews, diverted their attention for a season even from that on which they were so intensely set, namely, the persecution of the Christian Church; and hence, the disciples had rest.

Acts 24:25. From the very surface of this narrative we see how much more anxious Paul was for the salvation of Felix's soul than for his own deliverance from prison and from death. Now Josephus tells us that Felix was notorious for oppression, and was living in adultery with Drusilla, who was the wife of a foreign king. This leads us yet more to admire the apostle; it illustrates the peculiar propriety of his reasoning of righteousness, temperance, etc., and it shows the delicacy as well as fidelity of his preaching, in his seeking to produce conviction of sin, not so much by upbraiding Felix for his iniquity, or charging him with unrighteousness, intemperance, etc., as by reasoning with him on the loveliness of those graces of which he was destitute.

5. *Ecclesiastical history*, of course, provides us with more illustrations of Scripture than are to be found in profane history. For instance, we should have a very inadequate conception of the extent to which the Gospel was preached by the apostles, had we only sacred history to appeal to, the Acts of the Apostles noticing scarcely any other travels than those of St. Paul, and evidently not all of his. But from other sources we learn that the Gospel was preached in Idumea, Syria and Mesopotamia, by Jude ; in Egypt, Marmarica, Mauritania, and other parts of Africa, by Simon, Mark and Jude ; in Ethiopia by Candaces' Eunuch and Matthias ; in Pontus, Galatia, and the neighboring parts of Asia, by Peter ; in the territories of the seven Asiatic churches, by John ; in Parthia, by Matthew ; in Scythia, by Philip and Andrew ; in the northern and western parts of Asia, by Bartholomew ; in Persia, by Simon and Jude ; in Media, Carmania, and several eastern parts, by Thomas ; in Italy (perhaps in Spain and Gaul, possibly even in Britain), by Paul, or some of his fellow-laborers. In many of these places churches were planted within thirty years after the death of Christ, a period nearly ten years earlier than the destruction of Jerusalem ; thus rapidly did this least of all seeds grow up and wax a great tree, and spread out its branches and fill the earth (Mark 4 : 31, 32).

Nor is this the greatest benefit to be derived from such a study. It may also enable us, on disputed points, to find out the opinions of good and wise men, who lived before such points had become subjects of controversy.

6. *Manners and customs of the Jews. Houses, roofs, etc.* "When thou buildest a new house, then thou shalt make a battlement," etc. (Deut. 22 : 8). Are we surprised that this should be the subject of a divine command ? A knowledge of the manners and customs of Eastern countries will explain it. The roofs of their houses were (as they are to this day) flat, and very much used for taking fresh air. It was on the roof of his palace, which commanded a view of Babylon, that Nebuchadnezzar uttered his boast, and heard the denunciation of heaven against it (see the marginal reading to Dan. 4 : 29). Here they enjoyed the cool, refreshing breezes of the evening, and conversed with one another. Here they offered up their devotions, as we see in the case of Peter. Ahaziah probably met with the accident which led to his death, by falling through an opening in the roof on which he was walking. From Nehemiah 8 : 16, we learn that the Feast of Tabernacles was kept by the people making themselves booths, every one upon the roof of his house. How needful, therefore, that the roof should have battlements !

In our Lord's prophecy of the destruction of Jerusalem (Matt. 13 : 15), to express the urgency of the danger and the necessity of immediate flight, he says : "Let him that is on the house-top not go down into the house, neither enter therein," etc. How, then, could he escape ? By the staircases on the outside, leading from the top of the house to the street.

Dress. The upper garment in Eastern countries was an oblong piece of cloth, square at the corners, having a hem or border all around. It was something like the plaid of a

Scotch Highlander, and was about five yards long by five feet wide. This, on ordinary occasions, they threw loosely over them ; but when setting out on a journey, or preparing for any work which required great exertion, they tucked it up with a girdle. Thus Elijah girded up his loins and ran before Ahab ; and thus Elisha, urging Gehazi to make haste, bid him gird up his loins and go. Girdles were usually much ornamented, so as to be an important article of traffic. This explains why Elijah and John the Baptist, whose peculiar offices called them in an especial manner to show abstraction from the world, are described as wearing leathern girdles, *i.e.*, girdles of the commonest kind, altogether unornamented. In Exodus 29 : 5, is an account of Aaron's girdle ; and in Acts 21 : 11-13, Paul's girdle is mentioned with a very affecting display of his ardent love to the Lord Jesus. In Eph. 6 : 14 is a figurative allusion to the military girdle—"girt about with truth," denoting that as the girdle to the soldier, so godly sincerity to the Christian affords both ornament and strength (see 2 Cor. 1 : 12 ; 1 Tim. 1 : 5, 19 ; Psa. 25 : 21).

When about to exert their strength by the use of their arm, they removed the heavy folds of this loose dress, and they thus laid the arm bare, or revealed it. This will explain such passages as the following : "The Lord hath made bare His holy arm ;" *i.e.*, hath discovered and put forth his great power which for a long time seemed to be hid and unemployed ; again, "To whom hath the arm of the Lord been revealed ?" *i.e.*, who observes that he is about to exert his power ? When this outer garment was thrown off, the persons were said to be "naked," though they had on an inner garment, or close bodied frock (1 Sam. 19 : 24 ; Isa. 20 : 2 ; Micah 1 : 8). It was the outer garment that our blessed Lord laid aside, when, the evening before his crucifixion, he gave that remarkable instance of his love for his apostles, which was to be to them both an example of humility and an emblem of his atonement (John 13 : 1-8).

In that most touching farewell which Paul took of the Ephesian elders, when, at parting, "they all wept sore," one of the solemn appeals which the apostle makes, as proving his sincerity, is that he had coveted no man's apparel; *i.e.*, no man's *clothes*. The force of this is lost, if we do not know that in the East an important part of a man's wealth is in the apparel, the changes of raiment which he possesses. This explains the metaphors used in Matt. 6 : 19 ; James 5 : 2 ; and Job 27 : 16. Changes of raiment are, therefore, among the most valued presents in the East (see Gen. 45 : 22 ; 2 Kings 5 : 22).

Jer. 36 : 23, 24. When Jehoiakim had showed the utmost contempt and defiance of God by cutting with a penknife and casting into the fire the prophecy against him, it is mentioned, as an awful proof of the hardness of their hearts, that he and his servants did not rend their garments. The meaning is, they gave not even any outward sign of sorrow, alarm or repentance ; because in Eastern countries, rending the garment is the usual mode of expressing such feelings.

Josh. 5 : 15. "Loose thy shoe from off thy foot, for the place is holy." This was the highest acknowledgment of the divine presence customary among Eastern nations.

Matt. 10 : 10 ; Mark 6 : 9. Our blessed Lord, when giving his first commission to his apostles, bids them take sandals, not shoes. A knowledge of Eastern customs is necessary to enable us to see the meaning and propriety of such a direction on so solemn an occasion. The sandal was only the sole of a shoe fixed to the bottom of the foot ; it was usually made of rough material, sometimes even of rushes or the bark of palm trees. Shoes, on the contrary, were made of leather, and were intended for more delicate use. This explanation will show the great moral lesson implied by this injunction; the spirit of which appears to be, "Go in the readiest, plainest manner. Do not be studious of ease; be self-denying, humble. Go as you are, depending on my providence for your protection, and upon my blessing for your reward."

7. Some knowledge of the ideas and opinions prevalent among the people to whom the inspired writings were addressed, or among surrounding nations, is often important.

The precepts of the sermon on the mount become more impressive from the following facts. The Pharisees held that the thoughts of the heart are never sinful (Matt. 5 : 28); the Scribes, that the gifts which Jewish worshippers were required to place upon the altar, expiated all offences which were not amenable to the judge (verse 24). All maintained, says Maimonides, that oaths by heaven or by earth might be taken collusively, and had not the solemn obligation of oaths in which the name of God occurred (verse 34). It was also maintained (Buxtorf) that the prayer which is long shall not return empty. For sources of information on the opinions of the ancient Jews, read the Targum and Talmud.

8. A knowledge of the religious opinions of the nations by whom the Israelites were surrounded, is also often useful.

The plagues of Egypt were all inflicted on objects of Egyptian worship, and thus they became a rebuke to idolatry as well as an evidence of divine power.

VARIOUS OTHER MANNERS AND CUSTOMS.

D'Arvieux gives a remarkable instance of an Arab who, having received a wound in his jaw, chose to hazard his life rather than suffer the surgeon to take off his beard. To have the beard plucked was considered a greater disgrace than it is among us to be publicly whipped and branded with a hot iron. This will explain various passages of Scripture (2. Sam. 10 : 4, 5 ; Isa. 7 : 20 ; 1 : 6), where the metaphor is used to express the utter contempt and detestation to which our blessed Lord, in love to sinful man, surrendered himself.

"Neither do men put new wine into old bottles" (Matt. 9 : 17). Why not? Because their bottles were made of skin, not glass, and hence, like those of the Gibeonites, might become rent (Josh. 9 : 13). "I am become like a bottle in the smoke" (Psa. 119 : 83). A leathern bottle thus placed would become shrivelled and useless, and in the same manner had sorrow so dried up the beauty and strength of the Psalmist that he seemed to himself to have become useless and despicable. "Put thou my tears into thy bottle" (Psa. 56 : 8). Mourners' tears were put into a bottle as a remembrance of affection. So David prays that God will remember his sorrow.

"Here is Elisha the son of Shaphat, which poured water on the hands of Elijah" (2 Kings 3 : 11). When Elisha was made the instrument of delivering three kings and their armies from destruction, he was introduced to them as one who had poured water on the hands of Elijah. In the East the hands are washed by the servant, who, while the master holds them over a basin, pours water upon them.

Hence the phrase denotes that Elisha had been the servant and disciple of Elijah.

"He that loveth oil shall not be rich" (Prov. 21 : 17). Why not? Oil was much used in rich feasts; it implies, therefore, that they who indulge in luxuries seldom become rich. "Often those who once could not live without dainties have come to want necessaries."

"They sat down at thy feet" (Deut. 33 : 3); *i.e.*, they received instruction from thee. So Isaiah, speaking of Abraham, says that God "called him to his foot." Martha had a sister "who also sat at Jesus' feet." Saul of Tarsus was "brought up at the feet of Gamaliel." Scholars in Eastern countries sat at the feet of their masters, and the place would remind them of the humility which became them as learners.

"Behold a woman . . . stood at his feet behind him weeping, and began to wash his feet with tears," etc. (Luke 7 : 37). How could the woman, while Jesus sat at meat, wash his feet when she was standing *behind* him? Because they did not sit, as we do, at table, but reclined with their feet on a couch, which is sometimes called in Scripture a bed : see the account of Ahasuerus' ostentatious feast. So also John is spoken of as leaning on Jesus' bosom. They used to lie so that the shoulders of one were turned toward the breast of the other; all their right hands were turned toward the dishes, and they leaned on their left shoulders.

"Thou shalt not muzzle the ox when he treadeth out the corn" (Deut. 25 : 4; 1 Cor. 9 : 9; 1 Tim. 5 : 18). We use a flail, but they turned in oxen on the barn floor to tread it out. The Moors and Arabs continue to tread out their corn in this way.

Isa. 32 : 20. The prophet, looking forward to the time of the Gospel, when the Spirit should be poured out from on high, says : " Blessed are ye that sow beside all waters, that send forth thither the feet of the ox and the ass." These expressions exactly answer to the manner of planting rice. While the earth is covered with water, they cause it to be trodden by oxen and asses, etc., and after the ground underneath has been thus prepared, they sprinkle the rice on the surface of the water.

" The grass, which to-day is and to-morrow is cast into the oven," etc. It is usual in Eastern countries to employ the stalks of flowers, myrtle, rosemary, etc., to heat their ovens. This affords a clear comment on the words of our Saviour, by which he so beautifully enforces repose on God's providence. The scarcity of fuel, especially wood, in most parts of the East, is so great that they supply it with everything capable of burning. Vine twigs are particularly mentioned as so used, and women and children are employed to gather them and lay them in store for use (see allusions to this in Isa. 27 : 11 ; John 15 : 6).

" Two women shall be grinding at the mill " (Matt. 24 : 41). In those countries, and in that age of the world, the immense advantage of employing wind and water for the turning of mills was unknown ; their corn was ground by a hand-mill, turned chiefly by female slaves. This shows the deep degradation imposed on Samson, and threatened to Babylon, " Come down," etc., " take the mill-stones and grind," etc. It was a *woman* who cast a piece of mill-stone upon Abimelech's head. They usually ground it at break of day, hence the noise of mill-stones was a token of a populous and thriving country (see, in reference to this, Jer.

25 : 10 ; Rev. 18 : 22). "The sound of the mill-stone shall be heard no more at all in thee."

"The smoking flax" (Matt. 12 : 20), *i.e.*, the wick of a candle newly lighted, or just ready to expire from want of oil. The Jews used flax as we do cotton for candles or lamps. Thus the Saviour encourages the first rising of holy desire in the young convert, and revives the dying graces of the returning sinner, persevering in his work of mercy till he bring them to heaven.

"Shake off the very dust" (Luke 9 : 5). We have an instance of their doing so at Antioch; thus expressing utter renunciation, so as to have nothing with them in common.

Jer. 36. That which in verse 18 is called a book, is in verse 23 called a roll. As they were ignorant of the art of printing, which was not discovered till 2,000 years afterward, their books consisted of pieces of parchment rolled upon two sticks (see Luke 4 : 17, where the Greek might more properly be translated, "unrolled the book ").

"And about the eleventh hour he went out . . . and saith unto them, Why stand ye here all the day idle ?" At eleven o'clock, according to our method of computing time, not half the day is gone ; but the Jews reckoned the hours from sunrise, making noon the sixth hour, and the time of sunset the twelfth hour, so that at the eleventh hour the day was nearly past. This fact adds to the force of Peter's reasoning, " seeing it is but the third hour of the day," that is, about nine o'clock in the morning. This was the ordinary time for their morning sacrifice and prayer, before which time they did not eat or drink anything. The earliest mention of hours in the sacred writings occurs in the prophecy of Daniel ; and as the Chaldeans, according to

Herodotus, were the inventors of this division of time, it is probable that the Jews derived their hour from them.

"Now there was darkness over all the land, from the sixth hour unto the ninth hour" (Matt. 27 : 45), *i.e.*, from noon till about three o'clock ; the passover being always kept at the full moon, this could not arise in the ordinary course of nature from an eclipse of the sun.

"And in the fourth watch of the night Jesus went unto them, walking on the sea" (Matt. 14 : 25), *i.e.*, in the last of the four divisions, and shortly before daybreak. The Jews originally divided the night into three watches : the *first*, or beginning of the watches, is mentioned in Lam. 2 : 19 ; the *middle* watch, in Judges 7 : 19 ; and the *morning* watch, in Exo. 14 : 24. But in the time of our Lord they had learned from the Romans to divide it into four watches; a practice which they still retain. See Mark 13 : 35, which contains a solemn admonition to be ever living in a state of preparation for death, from the suddenness with which it may overtake us. The four divisions of the night are here alluded to—the "even," the "midnight," the "cock-crowing" and the "morning."

Isa. 5 : 10. In God's awful denunciation against the covetousness of the Jews, it is said, " Ten acres of vineyard shall yield one bath, and the seed of an homer shall yield an ephah." A bath was about seven gallons and a half, so that an acre of land would not yield a gallon of wine. An ephah was but one-tenth of an homer ; so that instead of the seed yielding, as it often did in that fruitful country, a hundredfold, nine-tenths of the seed would be lost. Thus, vain is man's effort without God's blessing. 2 Kings 5 : 5, 16—" 6,000 pieces of gold," or, as the Arabic reads, " 6,000 shekels of gold." We see more fully the disinterestedness of

Elisha in rejecting Naaman's present when, by calculating, the amount appears to be, in modern currency, nearly or quite $50,000, and which formed only part of the property he had brought to obtain his cure. This was the "hour of temptation," which indeed proved fatal to Gehazi.

Matt. 18 : 23. Much light is thrown upon the parable of the debtors, by our knowledge of the fact that a talent is 750 ounces of silver. And according to Prideaux's computation the 10,000 talents referred to in this parable, if talents of gold, would amount to £72,000,000 sterling; an immense sum, showing the number and weight of our offences against God and our utter incapacity of making him any satisfaction, and marking, therefore, still more clearly the sin of not forgiving the small offences of our fellow-creatures.

Matt. 20 : 2. A Roman penny (or denarius) was equal to about fifteen cents of our money. This, by giving us the ordinary daily wages of an agricultural laborer at that time, enables us to form a better estimate of the relative value of money then and now : thus, "Why was not this ointment sold for three hundred pence?" etc., a sum equivalent to the wages of a laborer for 300 days, and certainly, therefore, sufficient to excite the covetousness of one who was content to betray the Son of God for thirty pieces of silver, not half that amount; for the thirty pieces of silver, or thirty shekels, were but fifteen or twenty dollars, the price that was paid for a slave when killed by a beast. How striking a fulfilment of the prophecy, "He is despised and rejected of men." What a motive to us to love him! (See 2 Cor. 8 : 9.)

ON THE DIFFICULTIES AND SEEMING CONTRADICTIONS
OF THE BIBLE.

Since so much knowledge is proved to be necessary to a right understanding of the Bible, we may easily believe that difficulties, or seeming contradictions, which occur to us in reading it, most probably arise from our ignorance or inattention; and this admits of abundant illustration.

"The Lord was with Judah, and he drave out the inhabitants of the mountains, but could not drive out the inhabitants of the valley, because they had chariots of iron" (Judges 1 : 19). Voltaire scoffs at this, as if it implied that the Lord of heaven and earth is represented as being baffled by the chariots of iron; whereas the term "he" refers to Judah, not to the Lord. Judah's faith failed him, and he found that according to his faith so was it unto him; weak in faith, he was weak in power. Yet Voltaire was one of the most acute of infidels. But the frivolity of such objections, made by such men, shows how hatred of the truth blinds the mind to the perception of it.

"Answer not a fool according to his folly" (Prov. 26 : 4). The next verse is, "Answer a fool according to his folly." But a little attention to the reason given in each case removes the seeming contradiction.

We ought not to answer a fool according to his folly so as to be like him; *i.e.*, so as to betray, in the manner of answering him, the same evil temper which he showed. This Moses did at Meribah; and David in his answer to Nabal; and the men of Judah and Israel in their disputes about David.

We ought to answer a fool according to his folly, lest he

be wise in his own conceit; *i.e.*, we ought to answer him in such a manner as to expose his folly. Thus Job answered his wife; and our blessed Lord's life affords abundant instances: as when he was attacked by the Scribes and Pharisees because his disciples transgressed the tradition of the elders; when they desired of him a sign from heaven; when they questioned the authority by which he acted; and when they inquired of him as to the lawfulness of giving tribute to Cæsar.

2 Kings 16:9. The king of Assyria is said to have "hearkened unto Ahaz," but in 2 Chron. 28:20, we read that he "distressed him, and strengthened him not." Both statements are true. He did help him against the king of Syria, took Damascus and delivered Ahaz from the power of the Syrians. But the service was of little value, for the Assyrian monarch did not assist Ahaz against the Edomites or Philistines; and he distressed him by taking the royal treasures and the treasures of the temple, and rendered him but little service for so great a sacrifice.

Acts 9:7. In the account of Paul's miraculous conversion, it is said that the men who journeyed with him "heard a voice, but saw no man." In Acts 22:9, it is said they heard not the voice of him that spoke. The Greek word translated "heard," very frequently means "understood." They heard a voice, but not the words spoken; they heard a sound, but did not understand the meaning of it: just as we are told that Israel beheld Joseph's sons, while a few verses after, it is said his eyes were dim, so that he could not see; *i.e.*, he could see, but not distinctly—could not distinguish the features unless they came near (Gen. 48:8, 10).

"Now this man (*i.e.*, Judas) purchased a field" (Acts

1 : 18), but St. Matthew tells us that the chief priests bought the field with the money which Judas threw down in the midst of them. Many commentators remark that an action is sometimes said in Scripture to be *done* by a person who was the *occasion* of doing it. Thus, in one place it is said that "Jesus baptized;" in another that "Jesus himself baptized not, but his disciples." The passages are easily reconciled; his disciples baptized by his authority, but he did not baptize with his own hands.

Acts 16 : 12. Luke, in relating the first introduction of Christianity into Europe, speaks of Philippi in Macedonia as the chief city of that part of Macedonia, and a colony; while the 21st verse implies that it was a Roman colony. The silence of contemporary profane history as to that fact rendered it a difficulty, even to learned men, and threw the suspicion of inaccuracy upon Luke's narrative; but some ancient coins have been since discovered, on which Philippi is recorded under this character, particularly one which states that Julius Cæsar himself bestowed on this city the dignity and privileges of a Roman colony, which were afterward confirmed and augmented by Augustus.

Sometimes, though comparatively seldom, the translation might be improved, or the original will admit of another rendering, and thus the difficulty might be removed.

The Hebrews express their numbers by letters, and some of their letters are very much alike; hence, as Dr. Kennicott has shown satisfactorily, some seeming contradictions with regard to numbers have arisen, from one number being inadvertently written instead of another.

2 Sam. 12 : 31. David is said to have put the Ammonites under saws and under harrows of iron, etc., which gives the impression of great cruelty on his part. Were

there no answer to this, we must not shrink from charging him with whatever guilt might properly attach to the act, the Bible itself furnishing the principle by which to do so. But the original Hebrew admits of its being rendered instead of "under," "to" saws, etc., which implies nothing more than employing them as slaves in the most mean and laborious offices. The word translated "harrows of iron" may also be rendered "iron mines." It is indeed said that David cut them with saws; but seven of the Hebrew manuscripts collated by Dr. Kennicott have the word which means "he put them to saws," etc.

CHAPTER V.

THE EXAMPLES OF SCRIPTURE.

One of the most important means by which the Scriptures instruct us, is the example of others. But some caution is necessary in the application. For instance: 1. The cases may not be parallel. 2 Kings 9 : 31. "Had Zimri peace who slew his master?" said Jezebel to Jehu, inferring from this that success could not attend his enterprises; but Jehu had a divine warrant, Zimri had not, and it may here be remarked that an express command from God alters the whole nature of the case, and of the action; as in the instances of Abraham offering up his son, and Joshua destroying the Canaanites

2. On some points of duty there was not that clear revelation of God's will under the patriarchal and Mosaic dispensations that there is under the Gospel. This, while it gives a greater eminence to the piety of some of the Old

Testament saints, accounts in a measure for the failure of duty in others under circumstances where the same conduct in us would be much more sinful. Polygamy appears to have been one of these points.

This remark naturally suggests another.

3. The characters of persons are to be estimated by the opportunities they possessed of knowing their duty (Matt. 8 : 10 ; 15 : 28). The guilt of Judas was much greater than that of Pilate, as we know from our Lord's own words, "Therefore he that delivered me unto thee hath the greater sin ;" nor can we infer from the pardon of the dying thief that we can safely defer repentance to a death-bed. Capernaum was more guilty than Sodom, and presents a solemn warning to all who possess religious privileges and do not improve them (Matt. 11 : 23).

4. We ought to trace every act up to its principle, and having done so, to apply this principle to our particular circumstances. In Gen. 21 : 9, it is stated that "Ishmael mocked Isaac." In Gal. 4 : 29, the principle is developed. It was persecution of him that was born after the Spirit, contempt of God's promises and mockery of true religion. The mocking of Elijah toward the priests of Baal was a holy rebuke of irreligion, by which he more effectually exposed the gross folly, as well as wickedness, of the idolatry of Baal. Elijah's conduct in commanding fire from heaven was not dictated by any revengeful feeling, but by a desire to convince a wicked prince and an idolatrous people that the Lord was the true God, and that He alone ought to be applied to in time of trouble. The zeal of John and James, on the contrary, was without knowledge, passionate, persecuting; though to them it might seem to spring from a just regard to their Lord.

5. The silence of Scripture in not condemning any particular act, as for instance, the massacre of the people of Jabesh-Gilead and David's deceit to Abimelech, can never be construed into an approbation or even palliation of the act; for the same volume elsewhere furnishes the principles on which such actions are to be condemned, and often shows their sinfulness by recording the evil consequences which arise from them—a remark which may be applied to polygamy.

6. Much instruction may be obtained by observing the conduct of individuals in particular cases, and by contrasting the behavior of different persons under similar circumstances. Take, for instance, the boldness of Micaiah and Jeremiah; the faithfulness of John the Baptist, constantly speaking the truth, boldly rebuking vice and patiently suffering for the truth's sake; the weeping of Elisha, of the Psalmist, of Jeremiah, of Paul, of our Lord—from which we learn that the wickedness of the ungodly should be a cause of grief and pity; the disobedience of Saul in sparing Agag, the king of the Amalekites, and that of Ahab in sparing Benhadad. The consequences in the two latter cases were remarkable; an Amalekite robbed Saul of his crown, and it was in battle with Benhadad that Ahab was killed. Again, contrast the conduct of Saul under reproof with that of Eli; the malice of Saul against his successor, David, with the kindness of Eli toward his successor, Samuel; the refusal of Peter, Paul and Barnabas, with the readiness of Herod to accept divine honors. The humility of John the Baptist, with the self-conceit of Simon Magnus, "giving out that he was some great one." The feelings of Ahaz when invaded by Rezin and Pekah, with those of his son Hezekiah when invaded by Sennacherib. The anger of

Jeroboam and Uzziah when reproved, with the submission and increased diligence of Jehoshaphat; the impatience of Moses, Elijah, Job and Jonah, who prayed that they might die, with the willingness of Paul to live and suffer. And, lastly, the repentance of Judas, with that of Peter. The one was worldly, the other was godly sorrow; love to Christ caused Peter to weep; remorse of conscience drove Judas to suicide. The different effects of a good and a bad conscience under the same outward circumstances appear by contrasting the conduct of Joseph's brethren with that of Paul and Silas when cast into prison. Compare also Isa. 57 : 20, 21, with 2 Cor. 1 : 12. By thus examining and contrasting the different conduct of different individuals, as given in the Holy Scriptures, we are able to obtain a better knowledge of human nature, and of our hearts and duties.

Note well (1) the particular examples given of the effects of God's grace. When it is said that "Enoch walked with God," this may be considered to contain the principle of all that is excellent in character. But in the Bible, facts are accumulated illustrating this principle; details are given which exhibit the graces imparted to men by the Spirit of God, under every variety of circumstance. The sacred historian passes by those which the world calls great events, and which are the usual subjects of history. While the mighty empires of Babylon and Nineveh, and the progress of the arts and sciences in Egypt, are overlooked by him, incidents in the lives of obscure individuals are recorded. Thus more is said about Abraham's servant than about Nimrod, the great conqueror, who built Babylon and Nineveh. Details of the domestic lives of Abraham, Isaac, Jacob, Naomi, and Ruth, etc., are presented to us, because in these are illustrated the effects of God's grace on the human heart under circumstances where we most need the illustration of it—as in the relations of parent, child, brother, husband and wife, mother-in-law and daughter-in-law, master and servant, and in the duties, temptations and afflictions which arise out of these relations. The character of Noah presents a bright example of perseverance in well-doing. He appears, as Bishop Horne remarks, like the lily among thorns, diffusing its sweetness in the desert—a light burning and shining amid the darkness of sin. In the character of Job we are taught patience; in that of Moses, meekness; in that of Caleb, decision. Hannah is a pattern to mothers; Samuel and Josiah, to children; Joseph, to young men; Barzillai, to the aged; Eliezer, of Damascus, to servants; Daniel, to those under authority. Nehemiah and Esther are objects of imitation for their patriotism; Jonathan, as a friend in his conduct toward David, and as a son in his conduct toward Saul. He did not forget what was due to his father, even when that father was unjustly seeking to destroy David. David's conduct to Saul shows us how to overcome evil with good. So that there is gradually presented to us, embodied in the example of some one recorded in the Bible, an illustration of every duty to which we are called. And this remark applies still more strongly to the New Testament, in which is presented to us the perfect example of our Lord, and in which we are exhorted, by the assistance of divine grace, to attain to all excellence by following the "blessed steps of his most holy life."

2. *The particular examples given of the cause and effects of sin.*

(1) The power of sin, even in the true servants of God. Observe the want of confidence in God displayed by the

father of the faithful—Abraham; the impatience of the most patient—Job; the irritability of the meekest—Moses; the grievous fall of him who had shown such early, long-tried and eminent devotion, and who was so distinguished a type of the Messiah—David; and, lastly, the idolatry of the wisest of men.

(2) The various forms of sin in the wicked. Thus we find envy in Joseph's brethren; hatred in Esau; malice in Saul; slander in Doeg and Ziba; contempt for God's ministers in Korah; sedition and rebellion in the demagogue Absalom, who "preached political freedom in the chains of moral bondage;" ambition in Abimelech; revenge in Athaliah; covetousness in Achan and Gehazi; pride in Nebuchadnezzar; neglect of warnings in his grandson Belshazzar; daring impiety in Pharaoh and Hiel, who, like Ahaz, trespassed yet more in their affliction. Adonijah is represented as a spoiled child, harassing his father when he most needed his comfort. Ahasuerus is capricious; Zedekiah, indecisive, consulting Jeremiah, but wanting resolution to follow his directions; Rehoboam is headstrong; Ahithophel, worldly wise; Johanan, hypocritical; Sanballat and Tobiah are scoffers; Joab appears as a brave soldier, and in many instances a faithful servant—in the taking of Rabbah, preferring David's glory to his own; not deserting him (when almost all others did) to join Absalom; fearlessly expostulating with David against the sin of numbering the people; yet "a doer of evil;" co-operating with David in the murder of Uriah; assassinating Abner and Amasa through jealousy of their merit and power; and, in direct opposition to the appointment of God, siding with Adonijah against Solomon. Jehoram, king of Israel, is found cleaving to the sin of Jeroboam, though he had put away the image of

Baal, and neglecting the advice of Elisha, though he was curious to hear of his miracles; while in another age of the Church, Herod feared the Baptist, and heard him gladly, although he refused to put away his brother's wife (Mark 6 : 16-20).

(3) The progress of sin; as in Saul and Amaziah. Contrast Saul's humility, his command of temper, and his spirit of forgiveness, with his wounded pride, his violence of temper, and his spirit of murder against David, Jonathan and the priests. Observe how deep, at one time, were his convictions, and yet he perished at last in his iniquity; and with regard to Amaziah (see 2 Chron. 25 : 2, 9, 10, 14-27). From these examples we may learn that no former acts of righteousness, no former sacrifices of self-interest for conscience' sake, will avail us as an excuse for indulging afterward in sin.

(4) The vain excuses made for the commission of sin, particularly by laying the blame on others; as in the case of Adam and Eve, Aaron, Ahab and Jehoram.

(5) The self-deceit which accompanies sin; as in David and Balaam. David showed a quick susceptibility to the injustice of others, while unconscious of his own far greater injustice; and Balaam expressed this pious wish, "Let me die the death of the righteous, and let my last end be like his," at the very moment when he was running greedily after the wages of unrighteousness; thus showing that men can think on the most solemn subjects without any change of life, and that passive impressions (that is, impressions not followed up by action) serve only to harden the heart.

(6) The prejudices which oppose the reception of truth; as in the conduct of Naaman toward Elisha, of the Scribes and Pharisees toward our Lord, of the Jews toward the

apostles, and of the Athenians and Ephesians toward Paul.

(7) The force of habit; as in Ahab, who humbled himself at the preaching of Elijah, and yet returned to idolatry; and in Felix, who trembled at the preaching of Paul, and yet did not give up his evil practices (Acts 24 : 25, 26).

(8) The corrupt motives of right conduct; as in Jehu destroying the prophets of Baal (2 Kings 10; see Hosea 1 : 4).

(9) The manner in which circumstances develop the human character and show how little men are acquainted with themselves; as in Hazael, when raised to the throne, and in Joash, king of Judah, after the death of his uncle, Jehoiada.

(10) The evil of ungodly connections; as in the case of Esau marrying with those who were under the curse of God; and in that of Solomon, whom "outlandish women" caused to sin. Jehoshaphat's connection with Ahab by the marriage of his son with Athaliah, nearly led to the destruction of his whole family; and if Ahab had not had Jezebel for his wife, he might never have been guilty of the murder of Naboth.

(11) The danger of worldly prosperity. That which should call forth gratitude and increased devotedness to God sometimes produces forgetfulness of him; as in the case of Rehoboam, Uzziah and Hezekiah.—*Nicholls.*

To make the truth taught in these examples (Scripture) complete, we must trace the evidence of their weakness. They failed in the very parts of their character which were strongest. Abraham through fear (Gen. 20 : 2); Job through impatience (Job 3 : 1); Moses through irritability and presumption (Deut. 32 : 51).

CHAPTER VI.

ANALYSIS OF THE BOOKS OF THE BIBLE.

Specific introductions to the books of the Bible are, as Bishop Percy has observed, "the best of commentaries, and frequently supersede the want of any. Like an intelligent guide, they direct the reader right at his first setting out, and thereby save him the trouble of much after inquiry; or, like a map of the country through which he is to travel, they give him a general view of his journey, and prevent his being afterwards bewildered and lost."

In the following analysis of the books of the Bible, we make no attempt to prove their genuineness and authenticity. We proceed on the firm grounded belief that the Scriptures are the Word of God. The reader will notice that the order pursued is not that of the Authorized Version, but a chronological arrangement, following to some extent the course of historical events.

For the greater part of the central and collateral truths contained in the following analysis of the books of the Bible we are indebted to that excellent work of Dr. Anderson, entitled, *Searching the Scriptures, in Order to Abiding Communion with God.*

GENESIS.

Written by Moses for the Hebrews. The contents of Genesis consist of history, covering a period of about 2,369 years, from the Creation to the death of Joseph. Up to chapter twelve we have the history of the world in general; then the early history of the chosen race, and establishment of a theocracy. From the first page of this book it has been truly said that a child may learn more in one hour than all the philosophers in the world learned without it in 1,000 years. This book is the foundation of all history, for we are indebted to the tenth chapter for all that we know about the origin of nations; yet it is remarkable how much larger a portion of it is occupied with the history of one family than with all other inhabitants of the earth. The object of the writer, under divine guidance, would seem to have been two-fold : one to solve the great problems which have perplexed men's minds, respecting the origin of things, and the existence of evil; and second, how the patriarchal church was grounded upon promise, and preserved the hope, in the woman's seed, of a predicted Redeemer.

Central and collateral truths in the book of Genesis :

THE ORIGIN OF THINGS.

Man's fall—Recovery—Covenant blessings.

This book abounds with lessons of trust, obedience, integrity, God's faithfulness and man's depravity, and shows how retribution surely follows deception and prevarication. This latter point is strikingly shown in Abraham, Isaac and Jacob, and in the treatment received by Joseph from Jacob's sons. Prevarication is twice shown in Abraham relative to his wife; once in Isaac, and several times in Jacob. Abraham and his wife, in the matter of Hagar, appear to have been in a hurry to secure the fulfilment of God's promise. God had not yet said that the seed should come through Sarah—only from Abraham. A foul temptation may have a plausible pretence. The dissimulation of Abraham is transmitted to his son Isaac; and in turn Isaac is deceived by the treachery of his wife and of his son Jacob.

In Genesis we have seven representative men. In Adam there is ruin; Abel, atonement; Noah, regeneration; Abraham, faith; Isaac, worship; Jacob, service; and in Joseph, glory. Here we have all the chain. The ruin is set off by the atonement, which leads to regeneration by faith, which begets sonship, and afterwards service and glory.

"Genesis centres about seven prominent persons in pairs, as types of the whole human race. 1st. Adam in connection with Eve, or human nature innocent, fallen, helpless, when the Lord God clothed them with coats of skins, which he made types of Christ and the Church. 2nd. Cain in connection with Abel, or the religion of Deism, opposed to redemption through the blood of Christ. 3rd. Enoch in connection with Noah, the former the type of the heavenly people translated before the judgments of the last days; the latter the type of the earthly saved remnant passing through the judgments. 4th. Abraham in connection with Lot, one walking by faith, and the other by sight. 5th. Ishmael and Isaac, or he that was born of the flesh persecuting him that was born of the Spirit; Isaac setting forth sonship. 6th. Esau and Jacob, or the flesh disowned and hated, while he that was elected by God's sovereign grace represents service and discipline. 7th. Joseph, rejected by his brethren, tells of suffering followed by glory in resurrection power, when the 'Saviour of the world,' as his Egyptian name signifies, received his Gentile bride, whose name means 'beauty.'"—*Brookes.*

"It is here recorded that the Deity, a being infinitely above all creatures, formed the world in the plenitude of his power, and that man, created upright, by transgression fell. Pantheism and the Manichean system, therefore, two

114   HELPS TO BIBLE STUDY.

original independent principles of good and evil, are repudiated by this narrative."—*Horne*.

Prophecies fulfilled.

Prophecies	Fulfilment.
Bondage of Abraham's descendants (Gen. 15 : 13).	(Gen. 46 : 3-7.)
Concerning Isaac (Gen. 18 : 10).	(Gen. 21 : 1.)

Biographies. Of the nine prominent biographies contained in this book, only three—Abel, Enoch and Joseph—are faultless. Joseph is a type of Christ—a most suitable biography for young men.

Joseph, it has justly been remarked, is a bright example in every relation. At the age of seventeen years he appears uncorrupted by the wickedness of his brethren, or the partiality of his father; discountenancing the sin of the former, and prompt in his obedience to the latter (37 : 2-13; 4 : 8, 11). Unjustly sold as a slave, he is faithful to his master (39 : 4-6). He flees youthful lust, although exposed to temptation (39 : 9). Persecuted, he, like Paul, finds in prison opportunities of usefulness (39 : 22 ; 40 : 7). Flattered by Pharaoh, he disclaims all ability of himself to interpret the dream, and avows before a heathen court the power of God (41 : 16). At the age of thirty he is suddenly raised to the highest dignity, and yet becomes a pattern of industry and justice (41 : 38; 46 : 48). Though a courtier, he is truthful, and with noble simplicity avows the disreputable employment of his connections (46 : 31-34). As a brother, he exhibits unabated affection, not only for Benjamin, but to those who had hated him (43 : 29, 30; 45 : 14; 44 : 18-34 ; 45 : 4-13). As a son, though lord of Egypt, he manifests the most affectionate regard for his aged parent, who was now dependent upon him (46 : 29; 47 : 7). As a father, his piety appears in the names he gave his children (41 : 41, 51, 52), and his earnest desire for God's blessing for them in bringing them to Jacob's dying bed (48 : 1). For eighty years he lived in the midst of the greatest worldly grandeur, surrounded with every temptation to worldliness and idolatry, but his dying breath testified how entirely his heart and treasure were in God's promises (50 : 25; Heb. 11 : 22 ; 1 John 5 : 4).—*Nicholls.*

Connection with other parts of the Scriptures. The book of Genesis may properly be called a foundational one ; it stands intimately connected with other books of Scripture. There is a remarkable correspondence between the books of Genesis and Revelation; the paradise of God, the tree of life, the river, the crown of sovereignty on man's brow, seen in the former, re-appearing in the latter, and the blessings lost in the first Adam are restored in the last Adam in the very order in which they disappeared. There are seven prophecies of a Redeemer in this book (3 : 15 ; 12 : 3 ; 18 : 18; 26 : 24 ; 28 : 14 ; 49 : 10).

Study the third chapter of Genesis, noting thirteen marks of the fall, and find a gospel remedy for each one, through the atonement of Jesus. Note, also, the ever-increasing downward tendency of those who indulge in sin, as indicated in Rom. 1st chapter.

JOB.

Supposed to have been written by Job ; while others attribute its authorship to Moses—notably the beginning and ending of the book.

The most probable opinion fixes the date of this book as earlier than Abraham. The arguments in support of this theory are: 1. The long life of Job, extending to 200 years. 2. The absence of any allusion to the Mosaic law, or the wonderful works of God toward Israel in their departure from the land of bondage, and their journey to Canaan, which are constantly referred to by other writers, as illustrating the character and government of Jehovah. 3. The absence of any reference to the destruction of Sodom and Gomorrah; which memorable event occurred in the vicinity where Job lived, and which, as a signal and direct judgment of the Almighty upon the wicked, would hardly have been omitted in an argument of this nature. 4. The worship of the sun and moon being the only form of idolatry mentioned, which was, without question, the most ancient (chapter 31:26-28). 5. The manners and customs described, which are those of the earliest patriarchs. 6. The religion of Job is of the same kind as that which prevailed among the patriarchs before the Mosaic economy. It is the religion of sacrifices; but without any officiating priest or sacred place. 7. To these arguments Dr. Hales has added one derived from astronomy, founded on chapters 9 : 9, and 38 : 31-32. He states that the principal stars there referred to, appear, by a retrograde calculation, to have been the cardinal constellations of spring and autumn, about B. C. 2130, or about 184 years before the birth of Abraham. 8. The most ancient kind of writing, by *sculpture*, is mentioned in Job 19 : 24. 9. The manner in which wealth is estimated, by *cattle* (43 : 12). 10. The slavish homage of prostration to princes, which prevailed from an early period in the East, was then unknown, no traces of such adoration being found in this book. 11. The most ancient species of idolatry is here mentioned, namely, Zebianism, or the worship of the sun and moon (31 : 26-28). 12. The language spoken by all the persons named in this book—Idumeans and Arabians—being *pure* Hebrew, we are referred on the question of its authorship to a period when this language had not yet branched into different dialects. The coincidences of names with some of the descendants of Ishmael and Esau, and supposed allusions to the destruction of Sodom (15 : 34 ; 28 : 15), are thought to refer to a date nearer the Exodus. The scientific and physical knowledge displayed in it, and references to artificial instruments of advanced civilization (41 : 7-13), have led some to assign it to the time of Solomon.

While agreement is nearly uniform, that the historical incident belongs to the patriarchal age, opinions differ as to the date of its composition. Assyrian tablets and monuments show that there were such animals and monsters known,—except the leviathan—and that astronomical knowledge was as far advanced as that displayed in the book of Job.

This book is interesting as containing the earliest record of patriarchal religion, as it was professed by one *not* probably of the seed of Abraham.

Central and collateral truths in the book of Job:

DIVINE DISCIPLINE.

Afflictions—Heart searchings—Rest in God.

Key thoughts: 1. The book of individual discipline for the learning of self. 2. "So God blessed the latter end of Job more than the beginning." Doctrines and lessons: 1. The Resurrection. 2. Repentance. 3. The Holy Spirit an active agent in the work of creation. 4. The personality and malice of Satan. 5. The world by wisdom knows not God. 6. The need of a daysman between God and sinners. 7. The unsearchable perfections of Jehovah. 8. "The end of the Lord, that the Lord is very pitiful, and of tender mercy." 9. "It is worthy of notice that if Job lived between the deluge and the call of Abraham, we have an additional proof that God has never left the world without witnesses to his truth. 10. Copy Elihu's humility, though able to speak best he spoke last. 11. Uncharitableness is of the devil (1 : 9, 10). Its origin, no less than its unloveliness, should put us on our guard against it. 12. What wisdom is needed to conduct controversy wisely, when even Job failed." 13. It teaches the innate depravity of the human heart, and the necessity of death to self and acquiescence in the divine will.

Prominent words in the book : "Almighty," "afflicted," "tongue."

Biographies. Eliphaz was of Teman in Idumea. This was originally the name of a prince of the posterity of Esau (Gen. 36 : 11-15). Bildad belonged to a people descended from Shuah, the last of the six sons of Keturah, the second wife of Abraham (Gen. 25). Zophar is called the Naamathite. Nothing further is said of his descent or place of abode. In their controversy with Job they uttered many deep truths, and some contradictory sentiments.

That Job is a real character is proved by the manner in which he is introduced by the prophet Ezekiel (14 : 14) and the apostle James (5 : 11). He was an inhabitant of Uz, in that part of Arabia bordering on Judea, and has been supposed to be descended from Uz, the eldest son of Nahor, Abraham's brother.

In Job we see the mighty power of grace to sustain the soul under the deepest afflictions. Behold his patience, his resignation and general integrity! But in the third chapter we see this eminent saint yields to impatience, and curses the day of his birth! How are we to reconcile this outburst of depravity with his previous profession and divine endorsement of his perfections? This difficulty may be met in two ways: 1. "Allowing his perfection to be evangelical—as in the Arminian balances—the divine indorsement was primarily announced; but afterwards he sinned, and gave place to impatience, and cursed his birth. Sanctified humanity is not impeccable.

2. "We deem it a better explanation to affirm that Job's perfection was a general indorsement of his moral standing. It was a perfection less than the *elimination of all depravity.* When Job cursed his birth he indisputably became sinfully impatient. It was an outburst of innate depravity. After this he did better; and God then indorsed him as more correct than his companion. Whoever undertakes to vindicate Job as being all the time a fully sanctified man undertakes a logical load that will break him down. We think it safer to limit Job's perfection to his age, *i.e.*, to the light —the dim light of the patriarchal dispensation. We do not like the common practice of referring to Old Testament samples to illustrate New Testament standard perfection." —*Rev. R. Gilbert.*

Connection with other parts of the Scriptures. The book of Job may be read in connection with Rom. 3 and Heb. 12: 1-14.

EXODUS.

Written by Moses for the Hebrews. "This book is divided into two parts—chapters 1-19, historical; and 20-40, legislative. It embraces the history of about 145 years, from the death of Joseph to the erection of the tabernacle in the wilderness of Sinai. The title of this book is peculiarly appropriate. Exodus means departure, and this book contains the account of the departure of the Israelites out from Egypt—an event which is the foundation of their whole history as a nation, and which is more frequently referred to than any other in their subsequent history."— *Nicholls*.

Central and collateral truths in the book of Exodus :

MAN'S REDEMPTION.

Bondage—Deliverance.

Key thoughts : The book of redemption types. The cruel bondage of sin. The mighty delivering power of God is manifested in the ten plagues and the crossing of the Red Sea. The tendency to speedy apostasy in human nature is shown (1) in the murmuring of the Israelites for water ; (2) then for bread ; (3) then for water again ; (4) and then making a golden calf, which led to the death of three thousand men. The success of importunate prayer is seen in the intercession of Moses for the Israelites. God must be obeyed. The superintending providence of God is shown in his care over Moses at his birth, his removal to Midian, and forty days' fasting on the mount.

" The many types of this book are fraught with lessons of the deepest significance. Turn to chapter 17 : 6 : ' Behold I will stand before thee there upon the rock in Horeb : and thou shalt smite the rock, and there shall come water out of it, that the people may drink.' Now turn to 1 Cor. 10 : 4, and get the New Testament interpretation of the above passage : ' They drank of that spiritual rock that followed them ; *and that rock was Christ.*'

"Manna is a type of the 'Bread which came down from heaven' (John 6:51), for nourishing the immortal soul. Moses was a type of Christ, in giving laws to the children of Israel."—*Cornell.*

"It is a remarkable circumstance that Christ, *our passover*, was sacrificed for us, and our deliverance from the bondage of sin completed, in the same month, and on the same day of the month, that the Israelites were delivered from the bondage of Egypt. Man did not intend this. Compare Matt. 26:5 with Acts 13:27."—*Nicholls.*

"There are more types of Christ in this book than in any other book of the Old Testament."—*Matthew Henry.*

"We think the leprous hand must signify in the antitype a regenerated life. We have no doubt but that the rod is a type of a thoroughly consecrated life; a life with all its occupations cast down at the feet of Jesus; then taken up again and used for him and his glory."—*Dr. Pentecost.*

The mixed multitude (Ex. 12:38) was composed of a multitude of Egyptians and others, not Israelites, who went out with Israel when Israel left Egypt. The lusting of this mixed multitude incited the people of Israel also to lust (Num. 11:4-7). At first (Ex. 15) all was well. It was something to be identified with this victorious people; but afterwards they rebelled and became a snare to the Israelites. Entire separation from all worldly associations is the only safe course for the people of God.

Promises or prophecies fulfilled. Here we have a fulfilment of the prophecy made to Abraham, that his seed should multiply and be afflicted 400 years, and in the fourth generation be delivered; also of a similar statement made by Joseph to his brethren.

Biographies. Moses—brought up in all the learning of

the Egyptians—renounced all his privileges and prospects to become the deliverer of his people; he had a clear call to his work, and forty years' training in Jethro's service; in temper very meek. Aaron—yielded to temptation and made a calf; his excuse for this sin was exceedingly shallow.

Connection with other parts of the Scriptures. The connection between the books of Genesis and Exodus is supplied in Exodus 1. Thus, at the close of Genesis, we have Jacob's family before us; and as Exodus takes up the history of Moses—a great grandson of Levi, who was Joseph's brother—we are at once informed as to our place chronologically at the opening of Exodus—about three generations, sixty to seventy years each (Matt. 1:17), or 200 years. This book gives deep spiritual light into many other parts of Scripture. There are forty-four references to this book by Christ and his apostles. The description of the plagues may be read in connection with Rev. 15:16; Israel's triumphant song with Rev. 15. From 2 Tim. 3:8, we learn that the magicians were Jannes and Jambres.

LEVITICUS.

Written by Moses for the Hebrews at Sinai. This is called the book of Leviticus, because it contains so much of the law, the administration of which was intrusted to the tribe of Levi; it consists almost wholly of words spoken by Jehovah from the tabernacle, and comprises the transactions of not more than a month. First, we have the offerings: 1. The burnt offering (Eph. 5:2); 2. The meat offering (John 4:34); 3. The peace offering (Eph. 2:14); 4. The sin offering, showing what man is (2 Cor. 5:21); 5. The trespass offering, showing what man does (1 Pet. 2:24); 6. The heave offering (Heb. 9 : 12) ; 7. The wave offering (Heb. 12 : 24; 1 : 7). Second, priestly consecration (8, 10). Third, separation unto the Lord (11, 12). Fourth, sinners cleansed and consecrated (13, 14). Fifth, "Be ye holy, for I am holy" (15-22). Sixth, the feasts : 1. The Sabbath (Heb. 4 : 9); 2. The passover (1 Cor. 5 : 7) ; 3. The firstfruits (1 Cor. 15 : 23) ; 4. Pentecost, (Acts 2), but evil present (Acts 5 : 1-10) ; 5. The trumpets (Mark 16 : 15, 16) ; 6. The atonement (Heb. 9 : 22) ; 7. The tabernacles (Titus 2 : 23). Seventh, looking on to the end (24-27), the last three chapters having been spoken in mount Sinai.

Central and collateral truths in the book of Leviticus :

ATONEMENT BY SACRIFICE.

Necessity of a Mediator—Worship and Service.

The Mosaic economy was pre-eminently one of physical and moral cleanness. God requires a clean people, inwardly and outwardly. Jehovah requires implicit obedience in all things. He shows us the absolute need of separation from all worldly alliances. The sacrifices were types of the great sin-bearer—"shadows of good things to come." The purity required of the Levitical priests teaches the necessity of holiness as the great qualification for those who minister in holy things. When a man swears to a thing concerning which he has been kept in ignorance, when he finds it out, he shall be guilty and shall confess it (chap. 5 : 4, 5). O ye members of masonic lodges, consider this ! Nadab and Abihu were slain for offering strange fire ! (chap. 10.) Take heed ! Aaron and his sons were not to drink wine nor strong drink when going into the tabernacle of the congregation (chap. 10 : 9).

Connection with other parts of the Scriptures. Leviticus

is closely connected with Exodus at its beginning and with Numbers at its close ; for while the order for consecration of priests is given in the former, the ceremony itself is recorded in Leviticus ; and the exemption of the Levites from the military service and their special functions are given in Numbers. The epistle to the Hebrews and this book are intimately connected. Hebrews, especially chapters 5 to 10, is a Bible commentary on this book. The 26th chap. should be read with Deut. 28th chap. The preservation of the Jews as a distinct people to this day is a living comment on chap. 26 : 4.

For whom is this book peculiarly suitable? Unbelievers in sanctification and total abstinence from strong drink should read this book.

NUMBERS.

Written by Moses for the Hebrews in the land of Moab. This book contains both law and history.

Called Numbers in the Septuagint and Vulgate, from the double census of the Israelites, covering a period of thirty-eight years. It is the wilderness book, recounting the trials, conflicts and sins of the way, and it admits the following divisions : First, preparation for the journey, every man numbered, knowing his pedigree, having his place and work assigned, responsible to maintain holiness, separated unto the Lord, and presenting offerings all seen in the light of the sanctuary, and all needing the blood of the passover and the guidance of the cloud (1-9). Second, on the march, but failure at every step, first of "the mixed multitude," then of God's people, then of the faith of Moses, then of Miriam and Aaron, then of the ten spies, then of the whole congregation, then of Korah, Dathan and Abiram, making the priesthood of Christ in resurrection fruitfulness very precious to God (10:18). Third, provision for failure along the desert road (19). Fourth, sin, the cross and victory (20-24). Fifth, mingling with the world, and its consequences (25). Sixth, renumbered; Simeon losing heavily, and directions given for the possession of the land (26-34). Seventh, the wilderness book closes with the cities of refuge and a marriage (35-36).—*Brookes.*

Chap. 24 : 17-19, contains a remarkable prophecy of Balaam. His prophecy of the star of Jacob points to the "bright and morning star" which, through the tender mercy of God, was to visit us; and his mention of the sceptre points to the spiritual kingdom of him who must reign till he has put all his enemies under his feet (1 Cor. 15 : 25).

Central and collateral truths in the book of Numbers :

MAN'S REBELLION.

Unbelief and Conflict.

Key thought : The book of wilderness walk and Israel's warfare. The awful results of discontent and murmuring are manifested when the Israelites complained, and a fire burnt among them ; when they lusted for flesh, and God destroyed many of the people while eating it; when they murmured against Moses for destroying Korah and his family, and 14,700 died of a plague; when they murmured about the way, and fiery serpents destroyed them. The fearful sin of unbelief is shown when they should have marched straight into Canaan, but were sent to march forty years in the wilderness, and to die there. Notice also the mischievous influence of the unbelieving report of the spies and their awful death. Of covetousness, as in the case of

Balaam. Of jealousy, as in the cases of Aaron, Miriam and Korah. Miriam becomes a leper, and Korah was destroyed. The damning power of *one* sin is strikingly seen in the case of Moses being shut out from Canaan for his transgression at Kadesh-barnea. The marvellous power of prayer is shown when Moses prays for Miriam to be healed; when Moses and Aaron plead for the Israelites (chap. 14), and their guilt was forgiven; when they plead that not all the congregation, in the matter of Korah, should be destroyed; when they plead for water at Kadesh-barnea, and when Moses prayed for their delivery from fiery serpents. God's priests must first be consecrated before they enter upon their work, as seen in the case of the Levites. Their consecration is similar to the pentecostal baptism of the apostles. The cloud and pillar of fire teach that God would have us move only when he leads. That God will supply all our needs is indicated in his caring for the temporal wants of the Israelites. Always victory when God is obeyed, as shown in the wonderful conquest of so many kings, and the taking of their property, by the Israelites. The case of the man who was stoned to death for gathering sticks on the Sabbath teaches the much-needed lesson of keeping holy that day. Those who are honored of God are often envied, as was Moses and Aaron.

Biographies. Moses manifested a want of faith as to *how* the Israelites were to be supplied with flesh. In Exodus 32:10 the Lord said he would make of Moses a great nation, and now in chap. 14:12 he repeats it. He sins by "speaking unadvisedly with his tongue" at Kadesh-barnea. His piety and meekness seen in the case of Eldad and Medad; in the case of his brother's and sister's sedition, and in the matter of the plague. He is warned of his death.

Aaron sins against God with his sister. It does not appear, however, that he was punished after he had confessed his sin to Moses. To stop murmuring and jealousy against him, God causes his rod to bud to let them know that he was really approved of God.

Balaam, a covetous man, causes the children of Israel to commit idolatry. He dies in battle.

Connection with other parts of the Scriptures. 1 Cor. 10 and Heb. 3 : 4 may be read with portions of the book of Numbers included between chaps. 11 and 26. This book throws much light on the doctrine of holiness. For an inspired practical comment on the history of the Israelites in the wilderness, see Psa. 78, 105, 136, and 1 Cor. 10. If you desire further to know what the wilderness means, you must read 3rd and 4th chapters of Heb., and there you will see that the wilderness life means a life of unbelief and sin. Turn further to Heb. 11, the whole forty years is left out of that recorded history of faith. O ye that plead for a wilderness state as the experience of justified souls, note this !

Fulfilment of prophecy. This book wonderfully displays the faithfulness of God in his promise to Abraham, that his seed should be as the stars of heaven. At the close of their journey their number was found to be scarcely less than when they went into the wilderness. They left that wilderness amounting to more than two millions.

For whom is this book peculiarly suitable ? For careless and disobedient professors of religion. For those who make light of sin. For those who are not obeying God by marching into the land of Canaan—*i.e.*, perfect love.

DEUTERONOMY.

Written by Moses for the Hebrews, in the land of Moab. Deuteronomy means the "law repeated"; and this fifth and last book of the Pentateuch is so called because it contains a repetition of the law, which was a second time delivered by Moses, with some omissions, additions and explanations. The additions are such as were peculiarly adapted to their state, when just entering the promised land. The explanations tend to illustrate the holiness of heart required by the Mosaic law. As the book of Leviticus would instruct them in the forms of their worship, so may this book be considered as instructing them in what spirit they should perform it. For instance, chap. 10 : 16 explains the spiritual intention of circumcision, that it has reference to the purifying of the heart from sin; and (compared with 30 : 6) taught them, while referring all holiness to God's grace, to look for that grace in the diligent use of every means appointed by God for imparting it. Compare chap. 10 : 16, and 30 : 6, with Phil. 2 : 12, 13. Though this book is chiefly a repetition of laws, it mentions some facts not recorded in either Numbers or Exodus (see 4 : 3, 4 ; 8 : 4 ; 29 : 5). The whole book may be said to embrace a history of about five weeks.

Central and collateral truths in the book of Deuteronomy :

CONSECRATION TO GOD.

Disobedience and Death—Obedience and Life.

Key thoughts : 1. The book of conduct for Canaan. 2. "Line upon line." Observe the very important use to be made of the prophetic ode of Moses—a portion of Scripture remarkably displaying the attributes of God. Observe also the prophecies uttered in this book concerning the Jewish nation; illustrating the moral use of prophecy—that is, the manner in which God presented the future before men, in order to influence their present conduct. Thus we see here foretold the success of the Israelites as consequent upon their obedience; God's blessing on their tribes; their apostasy and corruption; their punishments, dispersions and desolation; the idolatry and captivities of their kings; the rapid victories of the Romans, represented under the figure of an eagle, which was their standard; an enemy coming from the end of the earth, as in fact Vespasian and Adrian did, from Britain against Jerusalem; the miseries to be sustained by them when besieged (compare Deut. 28 : 52-58 with 2 Kings 6 : 28, 29 ; as also with the account which the Jewish historian Josephus gives of the taking of Jerusalem by the Romans, and their present conduct and condition, as exhibited to our own observation). This prophetic view of the whole history of the Jews, from their first redemption, after the Egyptian bondage, until their final conversion to Christianity, would not only prove a continual evidence to the Jews of the divine mission of their great law-giver, but is a confirmation of the inspiration of the Scriptures, and a most instructive display of the providence of God to every age of the Church.

Remarkable particulars contained in this book. 1. It was—with the obvious exception of the last chapter—not only written, but spoken by Moses to all Israel, immediately before his death. The peculiar propriety of so solemn an address appears, when we remember that the generation which had originally heard the law as delivered from Mount Sinai, with the exception of those under twenty years of age, had perished in the wilderness.

2. The general outlines of it, if not the whole book, were to be written upon stones, set up on their entering the promised land—a solemn memento of the terms on which alone they should retain possession of it (27 : 2, 3, 8).

3. The king—so far into futurity was Moses permitted to look therein!—was to write a copy of it with his own hand, and to read it all the days of his life (17 : 18, 19).

4. It was to be read publicly by the priests every seventh year, at the Feast of Tabernacles, in the hearing of all Israel (31 : 9-13).

5. It was by a reference to this book that our blessed Lord answered the suggestions of Satan; compare Matt. 4 : 4, 7, 10 with Deut. 8 : 3; 6 : 16, 13.

6. This law was to be *taught* by the parents *every day* to their children (6 : 7).

Connection with other parts of the Scriptures. This book is closely connected with, and is a sort of index to, all the preceding books of the Pentateuch. Compare chap. 18 : 15 with John 1 : 45; 6 : 14; Acts 3 : 22; 7 : 37. As the completion of the Mosaic dispensation, the advent of the Messiah is here more explicitly foretold than in the preceding books. The preparation which this prophecy made for the coming of Christ remarkably appears in the expectation of the Samaritans, who admitted no other books as inspired than those of the Pentateuch, but who to this day ground their expectation of the Messiah on this prophecy.

By comparing the law given in 21 : 22, 23, with Gal. 3 : 13, we find that it had a prophetic allusion to Christ, who was hanged on a tree and made a curse for us.

JOSHUA.

Supposed to have been written by Joshua—except a few verses describing his death—in Canaan, B. C. 1426 (chap. 24 : 26). There are evidences in the book of a different and much later hand (15 : 63). "The Jebusites dwell with the children of Judah at Jerusalem, unto this day." We learn from Judges 1 that this joint occupation of Jerusalem did not take place until after Joshua's death (verses 8-21).

Central and collateral truths in the book of Joshua:

THE REST OF FAITH.

Conflict—Faith and Victory.

Key thought: The book of warfare in Canaan. The evils of covetousness are vividly shown in the case of Achan. "It is remarkable," says Dr. Pentecost, "that the first sin that God signally punished upon the children of Israel entering Canaan was that of Achan, who coveted the wedge of gold and the goodly Babylonish garment; while the first sin that he punished after the descent of the Holy Spirit was that of Ananias and Sapphira, who kept back part of the price of their possession, while pretending to have given it all to the Lord." One sin hinders the work of God. Victory always follows obedience and faith. This is strikingly shown in the falling down of the walls of Jericho, and the slaying of thirty-one kings. In spiritual warfare God uses the most unlikely means, that the glory may be given to him. Read 1 Cor. 1 : 27-29. The crossing of the Jordan teaches utter death to self-life.

"The destruction of the Canaanites is a fearful admonition of the final issues of transgression at the great Day. Compared with the Israelites they were, probably, a disciplined, valiant people; but they seem to have made little effort to repel the invaders. Perhaps they trusted to the 'swellings of Jordan,' which at the time when Joshua entered Canaan —the vernal equinox—made the stream, as they supposed, impassable; or, perhaps, as one of their number expressed it, 'the terror of the God of the Hebrews' had fallen upon them. They were certainly fearfully wicked (Lev. 18 : 24-30; Deut. 9 : 4; 18 : 10-12). Their idolatry had, as idolatry ever does, augmented licentiousness and cruelty. The divine will they had once known, for they were descendants of Noah, and for centuries the light of an early revelation had lingered among them (Gen. 14). They had been warned—by the deluge, by the history of the cities of the plain, the destruction of Pharaoh, the recent overthrow of their eastern neighbors the Amorites, the passage of the Jordan, the capture of Jericho, the preservation of Rahab, and by the conviction of their own conscience. Their removal from Palestine, moreover, seems to have been essential for the preservation of the Israelites from the contaminating influence of idolatry, and they had the alternative of flight. In fact, many sailed to the distant shores of the Mediterranean, and there founded flourishing colonies, thus preserving to comparatively modern times, records of the God who fought against them. Some may object that the war in which they were exterminated was cruel, and that they might have been removed by famine or pestilence. To the *first* objection it is a sufficient reply that the cruelties thus practised were common to the age, and that in exterminating a very guilty people God did not direct milder usages than those which generally prevailed (Josh. 8). The *second* objection is answered by the fact that no plan could have made clearer or more impressive the power and righteousness of God, his infinite superiority to the idols of those nations, and his righteous hatred of the crimes which they had committed. It may be added, that by similar discipline the Israelites themselves were chastised. The general system involved in these events is strictly analogous to the course of moral government still exercised in the world; with this difference only, that *now*, men act as rods of God's anger by tacit permission; *then*, under his immediate authority."—*Angus*.

Prophecy fulfilled. The promise made by God to Abraham, Isaac and Jacob, that their seed should possess the promised land, is here fulfilled.

Biographies. Caleb, Joshua and Achan are the most prominent characters. The two former are noted for their faith and obedience. Joshua especially is characterized for his courage and fidelity. Notice the boldness of his faith in commanding the sun to stand still. Joshua is an instance of the remarkable influence which one holy man may be permitted to exercise over a whole nation.

Connection with other parts of the Scriptures. The book of Joshua is one of the most important writings of the Old Testament. It should never be separated from the Pentateuch, of which it is at once both continuation and completion. Between this book and the five books of Moses there is the same analogy as between the four Gospels and the Acts of the Apostles. Compare Joshua carefully with the epistles to the Ephesians and Colossians, and read them in connection with each other. The Red Sea shows what we are separated *from*, and answers to Rom. 6 : 7 ; the Jordan shows what we are separated *to*, and answers to Eph. 1 : 2, in the heavenlies now in Christ Jesus.

For whom is this book peculiarly suitable? For the

faint-hearted and "slow of heart to believe." Every "doubting Thomas" should read this book.

The phrases "be of good courage," "to this day," and "be strong," are of frequent occurrence in this book.

JUDGES.

It is not easy to determine on the authorship. It is probable that the earlier part was written by Samuel. The transposition of some of the chapters, as above given, is to meet the chronological order of historical events recorded. It comprises a period of about 300 years (or, according to the LXX—chronology quoted by Paul, Acts 13:20, 450 years). Seven periods of captivity, extending through 131 years, which God does not reckon in his chronology, as he takes note of time only when Israel are in his land, and seven prominent deliverers raised up to break the yoke of oppression.

The Judges here mentioned were not only magistrates, but some of them were prophets, and military chiefs, and avengers of the people. There were fourteen of these persons raised up, not in regular succession, but from time to time, to govern Israel, intermediate between Joshua and the kings.

Central and collateral truths in the book of Judges:

THE REST OF FAITH DISTURBED.

Idolatry and Defeat—Repentance and Deliverance.

Key thought: The book of failure in Canaan. *Retribution* is seen in the case of Adoni-bezek losing his thumbs and toes; in Abimelech, who was slain by throwing a piece of mill-stone upon him; and in the case of the Israelites' trouble and oppression for marrying into other nations, and for otherwise disobeying God. *The destructive power of sin* is shown in the slaughter of 40,000 Israelites, and all the tribe of Benjamin, except 600, as the result of the Gibeonites' sin. *That it is not mere numbers that win* is illustrated in the case of Gideon and his army, and in the singlehanded victories of Samson. Jephthah's case shows the folly of rash vows.

The book of Judges forms an important link in the history of the Israelites. "It furnishes us with a lively description of a fluctuating and unsettled nation—a striking picture of the disasters and dangers which prevailed without magistracy, when the highways were unoccupied, and travellers walked through by-ways; when a few prophets were appointed to control the people, and 'every one did that which was right in his own eyes.'"

"It exhibits the contests of true religion with superstition; and displays the beneficial effects which flow from the former, and the miseries of impiety. It is a remarkable history of the longsuffering of God toward the Israelites (Exodus 34 : 6 ; Ps. 103 : 13), in which we see the most signal instances of his justice and mercy alternately displayed. These things were written for our warning; none should *presume,* for God is just; none need *despair,* for God is merciful."—*Angus.*

The issue of worldly friendships. The league of the Israelites with the Canaanites issued in that people becoming thorns in their sides, and subjecting them to many grievous oppressions (chap. 2 : 3 ; 3 : 8, 14 ; 4 : 3 ; 6 : 2 ; 10 : 8 ; 13 : 1). Micah's sacrilegious agreement with Jonathan the Levite issued in the Levites robbing Micah of his ephod, etc. (18 : 20).

The Israelites, after the death of Gideon, remembered not the Lord their God, neither showed they kindness to the house of Gideon; thus instructing us that if a man casts off God he will soon cast off his friend, which is further seen in the case of Abimelech the usurper, and his friends the Shechemites. The blood of Gideon's sons is shed by the help of the Shechemites; the blood of the Shechemites is shed by Abimelech, who had thus employed them (9:24).

Samson's marriage feast with the Philistines was disgraced by fraud in his friend and treachery in his wife. His connection with Delilah is a yet more striking illustration of the fact "that the friendships which are begun in wickedness cannot stand" (see 2 Cor. 6:14-18).

Promises or prophecies fulfilled. The prophecy of the evils that should come on the Israelites, if they did not cast out the nations from the land, or if they went into idolatry, is here in part fulfilled.

Biographies. Those of Gideon, Jephthah and Samson are the most important. Samson's eyes were not put out till the Lord departed from him. The frequent retaliation of Samson on the Philistines, and his three times lying to Delilah and deceiving her, are worthy of serious consideration. On this point it should be borne in mind that these men—the Judges—sometimes acted under divine direction in executing judgment; for if this be lost sight of it will be impossible to approve of their conduct on some occasions. Some of them were called by God (3:9), and others elected by the people (11:5, 6).

Connection with other parts of the Scriptures. The books of Joshua and Judges bear the same relation to the four books of the Law that the Acts of the Apostles does to the four Gospels, but the former mark the decline of the Jewish, the latter records the progress of the Christian, Church. The corresponding Scripture in the New Testament is the second epistle to the Ephesians, Rev. 2:1-7; the seven churches in Asia answering in general to the seven stages of declension described in Judges.

Seven weak things in Judges:

Left hand..........	Judges 3:21	
The ox-goad	" 3:31	1 Cor. 1:27;
A woman..........	" 4:4	
A nail	" 4:21	
Piece of mill-stone..	" 9:53	
Pitcher and trumpet	" 7:20	2 Cor. 12:9.
Jawbone of an ass ..	" 15:16	

RUTH.

Supposed to have been written by Samuel, about the time when Gideon was called to be judge.

The book of Ruth contains the origin of David's family, and his descent from Judah. Compare chap. 4:18, with Gen. 38:29; Matt. 1:3.

It had been foretold to the Jews that the Messiah should be of the tribe of Judah; and it was afterward revealed further that he should be of the family of David. It was therefore necessary for the full understanding of these prophecies, that the history of the family of David in that tribe should be written before the prophecies were fulfilled, so that there might not be the least suspicion of fraud or design; and thus this book, these prophecies and the accomplishment of them, serve to illustrate and explain each other.

The events recorded took place in the time of the Judges (1:1), but the history was certainly written some time later

(4:7). Israel was grievously oppressed by the Midianites, who invaded the land, stripped them of their corn, and created an artificial famine; the only famine mentioned during the administration of the Judges.

This book comprises a period of ten years, and records the history of Ruth the Moabitess, who renounced her idolatry, married into an Israelitish family, and became united with the people of God. It traces the genealogy of David to a source not flattering to that sovereign; and this fact is one evidence of the truthfulness of the narrative.

Central and collateral truths contained in the book of Ruth:

THE SALVATION OF THE GENTILES.

The Bride—The Kinsman Redeemer—The Marriage— The Son.

Key thought: The book of typical prophecy, or godly households. This book, though brief, is remarkably rich in examples of faith, patience, industry and kindness. "It teaches the particular providence of God over our concerns; 'still out of seeming ill educing good.' Elimelech's misfortunes; his son's sin in marrying a Moabitess; the loss of her husband—all end in her own conversion, and in the honor of her adopted family. What changes ten years have produced! They have turned Naomi into Mara. She who went out full has come home again empty. Her fortitude and faith, however, sustain her; and in her trouble she shows equal wisdom and tenderness. When her daughters are told what they must expect if they accompany her to Canaan, Orpah weeps, but returns to her idols; and Ruth cleaves to her, indicating therein depth of affection and religious decision (1:16; 2;12). Her reward she received 'of the Lord God of Israel, under whose wings she came to trust.' Oh, the sure and bountiful payment of our God! Whoever forsook the Moab of this world for the true Israel, and did not at length rejoice in the change?"— *Brookes.*

The adoption into the line of the Messiah of Ruth, a Moabitess, seems also to be a preintimation of that great mystery, to be revealed under the Gospel, that the Gentiles should be fellow-heirs, and of the same body, and partakers of God's promises in Christ (Eph. 3 : 6-9). The pious amiability of Boaz, the pattern chief of a tribe, contrasts favorably with the prominent characters among the Judges— Abimelech, Jephthah and Samson. Learn further, that good people, like Naomi, may be very much afflicted for a time, yet God will be their comfort.

Connection with other parts of the Scriptures. This book may be considered as an appendix to the book of Judges, which precedes it, and an introduction to the two books of Samuel, which follow it ; as the chief subject of those books is David. Read this book in connection with Judges 6, 7, 8.

For whom is this book peculiarly suitable? For households generally. Mothers-in-law and daughters-in-law may learn much from this story.

Of the rich Boaz the Chaldee reads, *mighty in the law.* If he was both, it was a most rare and excellent conjunction ; to be mighty in wealth, and to be mighty in the Scriptures too, is to be mighty indeed. He was the grandson of Nashan, prince of Judah in the wilderness, and son of Salmon, probably a younger son, by Rahab, the harlot of Jericho.

140   HELPS TO BIBLE STUDY.

I. SAMUEL.

The first twenty-five chapters are supposed to have been written by Samuel, and the remainder by the prophets Nathan and Gad (see 1 Chron. 29 : 29).

This book comprises a period of about 115 years. This and the four succeeding books show God's dealings with his people under a monarchy. This volume contains the account of the change of government from judges to kings, to the death of Saul, who was the first of the kings.

Central and collateral truths in the first book of Samuel:

THEOCRATIC GOVERNMENT DISHONORED.

Saul—Disobedience—Rejection—Death.

Key thought: Royal government in the hands of Saul. His disobedience, rejection and death. God calls the young—*e.g.*, Samuel. Neglect of parents in punishing their children is a sore evil, and always results in calamity, as seen in Eli not restraining his sons. God may give us our requests, but trouble ensues. He gave the Israelites their request for a king, but he sent leanness into their soul (see Psalms). The ill government of Samuel's sons caused the Israelites to wish for a king ; so one sin leads to another. The evil result of impatience is seen in Saul offering sacrifice instead of waiting for Samuel. God's commands must be fully met ; partial obedience will not do, even though accompanied with sacrifices. We must not spare even the best, if God says destroy them, *e.g.*, Agag. God does not look merely upon the outward appearance—example, the selection of David from the sheepfold to be king over a great nation. Success does not depend on human might, but on faith in God, *e.g.*, David and Goliath. The envy of the human heart at the success and promotion of others beyond ourselves is shown in Saul hating David. David rises by pious, circumspect living. Through all the persecution of Saul toward David, he had the presence and help of Jonathan; so God always tempers good with evil. Those who have God on their side, as did David, are bound to prosper. When men are God-forsaken, though they resort to other means for help, as did Saul when he applied to the witch of Endor, they always miserably fail.

Promises or prophecies fulfilled. Death of Eli's sons (1 Sam. 2 : 34 ; 1 Sam. 4 : 11). Death of Saul (1 Sam. 28 : 19 ; 1 Sam. 31 : 42).

Biographies. Eli was good in the main, but neglected his duty in reproving his sons, for which he was severely punished by death. Samuel, a most admirable character, wise, upright, holy and unselfish. Observe his piety, his obedience to Eli, and his strict regard for the truth. He is earnest and persevering as a minister, leading men to repentance. As a judge he feared God, was unselfish, and always sought the good of others. He lived to the noblest of purposes—the glory of God and the good of his country. Saul made a good beginning, but came to a miserable end. David, led step by step by God, was obedient, successful and very merciful to Saul his enemy. He communed with God, behaved " wise as a serpent, and harmless as a dove." The sons of Eli and Samuel both did mischief, and caused others to do wrong.

Connection with other parts of the Scriptures. Many of the events recorded in this book shed light on the Psalms of David, with which they should be carefully read.

1. David's shepherd life (1 Sam. 16; Psa. 19 : 23).
2. David's victory over Goliath (1 Sam. 17 : 18; Psa. 8 : 9).

3. Saul's effort to capture David, in his own home (1 Sam. 19 : 11; Psa. 59).

4. Jonathan's warning (1 Sam. 20 : 35-42; Psa. 11 : 64).

5. David's flight to Ahimelech the priest (1 Sam. 21 : 1-9, etc.; Psa. 52).

6. David's flight to Gath (1 Sam. 21 : 11; Psa. 56 : 70).

7. Escape from Gath (1 Sam. 22 : 1; Psa. 34).

8. David in the cave of Adullam (1 Sam. 22 : 1, 2; Psa. 57, 13, 40, 141, 142).

9. In the forest of Hareth (1 Sam. 22 : 5; 23 : 14, 16; Psa. 63 : 17).

10. Escape from Keilah to the mountains of Ziph (1 Sam. 23 : 10-13; Psa. 31 : 54).

11. David sparing Saul (1 Sam. 24 : 1-16; Psa. 7). An appeal against Cush, who had slandered him to Saul, saying, "David seeketh thy hurt."

12. The cave of En-gedi (1 Sam. 23 : 29; Psa. 35 : 36).

13. Wilderness of Paran. Incident of Nabal (1 Sam. 25 ; Psa. 53). Nabal means fool.

14. Ziklag (1 Sam. 27; Psa. 16 : 38, 39).

This book discloses a grand display of Christ, who is (1 Sam. 2 : 10) for the first time in Scripture spoken of as the Messiah, or anointed, and also as a king, before that office was established among the Israelites.

"Who does not see," says St. Augustin, "that the spirit of Hannah prophesied of the Christian religion, the city of God, whose king and founder is Christ? This is, indeed, the chief import of the hymn." Compare Hannah's song with that of Mary (Luke 1 : 46, 55).

II. SAMUEL.

Comparing this book with the books of Kings, we judge the author to have written during a time when the Mosaic law was forgotten, as he betrays no displeasure at its infringement, by sacrificing in high places, as is done by the writer of the Kings.

The scope of the books of Samuel is to continue the history of Israel; and to show the reason of the governmental change into a monarchy from the theocracy.

1. David establishes himself at Jerusalem as the seat of government. 2. The subduing of the Philistines, Ammonites, Edomites, Amalekites and the Assyrians; extending his kingdom to the utmost bounds of the land, thus fulfilling the promise made to Abraham (Gen. 12 : 2).

Central and collateral truths in the second book of Samuel:

THEOCRATIC GOVERNMENT ACKNOWLEDGED.

David—Obedience—Acceptance—Life.

Key thought: The book of royal government in the hands of David. In this book there is a remarkable number of cases in which retribution followed sin, and the same measure meted back to the offender.

Abner kills Asahel, and Abner is killed for this deed. Baanah and Rechab slay Ish-bosheth, Saul's son, and David orders them to be slain for doing so. David causes the death of Uriah, and he loses his child by Bath-sheba and Absalom also. Absalom slays Amnon and Joab slays Absalom. David numbers the people, and 70,000 die; illustrating the divine statement, that "pride goeth before destruction." David is very careful to ask counsel of God before making war, or taking any important step. He returns good for evil, as seen in his treatment of Mephibosheth, and tenderness to Absalom his rebellious son. The most devoted are in danger of falling. The curse of God will rest down on a nation, if it has done wrong, until that wrong is repaired or repentance shown, as seen in God sending a famine for three years on the Israelites for Saul's slaying the Gibeonites.

Prophecies fulfilled. The prediction that God would punish David for his adultery by raising up evil against him from his own house. Also that his wives should be given unto his neighbor, who would lie with them in the sight of all Israel before the sun. This was fulfilled by Absalom. And so far as this book goes, we see the sword did not depart from his house, as God had said. This book confirms the divine origin of the Pentateuch, by pointing out the fulfilment of a prediction there given (Deut. 17 : 14, 15).

Connection with other parts of the Scriptures. This book, like the first volume, is a key to many of the Psalms.

1. David king at Hebron (2 Sam. 2 : 17 ; Psa. 26 : 101).
2. David king at Jerusalem (2 Sam. 5 : 6-25 ; Psa. 21, 108, 110).
3. The Ark brought to Jerusalem (2 Sam 7 ; Psa. 132, 15, 24, 94, 138, 29).
4. Wars of David with Edom, Syria, etc. (2 Sam. 8 ; Psa. 60, 61, 44, 20).
5. David's penitence for the "great transgression" (2 Sam. 11, etc. ; Psa. 51, 32, 6, 69, 103).
6. Absalom's rebellion (2 Sam. 15-18 ; Psa. 4, first evening of flight ; 3, next morning, also the two Psalms next mentioned; 5, 143, 26, 28, 61, 144, 62, 143, 42).
7. Ahithophel's treason (2 Sam. 15-18 ; Psa. 55, 41, 109).

8. Victory over Absalom (2 Sam. 18 ; Psa. 43). David's prayer at Mahanaim, while Joab fought with Absalom in the woods.

9. Sheba's rebellion (2 Sam. 20, 21 ; Psa. 2, 84).

10. David's review of his many victories (2 Sam. 22 ; Psa. 18).

This book is incomplete, and requires 1 Chron. chaps. 22-29, to supplement it. These chapters bring out incidents connected with making arrangements for building the temple which are not found elsewhere. The reader will readily see the connection.

By noting the dates as found in all reference Bibles, it will be seen that these chapters fill up an interim in the history chronologically. They form a complete historical chain, and fill up the space between the books of Samuel and the books which follow. . . . . . . These two books of Samuel have a close connection with what follows in Bible history.

For whom is this book peculiarly suitable? For those who wish to see the hand of God in the history of nations, individuals and churches.

PSALMS.

Composed at different times and collected and arranged by Ezra and his companions. The composition of the Psalms extends over 1000 years of the national life, from Moses to Malachi, in which Hebrew history is set to music. The Psalms, both in the Hebrew and in the Septuagint, are divided into five books, and the close of each is indicated by a doxology; viz., Psalms 41:13; 72:18-20; 89:52; 106:48; 150:6. Book 1. Christ in covenant relation to his people, walking in communion, though in the midst of trials. Jehovah—the covenant title in redemption—occurring more than 270 times. God—creation title—not fifty times. Book 2. Christ in connection with his people, viewed as out of the land. Jehovah, occurring about thirty times, and God more than 200 times. Book 3. Christ in connection with Israel from the beginning of their history. Jehovah occurring about fifty times, and God about sixty times. Book 4. Christ coming to take the kingdom and to bless the Gentiles; the progress and results of his advent being celebrated. Jehovah occurring more than one hundred times, and God about twenty times. Book 5. Christ ruling over all, to prepare the Jews for his earthly reign. Jehovah occurring more than 230 times, and God about thirty times.

One of these Psalms was composed 1500 B. C. They describe largely in prophecy the inner life of the Lord Jesus Christ. Unless this fact is kept constantly in view, they cannot be read intelligently. Of the seventy-five quotations from the Psalms found in the New Testament, more than fifty represent Christ as the speaker, or are directly applied to him, while he himself affirms that he is the theme of their testimony (Luke 24 : 44 ; John 5 : 39).

In some of the Psalms David utters bitter curses against his enemies. The most remarkable in this respect are Psalms 69 and 109; but these, Peter applies as prophecies fulfilled in the punishment of Judas and of the Jews. This teaches us that we are to understand curses contained in the Psalms as threatenings uttered, or judgments foretold, by a prophet of God, against hardened and finally impenitent sinners; and that the feeling with which we should repeat them should be an awful sense of God's holiness and justice in the punishment of sin.

For a complete classification of the Psalms the reader is

referred to Townsend's *Harmony of the Old Testament*, and to Angus' *Hand-book of the Bible*. This book (Psalms) is valuable as supplying additional scraps of history unrecorded in other books.

Central and collateral truths in the book of Psalms:

EXPERIMENTAL RELIGION.

David—Sin and sorrow—Grace and triumph.

Key thought: The book of experimental holy song and Messianic prophecy. The following titles—of special Psalms —point out the leading idea of each: Psa. 1. Photograph of a happy life. 2. Messiah the Prince. 4. Evening hymn. 5. Morning hymn. 8. Song of the Astronomer. 12. Good thoughts for bad times. 19. Creation and redemption anthem. 22. The Psalm of the Cross. 23. Heavenly pastoral. 24. Ascension anthem. 45. Brief form of Song of Solomon. 46. Luther's Psalm. 62. The "only" Psalm. 70. Poor man's memorial. 90. Dirge for dying humanity. 98. Coronation. 103. A Bible in itself. 104. Hemboldt says of this Psalm, that it is the finest description of nature to be found.

Prominent words in this book: "Praise," "joy," "affliction," "deliver," "keep," "wait," "mercy," "prayer," "peace," "refuge," "tongue" and "trust."

For whom is this book peculiarly suitable? Specially for the saint. It is an epitome of the Bible adapted to the purposes of devotion. In the language of this book the prayers of the Church have been offered up from age to age.

How to be interpreted. "In studying the Psalms, two rules of interpretation are of prime importance: first, ascertain the author, the historical origin, and the obvious scope of the psalm; second, carefully consider the historical meaning of its terms and allusions, and ascertain from New Testament quotations, or from the general tenor of the Gospel, how it is to be applied, either to Christ or the Christian Church. Though, perhaps, every psalm is connected in its origin and allusions with an economy which was 'to vanish away,' all are no less closely connected in sentiment and applicability to the economy that 'abideth.' Wisely studied, the whole book may be made our own, and become to us the expression of the holiest feelings in the purest form."—*Angus*

THE TWO BOOKS OF KINGS.

Written by the high priests, or scribes and recorders, who were contemporary with the events (2 Sam. 8:17; 2 Kings 18:18). Who these successive writers were, we are informed in 2 Chron. 9:29, where we read, "The acts of Solomon, are they not recorded in the book of Nathan the prophet, and in the prophecy of Abijah, the Shilonite, and in the visions of Iddo the seer?" By Jewish tradition the writing of these books is ascribed to Jeremiah. This is favored by internal evidence, there being a very marked resemblance between the latter portion of 2 Kings—in the incidents of which Jeremiah was a participator—and the corresponding narratives in the book which bears his name, and in which some of the events are described more fully (compare 2 Kings 25:22 and Jer. 43:7). The view, that the two books of Kings were drawn up from various documents by one hand, is confirmed by the books themselves. This reviser was probably Ezra or Jeremiah.

The two books of Kings form but one book in the Jewish canon. They contain the records of the Hebrew nation from the accession of Solomon to the destruction of Jeru-

HELPS TO BIBLE STUDY. 149

salem. Angus says, twenty-six years after. They comprise a period of about 426 years; also several prophetic utterances. The writings of the prophets who lived before and during the captivity receive much elucidation from the contents of the two books themselves. The *first book of Kings* comprises the history of the Israelites for about one hundred and twenty-six years, and consists of two distinct and separate portions; the first relating to the history of the undivided kingdom under Solomon, and the second the history of the two separate kingdoms of Judah and Israel for about eighty years.

"The text of Samuel, Kings and Chronicles is in a worse condition than that of any other of the inspired writings. We must not, however, ascribe to the authors what is really due to the errors of the copyists."—*Angus.*

Both books contain several prophecies that are quoted by our Lord and the writers of the New Testament as canonical (see Luke 4 : 25-27 ; Jas. 5 : 17). Note the subjugation and removal by Assyria of the ten tribes, one hundred and thirty-four years before the overthrow of Judah. They embrace a period of four hundred and twenty-seven years.

Central and collateral truths in the first book of Kings, 1 to 11 :

THEOCRATIC GOVERNMENT ACKNOWLEDGED AND DISHONORED.

*Solomon—Obedience—Magnificence—Disobedience—
Darkness.*

Central and collateral truths, 12 to 22 :

IDOLATRY.

Divine Warnings—Punishment—Kingdom Divided.

Key thought: The book of royal government in the hands of Solomon and his successors.

Central and collateral truths, second book:

DIVINE JUDGMENTS.

Idolatry -- Rebellion—Overthrow—Captivity.

Key thought: The book of royal government in its decline. The events detailed in these books are of themselves very interesting. The account of the wisdom of Solomon; the rash and impolitic conduct of his son, Rehoboam; the disobedient prophet; the widow of Zarephath; Elijah and the prophets of Baal; Benhadad's pride and defeat; Elijah's ascension to heaven; Elisha's succession to his ministry, and the series of miracles he performed; the panic and flight of the Syrians; the predicted death of Ahab and Jezebel, and their children, are all pregnant with instruction. We perceive in these impressive histories the characters and the qualities of men painted with the utmost fidelity, and the *attributes of God* displayed with great effect. The particulars and circumstances are sketched out with a brief and lively description; and the imagination lingers with pleasure in filling up the outline presented to our view.

Both these books are full of deep lessons on the bitter evils of apostasy.

The fall of Solomon should teach us that the very highest endowments possessed by man are not sufficient to preserve one from falling into the gravest sin and folly; and that the way of the transgressor is always hard.

Prophecies fulfilled. These books contain the fulfilment of many prophecies on the departure of Israel from God. Note also the following:

HELPS TO BIBLE STUDY. 151

PROPHECY.	TEXT.	FULFILMENT.
Builder of Jericho,	Josh. 6 : 26	1 Kings 16 : 34
Birth of Josiah,	1 Kings 13 : 2	2 Kings 23 : 15
Death of a prophet,	1 Kings 13 : 22	1 Kings 13 : 30
Destruction of the house of Jeroboam,	1 Kings 14 : 10	1 Kings 15 : 29
Death of Jeroboam's son,	1 Kings 14 : 12	1 Kings 14 : 17
Destruction of Baasha's house,	1 Kings 16 : 3	1 Kings 16 : 11
Great drought in the reign of Ahab,	1 Kings 17 : 1	1 Kings 18 : 41
Syrian invasion,	1 Kings 20 : 22	1 Kings 20 : 26
Punishment for the murder of Naboth,	1 Kings 21 : 19	1 Kings 22 : 38
Destruction of the house of Ahab,	1 Kings 21 : 21	2 Kings 10 : 11
Death of Jezebel,	1 Kings 21 : 23	2 Kings 9 : 36
Miraculous supply of water,	2 Kings 3 : 17	2 Kings 3 : 20
Plentiful supply of food,	2 Kings 7 : 1	2 Kings 7 : 18
Death of the unbelieving lord,	2 Kings 7 : 2	2 Kings 17 : 17-20
Reign of Jehu's sons to the fourth generation,	2 Kings 10 : 30	2 Kings 15 : 12
Death of the king of Assyria,	2 Kings 19 : 7	2 Kings 19 : 35-37
Babylonish captivity,	2 Kings 20 : 17	2 Kings 24 : 10-16

Biographies. The characters of the kings of Judah may be thus briefly given: David, the devout; Solomon, the wise. After the revolt: Rehoboam, the simple; Abijah, the valiant; Asa, the upright; and Jehoshaphat, the religious. The reigns of these kings were long when compared with the wicked kings of Israel. The number of the good was nearly equal to that of the bad; but the reigns of the good were generally long, and the bad short (1 Kings 16 : 15).

Connection with other parts of the Scriptures. The two books of Kings are connected immediately with the two books of Samuel as their continuation. These books contribute to throw light upon the writings of the prophets who lived before, and at the time of, the destruction of Jerusalem.

THE TWO BOOKS OF CHRONICLES.

Written probably by Ezra, B.C. 525, after the return of the Jews from the Babylonian captivity. Internal evidence favors the supposition that Ezra was the author of Chronicles, since the style and Chaldaisms strongly resemble those of the book of Ezra. In this both Jewish and Christian writers agree.

The genealogical tables are valuable, since they record the unbroken line of the faithful people for about 3,500 years.

The cause of their compilation is naturally suggested by the first difficulties that would present themselves to the leaders of those who returned from the captivity, in allotting the various portions of territory to the families entitled to them according to the Mosaic law. And again, the maintenance of the temple service, and of the payment of tithes, etc., required strict legal proof of hereditary descent on the part of the officiating priests and Levites. These two great political questions necessitated the compilation of authoritative genealogical tables. The Chronicles are the beginning of the ecclesiastical history, which continues, in an unbroken thread, to the end of the book of Nehemiah.

The first book of Chronicles coincides, generally, with the second book of Samuel; at the same time, the beginning gives matter which is not to be found either in the books of Kings or Samuel, and which stretches back as far as the Pentateuch, Joshua, and Judges. Note especially the genealogical record showing that Jesus Christ was of the seed of

Abraham; also the particular reference to David's institution of the divine worship, his court, and his men of valor. The first portion of the second book (chapters 1 to 9) relates to the same events as the first portion of the first book of Kings; viz., the history of the undivided kingdom under Solomon, and the second portion to the history of Judah under its several kings, from the revolt under Jeroboam to the Babylonish captivity.

In the two hundred and fifty-four years of the monarchy of Israel, nine different families occupied the throne. Twenty kings, all descendants of David, for three hundred and eighty-eight years occupied the throne of Judah.

Central and collateral truths in the two books of Chronicles:

Those of the first book are the same as in the second book of Samuel. Key thought: The book of God's earthly elect, connected with the throne and the ark. The principal truths in the second book (1 to 9) are the same as in 1 Kings 1-11; and those in 10-36 the same as in 2 Kings. Key thought: The book of God's earthly government in the house of David.

These books have been held in low estimation and much neglected by Bible students and commentators, because they say that they contain few things which are not to be found in the preceding books. This, to some extent, is true; but it is equally true that they supply many circumstances omitted in the former accounts, with additions, and are written with a particular view, which was: First, to separate God's people from the mixed multitude that returned from Babylon; second, to ascertain the lineage of Judah, from which the Messiah should come; and third, to reestablish them on their ancient footing.

"Harmony of prophecy and foreknowledge with human freedom and responsibility are illustrated in the history of these kingdoms. Prophecy, on the subject of heathen nations, becomes most copious in the age when these nations seem to triumph the most."—*Angus*.

Prophecy fulfilled. The number of Abraham's seed (Gen. 15 : 5, 6); fulfilled in 1 Chron. 21 : 5, 6.

Connection with other parts of the Scriptures. The three double books of Samuel, Kings and Chronicles have much in common, though they have also characteristic differences. They treat, for the most part, of the same period, and should be read and compared together. A comprehensive view may thus be gathered of Jewish history, and much light will be thrown on brief and obscure expressions. Their differences of aim, however, are as marked as is their substantial identity. Samuel gives the history of the formation of the kingdom, and a biography, even more than a history, of the first kings. The books of Kings, on the other hand, give a history of the theocracy under regal government, and are rich in brief allusions to the character, sins and consequent punishment of the rulers and of the people. The books of Chronicles, again, have special reference to the forms and ministry of religious worship, to the genealogies and consequent possessions of the various families and tribes, and to other topics connected with the return. Hence, genealogical tables; hence, also, the prominence given to the pious care in establishing public worship, of David, Solomon, Hezekiah and Josiah.

The second book concludes with an intimation of the decree of Cyrus for the restoration of the Jews, and the rebuilding of the temple.

Additional light is thrown on the Psalms:

1. The pestilence withdrawn (1 Chron. 20 : 14-30; 21 : 1 ; Ps. 30).
2. The building of the temple committed to Solomon (1 Chron. 28, etc.; Ps. 65, 67, 68).
3. David's review of his life (Ps. 145).
4. Giving the kingdom to Solomon (1 Chron. 29 ; Ps. 72, 91).

1 Chron. 20 : 1. This chapter goes on with the narrative in the eleventh and twelfth chapters of the second book of Samuel.

It is remarkable that the important episode of David's sin in the matter of Uriah, his reproof, and his repentance, are entirely omitted ; and this book of Chronicles passes immediately from the first verse of the eleventh to the twentieth verse of the twelfth chapter. It omits also the crimes of Amnon and Absalom, David's song, and passes to the eighteenth verse of the twenty-firsst chapter of the second book of Samuel, the last five verses of which, with some variations, conclude this chapter. This is due, perhaps, to the brevity of the history before the division of the kingdom; for he does not spare the sins of the pious monarchs that followed.

Ill treatment of the prophets. 2 Chron. 16 : 10, Asa, king of Judah, imprisons the seer who had told him God was displeased with him for having relied on Syria instead of Jehovah. 2 Chron. 18 : 7, Ahab hates Micaiah for the same reason. Micaiah was smitten and imprisoned by Zedekiah for his message. 2 Chron. 25 : 21, Zechariah was stoned to death for reproving Joash, king of Judah, and his people for idolatry. 2 Chron. 17 : 7, certain prophets were called princes (?) !

From 1 Chron. 21 : 1, we learn that it was Satan who tempted David to number Israel. The place where David made an altar to God on the occasion of the pestilence—Ornan's threshing floor—was afterwards selected as the site for the house of God (see 2 Chron. 2 : 1). It is noteworthy, that in 1 Chron. 28 : 12, we find that the pattern of the house of God which David had, was given him by the Spirit (see verse 19, same chapter). Solomon was twice anointed king (chap. 29 : 22). The second book gives only the history of the kings of Judah—not one of Israel.

SOLOMON'S SONG.

It was written probably by Solomon, in the early part of his reign. This poem is said to be the only remaining one of the 1,005 songs composed by Solomon. In the Hebrew idiom it is called *the* song of songs, or the best of them all. Both Jewish and Christian tradition agree in this. It is not quoted in the New Testament; but it formed part of the Jewish Scriptures. This book gives a description of wedded love. It is applied by Jews and Christians to the history of the chosen people of God, and their relation to him. It is said by others, that the more probable time of its compilation is the period of Rehoboam's reign; and that it refers to an overture of peace between the two kingdoms. A sublime and mystical allegory referring to the Lord Jesus Christ and his union with a pure Church.

Central and collateral truths in the Song of Solomon :

UNION WITH CHRIST.

Individuality—Completeness—Perpetuity.

Key thought: The book of one who found the object too great for his heart. Looking at this song from the position of the Old Testament, its ground idea is, "Thy Maker is thy husband." Identical with this is the New Testament idea, "The bride, the Lamb's wife."

"Much of the language of this poem was misunderstood by early expositors. Some have erred by adopting a fanciful method of interpretation—attempting to give a mystical meaning to every minute circumstance of the allegory. In all figurative representations there is always much that is mere costume. It is the general truth only that is to be examined and explained. Others, not understanding the spirit and luxuriancy of Eastern poetry, have considered particular passages as defective in delicacy—an impression which the English version has needlessly confirmed; and so they have objected to the whole; though the objection does not apply with greater force to this book than to Hesiod and Homer, or even to some of the purest of our own authors. If it is remembered that the figure employed in this allegory is one of the most frequent in the Scriptures— that in extant oriental poems it is constantly employed to express religious feeling—that many expressions which are applied in our translation to the person, belong properly to the dress—that every generation has its own notions of delicacy, the most delicate in this sense being by no means the most virtuous—that nothing is described but chaste affection—that Shulamith speaks and is spoken of collectively, and that it is the general truth only which is to be allegorized—the whole will appear to be no unfit representation of the union between Christ and true believers in every age. Properly understood, this portion of the Scripture will minister to our holiness. It may be added, however, that it was the practice of the Jews to withhold the book from their children till their judgments were matured." *Angus.*

Connection with other parts of the Scriptures. Throughout the Bible the union of Christ and his Church, or of God and his ancient people, is represented under the same endearing relation as that which this book discloses (see especially Psa. 45; Isa. 55 : 4, 6; 62 : 5; Jer. 2 : 2; 3 : 1; Ezek. 16 : 10, 13; Hos. 2 : 14-23; Matt. 9 : 15; 22 : 2; 25 : 1-11; John 3 : 29; 2 Cor. 11 : 2; Eph. 5 : 23-27; Rev. 19 : 7-9; 21 : 2-9; 22 : 17).

PROVERBS.

This book was written chiefly by Solomon, probably in the early part of his life. The object of this book is stated "to give subtilty to the simple, to the young man knowledge and discretion." The language is poetical, and the matter is strongly ethical. It is a manual of practical rules of life, as the book of Psalms is a manual of devotion.

Central and collateral truths in the book of Proverbs :

WISDOM.

Piety—Integrity—Purity.

Key thought: The book of wisdom for the world. Wisdom is here used in the sense of piety. This book shows in vivid colors the evils of intemperance; the snares of riches and of evil women; the mischief of sloth; the sin of pride, and of oppressing the poor. It further points out the causes of poverty; shows the value of industry and of a good wife, and gives much instruction on the proper training of children.

Connection with other parts of the Scriptures. The Proverbs are frequently quoted in the New Testament (see Matt. 15 : 4; Luke 14 : 11; Rom. 12 : 16, 17, 20; 1 Thess. 5 : 14; 1 Pet. 4 : 8; 5 : 5; James 4 : 6).

HELPS TO BIBLE STUDY. 159

Notice especially the invitations and counsels to mankind by Christ in the character of wisdom, and study each maxim in the light of Scripture examples. For instance: "Trust in the Lord with all thine heart; and lean not unto thine own understanding. In all thy ways acknowledge him, and he shall direct thy paths" (Prov. 3:5, 6). For Scripture examples in illustration, see 2 Chron. 14 (Asa); 2 King 14:14 (Hezekiah); 1 Sam. 30:6-8 (David); Ezra 8:21-23 (Ezra); Abraham's servant, Gen. 24:12-27; Nehemiah 2:4. Again: Prov. 4:14, "Enter not into the path of the wicked." Gen. 13:10-13 (Lot); 1 Sam. 23:1 (David).

Prov. 1:7. "The fear of the Lord is the beginning of knowledge; but fools despise wisdom and instruction." Rehoboam, 1 Kings 12:13; Eli's sons, 1 Sam. 2:25; Athenian philosophers, Acts 17:18.

Prov. 1:10. "My son, if sinners entice thee, consent thou not." Adam, Gen. 3:6; Balaam, Num. 22; Jehoshaphat, 1 Kings 22:4; prophet of Judah, 1 Kings 13:15-19, 24; Micaiah's firmness, 1 Kings 22:13, 14.

Prov. 1:32. "The prosperity of fools shall destroy them." The Israelites, Deut. 32:15-25; Hos. 13:6; Tyre, Ezek. 28:2, 16, 17; Sodom, Ezek. 16:49.

Prov. 4:18, 19. "The path of the just is as the shining light." The wise men, Matt. 2:1-13; Nathanael, John 1:46-51; the eunuch, Acts 8:27-40; Cornelius, Acts 10; Paul, 2 Cor. 3:18. "The way of the wicked is as darkness; they know not at what they stumble." Ahab, 1 Kings 18:17; the Jews, Ezek. 18:29; Jer. 5, 19, 25. Also their ignorance that the cause of their present miseries is their rejection of the Messiah (Deut. 28:29).

Prov. 5:22. "His own iniquities shall take the wicked

himself." Agag, 1 Sam. 15 : 33 ; Adoni-bezek, Judges 1 : 7 ; Haman, Est. 7 : 10 ; Judas, Matt. 27 : 3-5.

Prov. 9 : 8. "Rebuke a wise man, and he will love thee." David loved Nathan ; Peter loved our Lord, John 21 : 17 ; the two disciples constrained their reprover to abide with them, Luke 24 : 25, 29.

Prov. 10 : 2. "Treasures of wickedness profit nothing." Tyre, Ezek. 26 : 15 ; 27 ; 28 ; the rich man, Luke 16 : 23. "But righteousness delivereth from death." Noah, Gen. 7 : 1, with Heb. 11 : 7 ; Dan. 5 : 6 ; Belshazzar contrasted with Daniel.

Prov. 10 : 7. "The memory of the just is blessed." Elisha, 2 Kings 13 : 21 ; Jehoiada, 2 Chron. 24 : 15 ; Dorcas, Acts 9 : 36 ; Mary, Mark 14 : 9. "But the name of the wicked shall rot." Absalom, 2 Sam. 18 : 17 ; Jehoiakim, Jer. 22 : 18, 19 ; Jezebel, 2 Kings 9 : 37 ; Jeroboam, son of Nebat, 2 Kings 13 : 14, 15.

Prov. 10 : 24. "The fear of the wicked, it shall come upon him." The Canaanites, Josh. 5 ; Belshazzar, Dan. 5 ; Ahab, 1 Kings 22 ; Haman, Est. 7 : 7-10. "But the desire of the righteous shall be granted." Hannah, 1 Sam. 1 ; Est. 4 : 16 ; 8 : 15-17 ; Simeon, Luke 2 : 29, 30 ; Psa. 37 : 4 ; John 16 : 23, 24.

Prov. 10 : 25. "As the whirlwind passeth, so is the wicked no more." Elah, 1 Kings 16 : 9 ; Zimri, 1 Kings 16 : 18, 19. "But the righteous is an everlasting foundation." Abraham, Gen. 17 : 1-8 ; David, 2 Sam. 7 : 16 ; Matt. 7 : 24, 25.

Prov. 11 : 2. "When pride cometh, then cometh shame." Miriam, Num. 12 : 10 ; Uzziah, 2 Chron. 26 : 16-21 ; Nebuchadnezzar, Dan. 4 : 30. "But with the lowly is wisdom." Daniel, Dan. 2 : 30 ; Joseph, Gen. 41 : 16.

Prov. 11 : 5, 6. "The righteousness of the perfect shall direct his way: but the wicked shall fall by his own wickedness. The righteousness of the upright shall deliver them: but transgressors shall be taken in their own naughtiness." Haman, Est. 7 : 10 ; 8 : 7 ; Daniel's accusers, Dan. 6 : 24 ; Ahithophel's death, 2 Sam. 17 : 23, contrasted with David's restoration to his throne.

Prov. 11 : 10. "When it goeth well with the righteous, the city rejoiceth." Mordecai, Est. 8 : 16. "When the wicked perisheth there is shouting." Sisera, Judges 5; Athaliah, 2 Kings 11 : 13, 20; Rev. 19 : 1-3.

Prov. 11 : 21. "Though hand join in hand, the wicked shall not be unpunished." Tower of Babel, Gen. 11 : 4; the kings who combined together, Josh. 9 : 1, 2; Adoni-zedec, Josh. 10. "But the seed of the righteous shall be delivered." Mephibosheth, 2 Sam. 21 : 7; Solomon, 1 Kings 11 : 12, 34; Abijam, 1 Kings 15 : 4; the Israelites often, Exo. 3 : 15, 17; 2 Kings 8 : 19.

Prov. 11 : 25. "The liberal soul shall be made fat, and he that watereth shall be watered also himself." Abraham, Gen. 13 : 9; 14; widow of Zarephath, 1 Kings 17 : 10; the Shunammite, 2 Kings 4.

Prov. 12 : 5. "The counsels of the wicked are deceit." Geshem, Neh. 6 : 2; Ishmael, Jer. 41 : 1-7; Daniel's accusers to Darius, Dan. 6 : 8; Herod's to the wise men, Matt. 2; the Pharisees respecting the tribute money, Matt. 22 : 15 ; the Jews lying in wait for Paul, Acts 23 : 15.

Prov. 12 : 11. "He that followeth vain persons is void of understanding." Followers of Abimelech, Judges 9; and of Absalom, 2 Sam. 15; of Theudas and Judas, Acts 5 : 36, 37.

Prov. 12 : 13. "The wicked is snared by the transgression of his lips; but the just shall come out of trouble."

Adonijah, 1 Kings 2 : 23; Daniel's accusers, Dan. 6 : 24; the Jews, Matt. 27 : 25.

Prov. 12 : 15. "The way of a fool is right in his own eyes." Lot's sons-in-law, Gen. 19 : 14; Pharisees, John 9 : 34. "But he that hearkeneth unto counsel is wise." Moses, Exo. 18 : 19-24; Apollos, Acts 18 : 24-26; Pharaoh, Gen. 41 : 37-45; Jacob, Gen. 43 : 11; Nathanael, John 1 : 46, 47.

Prov. 12 : 19. "The lip of truth shall be established for ever." Caleb and Joshua, Num. 13 : 14; Nathan to David, 2 Sam. 7 : 12-17; with Luke 1 : 32. "But a lying tongue is but for a moment." Gehazi, 2 Kings 5; Ananias, Acts 5.

Prov. 12 : 25. "Heaviness in the heart of man maketh it stoop, but a good word maketh it glad." Nehemiah, Neh. 2, 12; the woman that was a sinner, Luke 7 : 38, 50; Mary Magdalene, John 20 : 11-18; Luke 24 : 17-32.

Prov. 13 : 7. "There is that maketh himself rich, yet hath nothing." Haman, Est. 5 : 13; church of Laodicea contrasted with the church of Smyrna, Rev. 3 : 17; 2 : 9; Ahab, 1 Kings 21 : 4, 16, 22. "There is that maketh himself poor, yet hath great riches." Matthew, Luke 5 : 27, 28; Paul, 2 Cor. 6 : 10; Phil. 3 : 8.

Prov. 13 : 24. "He that spareth his rod hateth his son: but he that loveth him chasteneth him betimes." Eli, 1 Sam. 3 : 13; David, 1 Kings 1 : 5, 6.

Prov. 14 : 6. "A scorner seeketh wisdom, and findeth it not." Athenian philosophers, Acts 17 : 18; Herod, Luke 23 : 8; the Jews looking for the Messiah, and yet rejecting Christ, Acts 13 : 41; John 9 : 29. "But knowledge is easy to him that understandeth." David, Psa. 119 : 18, 98-100; Jas. 1 : 5; Matt. 11 : 25.

Prov. 14 : 8. "The wisdom of the prudent is to understand his way." Job 28 : 28 ; Deut. 4 : 6 ; Ecc. 12 : 13. "But the folly of fools is deceit." Gehazi, 2 Kings 5 : 20, 27 ; Daniel's accusers, Dan. 6 : 24 ; Ananias and Sapphira, Acts 5 : 1-11.

Prov. 14 : 32. "The wicked is driven away in his wickedness." Hophni and Phinehas, 1 Sam. 4 : 11. "But the righteous hath hope in his death." Jacob, Gen. 49 : 18 ; Stephen, Acts 7 : 55-60 ; Paul, 2 Tim. 4 : 6-8 ; Peter, 2 Pet. 1 ; 14 : 16 ; 3 : 13.

Prov. 15 : 1. "A soft answer turneth away wrath." The Reubenites, Josh. 22 : 15, 21-30 ; Gideon, Judges 8 : 1-3 ; Abigail, 1 Sam. 25 : 23. "But grievous words stir up anger." Rehoboam, 2 Chron. 10 : 13 ; Saul and Jonathan, 1 Sam. 20 : 30-34.

Prov. 15 : 10. "Correction is grievous to him that forsaketh the way." Asa, 2 Chron. 16 : 10 ; the Jews, Isa. 1 : 5 ; Jer. 5 : 3 ; John 8 : 40. "And he that hateth reproof shall die." Amaziah, 2 Kings 14 : 11 ; 2 Chron. 25 : 27 ; the Jews, 2 Chron. 36 : 15-17 ; Luke 19 : 42, 43.

Prov. 10 : 15. "The destruction of the poor is their poverty," inasmuch as it exposes them to injuries and abuses. But sometimes poverty is a protection, as it appears in the tremendous judgment inflicted upon the Jews by Nebuchadnezzar ; where we are told he burnt every great man's house, taking all that had property captive, but leaving the poor of the land to be vine dressers (2 Kings 25 : 9, 12).

Prov. 11 : 15. "He that hateth suretyship is sure" (see also 17 : 18). This is not a condemnation of suretyships under all circumstances, but a strong warning against undertaking them rashly.

Prov. 18 : 22. "Whoso findeth a wife, findeth a good thing, and obtaineth favor of the Lord." Manoah found it so; but Ahab, Job and Jehoram did not.

Prov. 22 : 6. "Train up a child in the way he should go: and when he is old he will not depart from it." Pious principles instilled in early youth *seldom* fail of operating in old age. Moses, Samuel, Timothy are instances of it. Yet wicked Ahaz, one of the most dreadful examples recorded in Scripture of sin and of its consequent punishment, was the son of a wicked father, and the father of a wicked son. Jeroboam had a pious son, Abijah; and Samuel a Joel and Abiah, who became unjust judges, though we have no intimation, as in the case of Eli, that he had been too indulgent to them.

Rules for applying the Proverbs. 1. Like all general laws, some of them have occasional exceptions. Not all are unlimited or universal. For example, Prov. 10 : 27 : "The fear of the Lord prolongeth days: but the years of the wicked shall be shortened." Such is often the case, but Abel was murdered, and the life of Cain prolonged. Jonathan and Saul—the one like a very brother of David, the other an apostate—perished in the same battle. "The corn cut down with the weeds, though to better purpose." Men are less likely to harm us.if we are followers of that which is good, and yet persecution because of our goodness is supposed (1 Pet. 3 : 13). In truth, God has to teach us a double lesson—that he *certainly* will punish, and that he will punish *hereafter*. The shortening of the years of the wicked—present punishment—teaches the first, the lengthening of their years—the postponement of punishment—the second. Hence both the exception and the rule. Prov. 16 : 7. "When a man's ways please the Lord, he maketh even his enemies to be at peace with him." So it was with Abraham and the Israelites, with Solomon and Jehoshaphat; so it was not with David or Paul. 2. The force and significancy of these maxims will most clearly be seen and felt, if they are studied in the light of Scriptural examples. They are comprehensive laws, understood best when examined in particular cases.

We are not generally to expect any connection, either of sense or sentences in this book; but this is like a quantity of pearls, loose and unstrung.

Proverbial instruction is common in the early history of most nations, and especially in the East. This style of communication excites attention, exercises ingenuity, is favorable to habits of reflection, and fastens truth on the memory in a form at once agreeable and impressive. The elegance and force of the Proverbs of Solomon are increased by the poetic parallelisms in which they are written. Nearly every sentence is antithetical or explanatory, and attention to corresponding clauses will often fix the reading and determine the sense.

ECCLESIASTES.

Written by Solomon, probably at the close of his life, after his lapse into sin (1 Kings 11 : 1-13). Chapters 1 to 6 show the vanity of all earthly pleasures and occupations; chapters 7 to 12 show the nature, excellence and benefits of true religion. In this book wisdom is used in the sense of science or sagacity.

Central and collateral truths in the book of Ecclesiastes:

VANITY.

Pleasure—Riches—Ambition.

Key thoughts: (1) The book of one who found the world

too small for his heart. (2) "Vanity of vanities; all is vanity" (chap. 1 : 2). This is its first lesson. "Fear God and keep his commandments"—is its last. The main object is to show the utter insufficiency of earthly objects of desire and pursuit to confer real happiness. The inscrutableness of many of the arrangements of Divine Providence in this life, together with the universality of divine control in the affairs of men, is also set forth; also the numerous and bitter disappointments often experienced in the failure of human purposes and plans. The need of the Gospel, rather than the Gospel itself, is proclaimed in this book. Note especially the beautiful description of the infirmities of old age in the last chapter. Use temporal things, but desire eternal. To seek God is to desire happiness—to find him is that happiness.

Connection with other parts of the Scriptures. We believe that this book is not directly quoted by our Lord and his apostles, yet there are several references to it in the New Testament. The book is interesting, as it supplies satisfactory evidence of the fact that, toward the close of his life, Solomon repented of his unholy practices and licentious principles, if in such a course, as is probable, he had imbibed them.

For whom is this book peculiarly suitable? Let the young, learning from it the guilt and danger of yielding to the imaginations of the heart (11 : 9), remember their Creator in the days of their youth; old age, even if they reach it, being a very unfit season to begin so important a concern as the salvation of the soul.

It is a strange proof of the depravity of our nature that modern infidels—Frederick the Great, Voltaire and others—have warmly praised those parts of Ecclesiastes in which

Solomon records the false principles which his folly had for the moment led him to maintain. The true wisdom of the book they entirely disregard. It is necessary to keep the eye steadfastly fixed on the purport of the discourse, and to discriminate what the author delivers in his own, and what in an assumed character.

PROPHETICAL BOOKS.

Prefatory Note.—Jonah, Joel, Amos, Hosea, Isaiah, Micah, Nahum, Zephaniah, prophesied before the captivity; Jeremiah, Habakkuk, Ezekiel, Daniel, during it; and Haggai, Zechariah, Malachi, after the restoration. Prophets: this general appellation was given to these twenty-one books, because they were *written* by prophets, who, as the teachers of the people, were naturally the *annalists* also; *e.g.*, Samuel, Nathan, Gad, Iddo, Isaiah, Jeremiah. Explanation of terms in the prophets: Jewry, country of Judea; Nineveh, the capital of Assyria; Tyre and Sidon, the two principal cities of Phœnicia; Babylon, the capital of Chaldea. Babylonia had three meanings: 1. The country around Babylon. 2. The country of Chaldea. 3. Rome. Arabia, country of Arabians, or Arabs, descendants of Ishmaelites. Mohammed, an Arab; his countrymen who followed him were called Saracens. Ethiopia, the name of some countries where Cush or his posterity, the descendants of Ham, dwelt.

JONAH.

Supposed to have been written by Jonah, 862 B. C. He was the son of Amittai, a native of Galilee (2 Kings 14: 25). This fact is a proof of the falsehood of the statement of the Pharisees, that out of Galilee cometh no prophet (John

7 : 52). Jesus quotes from this book as of authority, hence no fable. The contrast between the Gentile sailors and the heathen Ninevites and the prophet is so greatly in favor of the former, as to stamp the narrative with truthfulness.

This book is mainly an historical narrative, recording Jonah's prophecy against Nineveh.

His first mission, chaps. 1, 2 ; his second mission, chaps. 3, 4.

Jonah succeeded Elisha as the messenger of God to the ten tribes about 180 years after Solomon. He is considered the most ancient of all the minor prophets whose writings have been handed down to us. He appears as a prophet to the Gentiles, being sent to Nineveh, which soon after this became the capital of the great Assyrian empire —a city equally distinguished for its magnificence and corruption. Nineveh at this time is supposed to have been much larger than Babylon, and the chief Gentile city of the world. Assyria is frequently mentioned in 2 Kings 15, and following chapters. It is necessary that the reader should first read this prophecy as an episode in the history, enabling him better to understand what follows.

Central and collateral truths in the book of the prophet Jonah:

DIVINE FORBEARANCE.

Disobedience—Disaster—Punishment—Obedience—Deliverance.

Sincere repentance is always successful. God gives timely warning before executing his judgments. Notice the particular providence of God as illustrated in this narrative. 1. God sent a great wind. 2. He prepared a great fish. 3. He spoke to the fish. 4. He prepared a gourd. 5. He prepared a worm. 6. He prepared a vehement east wind.

Biography. Jonah is the same prophet who is sent to Jeroboam 2 (see 2 Kings 14 : 25), in answer to the bitter cry of affliction that rose from Israel. God overruled Jonah's wicked disobedience : the men began to pray. After Jonah had been cast out, and the storm abated, the men feared the Lord exceedingly, offered a sacrifice unto the Lord and made vows. Jonah prayed, and was delivered. Nineveh was spared notwithstanding Jonah's disobedience. "It is deeply humbling and searching to our souls, to find that the man of God was exceedingly displeased and grieved by the divine forbearance and patience. He had cried : ' Yet forty days, and Nineveh shall be overthrown.' And the city still remained. Regard for his own reputation made him angry ; and he would rather witness the destruction of all the Assyrians than to see himself dishonored."—*Brooks.*

Connection with other parts of the Scriptures. The prayer of Jonah has a striking resemblance to many Psalms, *e.g.*, Psalms 69 and 42, also to Lamentations. Compare the book of Jonah with that of Nahum.

Type. The time of Jonah's continuance in the belly of the fish was typical of our Lord's continuance in the grave (Luke 11 : 30). And Jonah's deliverance was also a type of Christ's resurrection.

For whom is this book peculiarly suitable ? For those who shun a cross, or run away from their post of duty.

Miscellaneous notes. "Any one taught of the Spirit can readily see that the object of the Devil—in calling forth a sneer of incredulity at the deliverance of Jonah—is to lead men to reject the resurrection of Jesus ; for it is no more difficult to believe the one than the other. Science has shown that 'a great fish,' the true shark, exists in the Mediterranean. Yet when God speaks he is only to be treated as a liar. But such is man. It should be remembered that the narrative distinctly states that 'God prepared a great fish.' It is precious, too, to observe that he commiserated the little children in Nineveh, more than 120,000, and also many cattle."—*Brooks.*

JOEL.

Joel (whose God is Jehovah), son of Pethuel, tribe of Reuben, prophesied about the middle of the reign of Uzziah, king of Judah, B. C. 810-795, contemporary with Amos and Hosea. The prophecies of this book are addressed to Judah. The principal events predicted are : The Chaldean invasion, under the figure of locusts, etc.; the destruction of Jerusalem by Titus, described with such force and aggravation of circumstances as to be in some measure descriptive of that final judgment which every temporal dispensation of the Almighty must faintly prefigure ; the blessings of the Gospel dispensation ; the general outpouring of the Holy Spirit which was to accompany it ; the conversion and restoration of the Jews to their own land ; the destruction of the enemies of God, and the glorious state of the Christian Church which was to follow it. He exhorts them to repentance, fasting and prayer, and promises the favor of God to those who should be obedient. The whole book indicates that the prophet lived at a time when the people of Judah had not fallen into that extreme depravity which, in later times, drew down upon them such heavy chastisements. Uzziah had, indeed, begun to lift up his heart (2 Chron. 26 : 16); but the evil seems as yet rather a subject of prophecy than of history, though given in historical form.

In the Hebrew Bible this book is divided into four chapters, but if it is proper to make any break at all, it should occur at the 18th verse of the second chapter.

"It shall come to pass afterwards I will pour out my Spirit upon all flesh." When the apostle quotes this language on the day of Pentecost, he does not say the scene then witnessed was a fulfilment of the prophecy, but, "This is that which was spoken by the prophet Joel," and we know the signs accompanying the prediction were not witnessed, "blood, and fire, and vapor of smoke; the sun shall be turned into darkness, and the moon into blood, before that great and notable day of the Lord come." These signs did not follow the gift of the Spirit in Peter's day, because Israel was not then repentant and obedient; but, as God's Word is true, they shall surely be seen in a day yet future.

Hence the last chapter tells of the gathering of all nations about Jerusalem, where the judgment takes place which is described in Matt. 25 : 31-46. "The Lord shall also roar out of Zion, and utter his voice from Jerusalem; and the heavens and the earth shall shake: but the Lord will be the hope of his people, and the strength of the children of Israel." Their enemies will be overthrown, but amid the tokens of supernatural fertility, "Judah shall dwell forever, and Jerusalem from generation to generation."

Central and collateral truths in the book of the prophet Joel :

THE HOLY SPIRIT.

Humiliation—Prayer—Conflict—Victory—or

JUDGMENT AND BLESSING.

Temporary Calamities—Repentance—Promise of the Spirit—The Second Advent.

Key thought: The book of universal judgment and latter-day blessing for Judah.

Connection with other parts of the Scriptures. This book should be read with Acts 2, Rev. 6 and 14 chapters.

That Joel was contemporary with Amos is not merely seen in the fact that Amos begins his prophecy where Joel concludes his: *The Lord shall roar out of Zion,* but that he speaks of the same judgments of locusts and drought and fire that Amos laments, which is an intimation that they appeared about the same time, Amos in Israel, and Joel in Judah.

AMOS.

Amos (a burden), a shepherd of Tekoah and dresser of sycamore trees, and contemporary of Hosea, prophesied during the reigns of Uzziah and Jeroboam 2, and during the early part of Isaiah's ministry, B. C. 810-785. "Not a prophet or prophet's son," *i.e.*, not trained to that office, but called by an irresistible divine commission to prophesy. Amos saw his first vision "two years before the earthquake," which happened, as we learn from Zechariah, in the days of Uzziah (Zech. 14:5; Isa. 5:25). His name is not to be confounded with that of Isaiah's father, Amoz.

Amos directed his prophecies chiefly to the ten tribes of Israel, though not exclusively, for he denounces judgments also against Judah, and threatens the kingdoms that bordered on Palestine—as the Syrians, Philistines, Tyrians, Edomites, Ammonites and Moabites. He foretells in clear terms the captivity of the ten tribes, a prediction accomplished about sixty years after, when Shalmanezer, king of Assyria, destroyed the kingdom, and the awful calamities attending it; concluding with assurances that God would not utterly destroy the house of Jacob, but after sifting and cleansing it among the nations, he would raise it again to more than its former splendour and happiness in the kingdom of the Messiah, by the accession of Gentile subjects. He rebukes also the corruption of their manners, which kept pace with their prosperity; he charges the great men with partiality as judges, and violence toward the poor.

Central and collateral truths in the book of the prophet Amos :

DIVINE JUDGMENTS.

Sin—Punishment—Mercy—Restoration.

Key thought: The book of certain judgment upon the Gentiles and all Israel, with future restoration of the latter. The previous occupation of Amos illustrates the grace which selects its ministers "from the tents of the shepherds as well as from the palace of the sovereign," qualifying each for the duties to which he is called (1 Cor. 1 : 27, 29). Note: The idolatrous priest Amaziah complains to Jeroboam, who orders Amos to quit his kingdom, and, instead of prophesying against him, to prophesy against Judah. In the next chapter a famine of God's Word is threatened. No prophet has more magnificently described the Deity, more gravely rebuked the luxurious, or reproved injustice and oppression with greater warmth, or more general indignation.

Connection with other parts of the Scriptures. Compare chap. 11 : 11-15, with Acts 15 : 15. This book may be read in historical connection with 2 Kings 10, 16, 18, and 2 Chron. 26. His prophetic character is established by the testimony of Stephen, the first martyr, and James (Acts 7 : 42, 43 ; 15 : 15-17).

HOSEA.

Prefatory note. He is the first of the minor prophets whose books were written at various periods extending over

400 years. Called minor not as less in point of inspired authority, but simply in point of size.

Hosea, the writer of this book, prophesied during the reigns of Uzziah, Jotham, Ahaz and Hezekiah, but especially in the days of Jereboam 2, King of Israel, B. C. 800-725. He was contemporary with Amos, Micah and Isaiah, though he began to prophesy before the latter (Isa. 1 : 1 ; Hos. 1 : 1).

The prophecies of Hosea are directed almost exclusively to the ten tribes. He addresses them under the title of Israel; of Samaria, which has been since the days of Omri their capital; of Ephraim, the most distinguished of the tribes, to which Jeroboam, their first king, belonged. The great sin of that king in having set up the calves at Dan and Bethel, uninterruptedly persisted in by the Israelites during the course of 150 years, had spread every form of vice among priests and people: and though, when Hosea began to prophesy in the reign of Jeroboam 2, there was great outward prosperity, iniquity was fast working their ruin. Hosea, therefore, in the strongest terms, points out their guilt and danger, using the expressive figures of adultery and whoredom to reprove their idolatry, which implies the violation of their covenant with God, and the alienation of their affections from him. In the most earnest manner he calls them to repentance, showing how vain was their dependence on other nations, and their pursuit of happiness in departure from God; they were sowing the wind and would reap the whirlwind. He labored more than sixty years, but with very little success, and probably lived to see his awful threatenings executed in the captivity of the ten tribes. The principal events predicted in this book are —the captivity and dispersion of the kingdom of Israel;

the deliverance of Judah from Sennacherib—figurative of salvation by Christ; the present destitute state of the Jews; their spiritual restoration and union with the Gentiles in the kingdom of the Messiah; the call of our Saviour out of Egypt; and his resurrection on the third day; while the assurance of a final ransom to his people from the power of death and the grave is celebrated in the loftiest strains of triumph and exultation.

Central and collateral truths in the book of the prophet Hosea:

IDOLATROUS DISOBEDIENCE.

Rejection—Dispersion—Restoration.

Key thought: The book of Israel's moral condition—past, present and future. Note: For sixty long years Hosea continued these warnings and appeals—with but little success—a bright example of persevering fidelity under the greatest discouragements. Chaps. 6, 13, 14, will be found particularly useful to awaken those feelings of repentance and faith which become the Christian Church in every age. In chap. 2, ear-rings and jewels as ornaments are spoken of disapprovingly.

Connection with other parts of the Scriptures. Huetius observes that many passages in the prophecies of Jeremiah and Ezekiel seem to refer to the prophet Hosea, and to be borrowed from him, who wrote a good while before them. As Jer. 7 : 34 ; 16 : 9 ; 25 : 10, and Ezek. 26 : 13, speak the same with Hosea 2 : 11, so Ezek 16 : 16 is taken from Hosea 2 : 8. And that promise of *serving the Lord their God*, and *David their King* (Jer. 30 : 8, 9 ; Ezek. 34 : 23), Hosea had before (3 : 5). Ezek. 19 : 12, is taken from Hosea 13 : 15.

Thus one prophet confirms another; and all "these worketh that one and the self-same Spirit."

ISAIAH.

Written by Isaiah, who prophesied during the reigns of Uzziah, Jotham, Ahaz and Hezekiah, kings of Judah.

Central and collateral truths in the book of the prophet Isaiah:

MESSIAH.

Humiliation—Death—Triumph—Glory.

Key thoughts: 1. The book of comprehensive and magnificent history. 2. "The vision of Isaiah which he saw concerning Judah and Jerusalem." 3. Salvation. Prominent words: "Light," "darkness," "affliction," "salvation," "strength," "peace," "delight," "ashamed," "I will." Note God's great care for his people and for his messengers. Sixteen chapters refer to the Messiah. Hezekiah in deep affliction sends for Isaiah to pray for the nation. Sennacherib sends Hezekiah a threatening, blasphemous letter. Hezekiah spreads it before the Lord. God hears his prayer, and promises to put a hook in his nose and defeat Sennacherib, which he did, and smote one hundred and eighty five thousand of the Assyrians; Sennacherib himself being killed. Fifteen years were added to the life of Hezekiah in answer to his prayer. Hezekiah, on his recovery, shows the messengers of Merodach-baladan, king of Babylon, all his treasures, and all he had. Isaiah was sent to reprove him for this, and foretells the Babylonian captivity. This conduct was a mark of pride in Hezekiah, and became a temptation to his enemies. In 2 Chron. 32:31, we learn that

Hezekiah did this while God had left him to try what was in his heart.

In reading this and every other book of the prophets, particular attention should be paid to the sins which peculiarly call forth the indignation of God, that we may avoid them. Thus, besides the grosser sins of bloodshed, oppression, slaying the children in the valleys, in the clefts of the rocks, etc., may be noticed covetousness, 5 : 8; confounding the distinctions between right and wrong, 5 : 20 ; self-conceit, 5 : 21 ; disregard of God's providence, 5 : 12 ; 29 : 15 ; a heart intoxicated with success, and giving itself up to worldly pleasure, 47 : 8 ;' 22 : 13. So also the evil of pride in Babylon, 14 : 13 ; Moab, 16 : 16 ; Tyre, 23 : 9 ; Ephraim, 28 : 3 ; Shebna, 22 : 16-19 ; Sennacherib, 37 : 23 ; and the blessings of humility are very observable. Human philosophy thought humility incompatible with other virtues; the Bible declares all other virtues to be vices and defects without it.

Prophecies fulfilled. In the writings of Isaiah we find several prophecies which had an early or immediate fulfilment; and these, as they were fulfilled, confirmed the faith of the people in the more remote. Syria and Israel, for example, were to be conquered by Assyria before the infant son of the prophet could say, "My father." The glory of Kedar was to fall in one year, that of Moab in three years, that of Ephraim in sixty-five years, that of Tyre in seventy years, while the predicted prolongation of Hezekiah's life must have established the authority of the prophet, and illustrated the providence of God.

Connection with other parts of the Scriptures. Read in connection with Isaiah to know the actual state of the people of Judah at that particular time, 2 Kings 14-20; 2

Chron. 26-32. Observe also that chapters 36-39 of Isaiah are identical with 2 Kings 18-20.

Miscellaneous notes. "It may be well before entering upon the prophecies, to say that they must be studied in the light of two principles: First, they express the counsels of God with respect to his Son, and look on to the great crisis that is to usher in his second advent. Second, while many of the events which they predict may have had a fulfilment in the past, they can have their fulfilment only in that grand consummation toward which the Church and the world are so fast hastening. The five books known as 'the law,' give us the utterance of God's voice, showing what man ought to be, followed by the historical books, showing what man is under the best circumstances. 'The prophets' give us the utterance of God's voice, showing what man will be till Jesus comes. The five books known as 'the Psalms,' and including Job, Psalms, Proverbs, Ecclesiastes and the Song of Solomon, give us the utterance of man's voice, telling out the various phases of human experience. It is said that Isaiah was put to death, being sawn asunder, for contradicting or adding to the Mosaic law (Isa. 6:1; compare with Ex. 33:20)."—*Brooks.*

PROPHETS NEAR TO OR DURING THE CAPTIVITY.

MICAH.

Written by Micah, a prophet of Judah, who prophesied during the reigns of Jotham, Ahaz and Hezekiah, B. C. 758-699, and was contemporary with Isaiah, Joel, Hosea and Amos.

He foretells in clear terms the invasions of Shalmanezer and Sennacherib; the dispersion of Israel; the cessation of prophecy; the utter destruction of Jerusalem by Vespasian; nor less clearly the deliverance of Israel; the destruction of Assyria, and of the enemies Assyria represents; the birthplace of Christ, and his divine nature, for his goings forth are from everlasting; the promulgation of his Gospel from Mount Zion and its results, and the exaltation of his kingdom over all nations. He makes a striking reference to the history of Balaam, and begins his prophecy with the words uttered by his great namesake Micaiah, 150 years before (chaps. 1:2; 2 Kings 22:28).

His prophecies are divided into three sections, each marked by a formula, "Hear ye," each commencing with denunciation and ending with a promise.

As Samaria, Israel's metropolis, was taken first, and Jerusalem, Judah's capital, subsequently, in the introductory heading, Samaria is put first, then Jerusalem.

Central and collateral truths in the book of the prophet Micah:

JUDGMENT AND MERCY.

Sin and Punishment—Salvation and Peace.

Key thought: The book of judgment and future blessing of Jerusalem and Samaria.

Connection with other parts of the Scriptures. Compare generally with the prophecies of Amos, Hosea and Isaiah; and observe the identity between Micah 4:1-3, and Isa. 2:2-4. Also chap. 4:2, 7, with Luke 1:33; chap. 5:5, with Eph. 2:14; and chap. 7:18, 20, with Luke 1:72, 73. His language seems also quoted by Zephaniah 3:19; Ezek. 22:27, perhaps by Isa. 2:2-4; 41:15, and by our Lord, Matt. 10:35, 36.

Biographical note. One of Micah's predictions saved the life of Jeremiah, who would have been put to death for foretelling the destruction of the temple, had it not appeared that Micah had foretold the same thing above one hundred years before. He died in peace in the days of Hezekiah (Jer. 26 : 18, 89).

NAHUM.

Nahum probably prophesied in the period between Israel's being carried captive into Assyria by Shalmanezer and the destruction of Jerusalem by Sennacherib, B. C. 720-698.

At this period of perplexity and distress, when the fate of Samaria was present to the apprehension of Judah, when her own cities had been taken by Sennacherib, and Hezekiah had drained his treasure, and even despoiled the temple in the vain hope of turning away the fury of Sennacherib; then was Nahum, whose name signifies "comforter," raised up to console Judah, and to proclaim destruction to him that imagined evil against the Lord. His prophecy is one entire poem, with a sublime description of the justice and power of God, tempered with long-suffering, and forctells the destruction of Sennacherib's forces, and the subversion of the Assyrian empire, together with the deliverance of Hezekiah, and the death of Sennacherib. The destruction of Nineveh is then predicted in the most glowing colors and with singular minuteness. The prophet Zephaniah, who began to prophesy just before the fall of Nineveh, also refers to its destruction in chap. 2 : 13-15.

DIVINE ANGER.

Forbearance—Judgment—Ruin.

Key thought: The book of utter judgment upon proud

Assyria. This book is a striking illustration of the moral use of prophecy; by which is meant, that the prophecies of Scripture are not mere anticipations of the future, but are intended by confirming the faith of the true believer, to strengthen him for his present duties.

Connection with other parts of the Scriptures. Read this book in connection with Jonah, of which it is a continuation and supplement; the remission of God's judgments being illustrated in Jonah, and the execution of them in Nahum (compare Isa. 53 : 7; also Rom. 10 : 15, with Nahum 1 : 15).

Prophecy fulfilled. Nineveh, in Nahum's time, was the largest and most opulent city in the world. It was captured by Cyaxares B. C. 625 — an event which had been predicted by Jonah nearly 100 years before.

ZEPHANIAH.

Zephaniah (defended by Jehovah), son of Cushi, prophesied in the former period of Jeremiah's ministry, and in the early part of the reign of Josiah, B. C. 640-609.

Zephaniah prophesied with the same object as Jeremiah, viz., to declare that the great day of trouble, distress, desolation and darkness was at hand in the approaching captivity of Judah, and to point out the sins which were the cause of it. He denounces God's wrath against the nations which assisted in oppressing the Jews, or rejoiced over them in their calamities; and he foretells their present dispersion and ultimate conversion, when the name of God, through them, shall be glorified throughout the world. He describes the desolation of Nineveh with remarkable accuracy. No doubt this prophet assisted Josiah in his pious efforts to bring back the people to the worship and obedience of the true God.

Central and collateral truths in the book of the prophet Zephaniah:

DIVINE VENGEANCE.

Denunciation—Punishment—Mercy—Restoration.

Key thought: The book of unsparing judgment and blessing upon the remnant of Israel. Note the following impressive declaration: "He will search Jerusalem with lighted candles." Silver and gold are of no value in the day of God's wrath.

Connection with other parts of the Scriptures. Compare chap. 1 : 7, with Matt. 22 : 2-14; chap. 11 : 13-15, with Nahum 2, 3.

Fulfilled prophecy. By comparing Amos 1 : 6-8, and Zech. 9 : 5, with Zeph. 2 : 4-6, it will appear that the prophets made the following discrimination as to the fate of the four neighboring and chief cities of Philistia; viz., Gaza, Ashkelon, Ashdod and Ekron. They declared of Gaza that baldness should come upon it; that it should be forsaken, and bereaved of its king. At the present moment, amid ruins of white marble, showing its former princely magnificence, a few villages, badly built of dried mud, are the only abode of its inhabitants—amounting altogether to less than 2,000. Of Ashkelon and Ashdod they had said, "I will cut off the inhabitants from Ashdod : Ashkelon shall be a desolation—it shall not be inhabited:" and so it is. Gaza is inhabited, but Ashkelon and Ashdod are not; their ruins mark their site, but no human beings live there; they are the abode only of scorpions, though many hundreds of years after these prophecies were delivered they were among the most celebrated cities. But as distinct from Gaza, which was to be the abode of poverty, and Ashkelon and Ashdod, which were to exist, but be without inhabitant, it was foretold of Ekron, "it shall be rooted up," and such is the fact. Its very name is lost, nor is the spot certain on which it stood; though, at the time the predictions were uttered, it was equally flourishing with the rest.

JEREMIAH.

Written by Jeremiah, who prophesied during the reigns of Josiah, Jehoiakim and Zedekiah.

The word of the Lord came to Jeremiah when he was very young, in the thirteenth year of Josiah, or B. C. 628, so that he followed Isaiah at the distance of about 100 years. He delivered his discourses at particular times during a period of more than forty years; and hence the lack of chronological order and logical arrangement. Although his entire ministry was passed in the most trying circumstances, immediately preceding and immediately succeeding the Babylonian invasion and the fall of Jerusalem, he may be pre-eminently called the prophet of hope. He was regarded as the bird of evil omen by the rulers of Jerusalem, and was subjected to the greatest persecution. He saw the city besieged and taken, his warnings neglected, but fulfilled, his fellow-citizens carried captive, and Jerusalem a heap of ruins. In an adjoining cave he wrote his lamentations over it. A remnant rallied round him after the death of Gedaliah, and were forbidden by God, through his mouth, to flee into Egypt; but they accused him of falsehood, and, disregarding the divine command, carried him with them into that country, where, according to Jerome, he was put to death.

Central and collateral truths in the book of the prophet Jeremiah :

JUDGMENT AND MERCY.

Rebellion—Desolation—Captivity—Deliverance.

Key thought: The book of judgment upon Judah, nations, and latter-day glory. In Jeremiah we have an example of the strictest fidelity in reproving sin, united with the deepest compassion for the sinner. Note his sufferings. In chap. 20 we are told that he was put in the stocks for delivering God's message. In chap. 32 Zedekiah imprisons him ; in chap. 37 he is smitten, and again cast into prison ; and in chap. 38 he is cast into the dungeon, and sinks into the mire.

From his predictions may be clearly shown that the prophets, under the Mosaic law, foresaw its abrogation, and acknowledged it was intended to introduce the Gospel scheme. He speaks of the ark being no more remembered, of the abolition of legal ordinances, the propagation of a more spiritual religion, and says that the new covenant, which God would make with Messiah, would set aside the old one. He also foretells the call of the Gentiles, and the final restoration of Israel. He further describes the efficacy of the atonement—the excellence of the Gospel in giving holiness as well as pardon.

Connection with other parts of the Scriptures. For the first fulfilment of the prophecies respecting the return of the Jews, read Ezra and Nehemiah.

The book of Jeremiah differs from that of Isaiah in this respect, that while it was the leading object of Isaiah to attempt the reformation of the Jews, the awful nature of Jeremiah's message was to proclaim the near desolation of his country, now hardened in impenitence. This gives a peculiar feature both to his character and writings which has led to his being called the weeping prophet. His name translated is "He shall exalt Jehovah," and his whole life was spent in endeavoring to promote God's glory.

His prophecies were known to Daniel in Babylon (Dan. 9 : 2).

LAMENTATIONS OF JEREMIAH.

Written by Jeremiah after the captivity and taking of Jerusalem. This remarkable poem is a dirge consisting of five elegies, sung amid the ruins of Jerusalem. As in the Psalms, the sufferings of God's people are so linked with the sufferings of our Lord Jesus Christ, that he is to be kept in view all the time. The chapters of this book express, with most pathetic tenderness, the grief of Jeremiah for the desolation of Jerusalem and the captivity of Judah, the miseries of famine, the cessation of all religious worship, and the various other calamities by which his countrymen had been visited according to his predictions.

Central and collateral truths in the book of Lamentations :

UNUTTERABLE WOE.

Calamities and sorrows—Humiliation and prayer.

Key thought : The book of godly feelings in view of Israel's sorrows. "The use of this book, no doubt, was great to the pious Jews in their sufferings, furnishing them with language to express their natural grief, and helping to preserve in them a lively remembrance of their desolated Zion ; and as well for their children, who did not see it, who were in captivity. His leading object is to teach his countrymen neither to despise 'the chastening of the Lord,

13

nor to faint when they were rebuked of him,' but, turning to God with deep repentance, to look to him alone for deliverance. When we consider the ill-treatment which Jeremiah received from his countrymen, the spirit which he here displays is a striking illustration of the influence of the Holy Ghost on the heart of a true servant of God."
—*Angus.*

Connection with other parts of the Scriptures. This book is a kind of appendix to the prophecies of Jeremiah, of which, in the original Scriptures, it formed a part (compare Lam. 3 with Job 3 : 13-23).

For whom is this book peculiarly suitable? This book is eminently adapted to the afflicted and to those who mourn over the desolations of Zion.

HABAKKUK.

Habakkuk probably prophesied in the reign of Jehoiakim, king of Judah, in the time of Jeremiah, a short time before the siege and destruction of Jerusalem, B. C. 612-598.

Of all the nations that had most afflicted the Jews, and in them the Church of God, the chief were the Edomites, the Assyrians, the Chaldeans; and three of the prophets were raised up on purpose to pronounce the destruction of these nations. Obadiah, that of the Edomites; Nahum, that of the Assyrians, who had carried the ten tribes into captivity; and now Habakkuk, that of the Chaldeans, who completed the captivity of the remaining tribes. His predictions are in the form of a dialogue, and relate to the wickedness of the Jews, and their certain punishment by the Chaldeans; the captivity in Babylon with deliverance from it, and the ultimate destruction of the Babylonian empire. This book breathes a remarkable spirit of prayer.

It expresses the prophet's holy indignation at the iniquity of his countrymen, with earnest intercession for their welfare. The concluding prayer, in which he describes the wonders God had wrought for Israel in times past, was admirably calculated to inspire the pious among them with confidence in prospect of their approaching calamity.

Central and collateral truths in the book of the prophet Habakkuk:

THE CONFIDENCE OF FAITH.

Adversity—Calamity—Trust and joy.

Key thought: The book of Jewish spiritual exercise. From chap. 2 : 3, 4, we may observe the great principle which forms the true character of the true servant of God in every age—a passage quoted three times in the New Testament. This principle will enable us, like Habakkuk, to joy in tribulation.

Connection with other parts of the Scriptures. Compare chap. 1 : 5, with Acts 13 : 40, 41 ; and chap. 2 : 3, 4, with Rom. 1 : 17 ; Gal. 3 : 11 ; and Heb. 10 : 37, 38. See also Heb. 11 and Gal. 2 : 20.

Biographical notes. It is said that Habakkuk remained amidst the desolation of his country rather than follow his brethren into captivity. In the days of Eusebius his tomb was shown at Bela, in Judah.

OBADIAH.

Obadiah (servant of Jehovah). The time when he prophesied is uncertain, probably between the taking of Jerusalem and the destruction of Idumea, B. C. 588-583 and consequently contemporary with Jeremiah ; or at a much earlier period, and therefore contemporary with Isaiah and Hosea.

"This book, though quite short, is very important, as it predicts the utter destruction of the Edomites, or Idumeans, the descendants of Esau, the twin brother of Jacob, and the type of the unchangeable hostility of the flesh to that which is born of the Spirit. Although their name and identity are lost at present among some of the existing nations, God will search them out in the last days; and it is apparent that a more terrible destruction awaits them then than that which has overtaken them in the past.

"The prophet announces that the hand of the Lord will drag them from their munitions of rocks, though they exalt themselves as eagles, and set their nest among the stars— all this for their treatment of Jerusalem in the day of its calamity and sorrow. This shows that whosoever touches his people touches the apple of his eye; and it will be remembered in the day of the Lord that is near upon all the heathen (verse 15).

"Thus this book, however short, reaches on, like all prophecy, to the second advent of the Lord Jesus; and, like all prophecy, it promises both spiritual and national recovery and spiritual restoration to the now scattered children of Jacob. For, unlike the captivity which had just been inflicted on the chosen race, the prophet declares that Edom should be as though it had never been, and should be swallowed up forever—a prophecy which has been remarkably fulfilled—while Israel should spiritually rise again from her present fall; should repossess not only her own land, but also Philistia and Edom; and finally rejoice in the holy reign of the promised Messiah."—*Brooks.*

HELPS TO BIBLE STUDY. 189

Central and collateral truths in the book of the prophet Obadiah :

JUDGMENT AND MERCY.

Denunciation— Destruction— Restoration— Victory.

Key thought : The book of judgment upon Edom. From the doom of the Edomites we learn how hateful their dispositions are in the sight of God. " He that is not concerned that his brother should perish, is in great danger of perishing himself."

Connection with other parts of the Scriptures. Compare Obad. 1 : 9, with Jer. 49 ; 14-22 ; also with 2 Chron. 28 : 17 ; also verse 21 with Luke 1 : 33 ; Rev. 11 : 15 ; 19 : 6 ; Amos 1 : 11-12 ; 9 : 11-15 ; Joel 3 : 19, 20 ; Ezek. 35. It is a book that should be studied in connection with the following Scriptures : Num. 20 : 14-22 ; 24 : 17-19 ; Psa. 60 : 8-12 ; 137: 7 ; Isa. 11. : 11-14 ; Isa. 34. The following are a few of the many references which show the ill-treatment of the Jews by the Edomites : 2 Chron. 28 : 17 ; with Exo. 25 : 12, 13 ; and Obadiah.

Obadiah is a fuller statement, and virtually a commentary on the foregoing briefer prophecy of Amos as to Edom. Amos 1 : 11 ; 9 : 11-15, of which last five verses Obadiah is an amplification, and therefore placed next to Amos. So much of Obadiah is found in Jer. 49, that it seems antecedently more probable that Jeremiah should have quoted from Obadiah than that Obadiah should have incorporated so much of Jeremiah. Obadiah has many expressions very similar to Joel.

Prophecy fulfilled. The prophecy of the destruction of the Edomites was partially fulfilled by Nebuchadnezzar, and further by the entire subjugation of Edom by John

Hyrcanus, after which it vanishes from history; but its completion, in the possession of Idumea by the Israelites, must still be anticipated after the final return of that people to their promised inheritance, and, therefore, this book is the most favorite study of the Jews to this day.

EZEKIEL.

Written by Ezekiel, who prophesied for about 22 years, B. C. 595-574, during the early part of the captivity, both before and after the destruction of Jerusalem. He was contemporary with Jeremiah and Daniel. He was among the first captives who were carried away to Babylon by Nebuchadnezzar, and was probably settled with other exiles on the banks of the river Chebar, which was the principal scene of his predictions, though he was occasionally conveyed in spirit to Jerusalem.

The design of Ezekiel's prophecies was to instruct the captives, so that whilst Jeremiah was denouncing the judgments of God at Jerusalem, promising consolation to the faithful and threatening the disobedient and idolatrous with punishment, Ezekiel was pursuing the same course at Babylon, confirming the truth of Jeremiah's predictions as to the speedy destruction of Jerusalem, comforting the pious among the captive Jews with the assurance of their future restoration and of the divine judgments upon their cruel oppressors, and predicting the flourishing and happy state of the Church in the times of the Messiah. The predictions of Ezekiel are marvellously varied. He has instances of vision, 8-11; symbolical actions, 4 : 8; similitudes, 12 : 15; parables, 17; proverbs, 12 : 22; 18 : 1; poems, 19; allegories, 23, 24; and open prophecies, 6, 7, 20. Ezekiel's prophecy was largely for the *encouragement* of Israel. In the vision of dry bones it was intended, no doubt, to revive their hopes; and it may be considered as an earnest of a general restoration here promised to the *whole house of Israel.*

Central and collateral truths in the book of the prophet Ezekiel:

DESTRUCTION OF JERUSALEM.

Idolatry—Rebellion—Captivity—Restoration.

Key thought: The book of judgment upon Israel, and connected nations, with future blessing of Israel. Notice the self-denial and suffering to which Ezekiel was called in the discharge of his office, and yet his ardent love for his countrymen; the wickedness of the Jews at Jerusalem, immediately before their destruction, particularly illustrated by the conduct of Pelatiah, and his awful death, producing no change in their conduct; the deceit they practised on themselves in the commission of sin; the mention of disobedience to parents and profanation of the Sabbath, as among the sins which brought upon them God's wrath; the treatment of Ezekiel's ministry by the Jews in captivity; the conduct of the Jews in Judea, who, after the destruction of Jerusalem, instead of being awed by so terrible a visitation, persisted in the same sins, and confidently hoped to be enriched by the ruin of their brethren. These are views of human nature given by the Holy Spirit for our admonition. Observe also Pharaoh's pride, and God's notice of it. The vision of the dry bones, setting forth the restoration of the people of Israel, illustrates to us the only means by which our nature can be raised from the death of sin to the life of righteousness. But let us remember that, though God works in us to will and to do, we must seek his grace by sincere repentance. The elders of Israel, regarding iniquity in their hearts, were not heard. Of the prophecies and types respecting the Messiah's kingdom, may be particularly noticed—the prophecies in which Christ is spoken of in the character of a shepherd, and under the title of David, as being the person in whom all the promises made to David are fulfilled ; and the vision of the holy waters, issuing out of the temple, and their virtue ; a most beautiful emblem of the gradual progress of the Gospel, and of the influences of the Holy Spirit accompanying it.

Biography. Ezekiel was, like Jeremiah, a priest as well as a prophet. His name signifies " The power of God girding with strength." He was a man of great energy of mind, vigor of conception, and tenderness of heart, subordinating his whole life to the great work of his prophetic office, and was eminently fitted, both by natural disposition as well as by spiritual endowments, for the special department of service to which he was divinely called. The style of his writings is particularly vigorous and bold, picturesque in imagery, commanding in diction, manifesting at times sternness with dignity, and frequently referring to the spirit and form of the ceremonial law. We learn from an incidental allusion in chapter 24 : 18—the only reference which the prophet makes to his personal history—that he was married and had a house (8 : 1) in the place of exile, and that he lost his wife by a sudden and unforeseen stroke. Tradition says that he was put to death by one of his fellow-exiles, a leader among them, whose idolatries he had rebuked. In the Middle Ages what was called his tomb was shown, not far from Bagdad.

The lost ten tribes. The ten tribes, composing the kingdom of Israel, were taken captive into Assyria by Tiglath-Pileser, about 740 B. C. (see 2 Kings 17 : 6). For information on the deeply interesting subject of their identification the reader is referred to such works as *Lost Israel Found*, by Edward Hine, and *Fifty Reasons why the Anglo-Saxons are Israelites of the Lost Tribes of the House of Israel*, by Rev. W. H. Poole, D.D.

The 17th chapter of Ezekiel should be read in connection with Exo. 20 : 5. Tyrus is three times prophesied against thus: "It shall never be any more," "never be found again," "never shalt thou be any more." It is here prophesied that Egypt should be a base or tributary kingdom. This has been literally fulfilled. It is also prophesied that Israel and Judah shall be united (37 : 19).

Ezekiel and Daniel are the only writing prophets of the Old Testament who lived and prophesied anywhere but in the land of Israel, except we add Jonah, who was sent to Nineveh to prophesy.

DANIEL.

Written by Daniel, who prophesied during the captivity, for a period of more than seventy years; consequently he was contemporary with Ezekiel.

Chap. 2 predicts the course of the five great empires of the world, which should succeed each other in supremacy; viz., the Babylonian, Persian, Grecian, Roman and Christian. In chap. 7 the four worldly empires, under the figure of four beasts, are viewed in their religious aspects. In chap. 8 is foretold the struggle between the Persian and Grecian powers, and the rise of the corrupting influence of Antiochus Epiphanes (the little horn), which prepared the way for the final overthrow of the Jews by the Romans. Then follow the precise prophecies regarding the Messiah. In seven weeks (49 years) the city would be rebuilt; in sixty-two weeks (434 years) Christ would begin his ministry, and in the middle of one week (3½ years) he would be cut off. Chap. 10 foretells the opposition of the Persian power to the restoration of the Jews; while chap. 11 more eminently predicts the history of the four Persian kings, that of Alexander and his successors, till the conquest of Syria by Rome, followed by a forecast of the growth of the supremacy of Christ's kingdom to the end of the world. Chap. 7 gives an epitome of the world's history. This book expressly predicts the death of the Messiah, whom Daniel is the first to mention by name (9 : 25-26); he even mentions the year in which he would be cut off. The later verses of chap. 11 are certainly applied in 2 Thess. 2 to Antichrist, and the 1,260 years of chap. 12 are referred to in the Apocalypse, as the time after which a great deliverance is to be effected for the Church. The predictions of this book have much of the distinctness of history, and have long formed an important part of the evidence of Scripture. The prophecies of this book extend from the first establishment of the Persian empire, more than 500 years before Christ, to the general resurrection. The fulfilment of some of these prophecies gives us the greatest assurance that the rest will be fulfilled, and at the same time affords an unanswerable proof that the Bible is the Word of God. The book of Daniel was written in the darkness of the most terrible captivity the Church had ever suffered. " By the rivers of Babylon, there we sat down, yea, we wept, when we remembered Zion. We hanged our harps upon the willows in the midst thereof." But then the harp of prophecy was most inspired with hope; then the grandest revelations were made of the future glories of the Church, and of the providence of God controlling all events for good.

Central and collateral truths in the book of the prophet Daniel:

DIVINE OMNISCIENCE.

Rise and fall of empires—The everlasting kingdom—Messiah's conquest and glory.

Key thought: The book of Gentile political history. "Everywhere the providence of God is seen, working or overruling all for the good of his people. The history of the temptations of Daniel and his companions, their constancy and deliverance, is highly instructive, illustrating at once the mystery of the divine dispensations, and the spirit and fidelity with which good men submit to them. The promise of the rebuilding of the temple was given to a penitent and prayerful prophet—the promise more comprehensive than the prayer he presented. He asked concerning Jerusalem, the answer told also of Messiah the Prince. The glorious display of the great work of redemption was made to Daniel *when in the act of prayer.* The book shows, moreover, that the world is God's world; that God is the Judge; that he putteth down one and setteth up another. The manifestation of his glory in the salvation of man is the great purpose he is carrying on in it. The wisdom of God in overruling the punishment of the Jews to the spreading of the knowledge of himself among the Gentiles, is very striking. Their seventy years' captivity in Babylon, and the miraculous events recorded in this book, would prove before the world, what Nebuchadnezzar and Darius were forced to acknowledge, that the God of Shadrach, Meshach and Abednego, the God of Daniel, is the living God, the great King above all gods. See also Ezra 1 : 3, with regard to Cyrus. Learn, also, that the privilege of an intercourse with heaven is not confined to a secluded life, or to those that spend their time in contemplation; for who was more intimately acquainted with the mind of God than Daniel, a courtier, a statesman, and a man of business? If those that have much to do in the world plead it as an excuse for their lack of devotion to God, Daniel will condemn them."—*Sel.*

Connection with other parts of the Scriptures. Compare the book of Daniel with that of Revelation, and observe the intimate connection between the two. Compare Daniel 9 : 4, 21, etc., with Isa. 57 : 15.

Biography. "Of Daniel little is known beyond what may be gathered from his own writings. He was not a priest, like Jeremiah and Ezekiel; but like Isaiah, of the tribe of Judah, and probably of the royal house (Dan. 1 : 6 ; 3). He was carried to Babylon in the fourth year of Jehoiakim, B. C. 606, eight years before Ezekiel, and probably between the twelfth and eighteenth year of his age. There he was placed in the court of Nebuchadnezzar, and became acquainted with the science of the Chaldees, compared with whom, however, God gave him, as he records, superior wisdom. By Nebuchadnezzar he was raised to high rank and great power, a position he retained, though not uninterruptedly, under both the Babylonian and Persian monarchs. The first event which gained Daniel influence in the court of Babylon was the disclosure and explanation of the dream of Nebuchadnezzar. This occurred in the second year of the *sole* reign of that monarch, *i.e.*, in 603. Twenty-three years later, as Usher thinks, B. C. 580, his companions were delivered from the burning furnace, Daniel himself being probably engaged elsewhere, at the time, in the affairs of the empire. Ten years later occurred the second dream of Nebuchadnezzar, and during the seven years of his madness, Daniel, it is thought, acted as viceroy. The date of the events recorded in chap. 5 is B. C. 538, toward the close of the reign of Belshazzar, when it appears Daniel was in private life (ver. 12, 13). That night the king was slain and the dynasty changed. The dignity which Belshazzar conferred on Daniel in the last hours of his monarchy was confirmed by Darius and Cyrus. Daniel died at an advanced age, having prophesied during the whole of the captivity (1 : 21), and his last prophecy being delivered two years later, in the third year of the reign of Cyrus. Ezekiel mentions his extraordinary piety and wisdom (Eze. 14 : 14-20 ; 28 : 3)."—*Sel.*

Miscellaneous notes. "Daniel has been compared to Joseph, the one at the beginning, and the other at the end, of the Jewish history of revelation ; both representatives of God and his people at heathen courts ; both interpreters of the dim presentiments of truth expressed in God-sent dreams, and therefore raised to honor by the powers of the world, so representing Israel's calling to be a royal priesthood among the nations ; and types of Christ, the true Israel, and of Israel's destination to be a light to lighten the whole Gentile world, as Rom. 11 : 12-15 foretells."

The Chaldean name of Daniel was Belteshazzar, which was given him on the occasion of his being put in training to be a courtier (1 : 3-6).

EZRA.

Written by Ezra, a priest, after the Babylonian captivity. This book, like the Chronicles, consists of journals kept from time to time, which were afterwards collected, and either abridged or added to, as the case required, by a later hand. This later hand in the book of Ezra was his own, as appears in the last four chapters.

Ezra's writings are an important continuation of Jewish history after the return from the seventy years' captivity. They embrace a period of about eighty years from B. C. 536 to 456, dating from the time of the decree of Cyrus, at which the Chronicles conclude. The book of Ezra is the accomplishment of Jeremiah's prophecies concerning the return of the Jews from Babylon.

It is to be observed that between the dedication of the temple and the departure of Ezra, *i.e.*, between chapters 6 and 7 of this book, there is an interval of about fifty-eight years; during which nothing is here related concerning the Jews, except that, contrary to God's command, they intermarried with the Gentiles.

Central and collateral truths in the book of Ezra:

RESTORATION.

Temple rebuilt—Prosperity—Repentance—Reformation.

Key thoughts: (1) The book of ecclesiastical history upon the return from Babylon. (2) Separation, (see Joshua 23 : 11; Judges 2 : 3 ; 2 Chron. 25 : 10).

Among the remarkable dispensations of Providence recorded in this history, we may notice especially how wonderfully God inclined the hearts of several heathen princes—Cyrus, Darius and Artaxerxes—to favor and protect his people, and to aid them in the work of rebuilding their city and temple (1, 4, 6, 7). Mark, too, how God overruled the opposition of the Samaritan, the decree of Darius being much more favorable than that of Cyrus

(Ezra 1 and 5 : 6). There is also another display of God's special and discriminating providence in the fulfilment of his promises to his people. Whilst in the land of *Samaria* colonies of strangers had been planted, which filled the territory of Israel with a heathen race, so as to prevent the return of the ancient inhabitants, it appears that in the land of *Judah* full room was left for the return and restoration of the Jews.

Note, the Samaritans, who sought to help and join the Jews in building, on being refused, became their enemies and sought to hinder them. They wrote to Artaxerxes to order them to stop building, which order was granted. Another letter was written to Darius, who ordered the work to proceed, and their enemies to help them. So God makes the wrath of man to praise him.

Prophecies fulfilled. In the return of the Jews from Babylon we see the fulfilment of the prophecies of Isa. 44 : 28, and Jer. 25 : 12 ; 29 : 10 ; the former had predicted the name of their deliverer, and the latter the exact time of their deliverance, as well as the state of heart with which it should be accompanied.

Biography. Ezra was one of the captives at Babylon, where he was probably born. He was the grandson of Seraiah, the chief priest, who was slain at the taking of Jerusalem (2 Kings 25 : 18-21), and therefore a descendant of Aaron. He was a "ready scribe," or rather instructor in the law of God. He was a man of deep humility (9 : 10-15), of fervent zeal for God's honor (7 : 10 ; 8 : 21-23), deeply grieving over the sins of the people, and sparing no pains to bring them back to repentance (9 : 3 ; 6 : 10). He joined the Jews at Jerusalem many years after their return, going up thither with the second large company.

Unlike Nehemiah, Ezra seems to have remained at Jerusalem. He is said to have lived to the same age as Moses, 120 years, and is esteemed by the Jews as next to him for the services he rendered their religion. He appears to have exercised civil authority for nearly twelve years. We read of him in the next book as employed in his sacred duties, and zealously co-operating with Nehemiah, who succeeded him in the government, in promoting the reformation of the people. Ezra is supposed to have revised all the books of the Bible then extant, disposing them in their proper order, and settling the canon of the Scriptures for his time.

Connection with other parts of the Scriptures. This book harmonizes with the prophecies of Haggai and Zechariah, which it materially elucidates (compare Ezra 5 with Haggai 1:12, and Zech. 3:4).

PROPHETS AFTER THE CAPTIVITY.

HAGGAI.

Haggai was the first who prophesied after the return of the Jews from Babylon, B. C. 520-518.

This prophet is supposed to have been born during the captivity, and to have returned to Jerusalem with Zerubbabel. He appears to have been raised up by God to exhort Zerubbabel and Joshua, the high priest, to resume the work of the temple, which had been interrupted nearly fourteen years by the Samaritans and others artfully attempting to defeat the edict of Cyrus. But now that these hindrances were removed, the Jews had become lukewarm in this great public work, and more solicitous to build and to adorn their own houses than to labor in the service of God. He continued prophesying about four months, and his earnest remonstrance appears to have had the desired effect. He predicts the greater glory of the second temple; for it was to be honored with the presence and ministry of the Messiah, whom he designates as "the Desire of all nations." In the closing prediction, Christ himself is spoken of under the type of Zerubbabel; and the temporal commotions which preceded his first coming; viz., the subversion of the Persian monarchy by the Grecian, and of the Grecian by the Romans; and in the terrible destruction of Jerusalem and the ruin of the civil government of the Jews shortly after his ascension.

Central and collateral truths in the book of the prophet Haggai:

DIVINE ENCOURAGEMENT.

Reproof—Obedience—Promises—Triumph.

Key thought: The book of encouragement in rebuilding the temple. Here we may learn that worldliness brings its own punishment. They "looked for much" and "it came to little." Drought and mildew were sent to rebuke their neglect of what ought to have been their first work. Note, in his remarkable prophecy of the Messiah, he five times uses the formula, "saith the Lord of hosts."

Connection with other parts of the Scriptures. This book should be studied in connection with Ezra, Nehemiah and Zechariah.

ZECHARIAH.

Zechariah began to prophesy about two months after Haggai, in the second year of Darius Hystaspes, B. C. 520-510, and continued his prophecy about two years.

The prophet was contemporary with Haggai, and had the same general object as he, to encourage and urge the Jews to rebuild the temple. The Jews we are told, "prospered through the prophesying" (Ezra 6 : 14), and in about six years the temple was finished. With this immediate object were connected—as was the universal custom of the prophets —others more remote and important. He emblematically describes the four great empires—the chariots and horses probably representing the Babylonian, Persian, Macedonian and Roman empires; he foretells many circumstances respecting the future condition of the Jews and their destruction by the Romans; and with these he intersperses many moral instructions and admonitions. Notice especially the preciseness of the predictions connected with our Lord's entry into Jerusalem, and the exact sum of money to be paid for his betrayal. Also some important details concerning the second advent and the conversion of the Jews. Jerusalem a second time to be destroyed. The last part of his prophecy contains the history of the Jews and of the Church to the end of time.

Central and collateral truths in the book of the prophet Zechariah :

THE SECOND ADVENT.

Judgments—Deliverance—Triumph.

Key thought: The book of "the last days" connected with Israel.

Connection with other parts of the Scriptures. Compare Zechariah with those portions of Isaiah and Daniel which relate to the coming of the Lord and the times of the Gentiles. Should be studied with Ezra, Nehemiah and Haggai.

Miscellaneous notes. Next to Isaiah, Zechariah has the most frequent and plain allusions to the character and coming of Christ; and he even specifies some points which had not been noticed by Isaiah. Christ is here called the "Branch," "Shepherd," and "Joshua." The expression "Lord of hosts" occurs forty-seven times in the prophet Zechariah.

ESTHER.

Ezra is supposed to have been the author. Date, about 485 B. C. Some suppose that this book was written by Mordecai; but the more probable opinion—one which may account for the omission of the name of God—is that it is an extract from the records of Persia. This supposition accounts for the retaining of the Persian word *Purim* (9 : 24-32); for the details given concerning the empire of Ahasuerus; and for the exactness with which the names of his ministers, and of Haman's sons, are recorded; also for the Jews being mentioned only in the third person; and Esther being frequently designated by the title of the "Queen," and Mordecai by the epithet of "the Jew." It also accounts for those parentheses which occur in the course of the narrative, the object of which appears to have been to give illustrations necessary for a Jewish reader; and for the abrupt termination of the narrative, by one sentence relative to the power of Ahasuerus, and another concerning Mordecai's greatness.

But few, comparatively, of the Jews availed themselves of the privilege to return to the land of their fathers. Most of the existing race had been born in Babylonia; they had made the country their home, and had gathered round them comforts which were not easily abandoned. Not more than

50,000 persons had gone up under Zerubbabel. The second band, under Ezra—more than seventy years later—numbered in all about 6,000 persons. Yet later, other bands sought the city and temple of God. Still the great bulk of the people remained in the land of their exile.

The institution of the festival of *Purim*, and its continued observance to the present time, is an evidence of the truth of this book. It has always been received as canonical by the Jews, who hold it in the highest veneration.

Central and collateral truths in the book of Esther:

DIVINE INTERPOSITION.

Dangers averted—Deliverance secured.

Key thoughts: (1) The man whom the king delighted to honor. (2) The book of God's secret government toward Israel.

The book of Esther shows how these Jews—though scattered among the heathen—were preserved, even when doomed by others to destruction. Though the name of God is not found in the book, his hand is plainly seen, anticipating threatened evil, defeating and overruling it to the greater good of the Jews, and even of the heathen (1; 2: 4-10). Nor was it the safety of the Jews in Babylon only that was in peril; if Haman had succeeded, as the power of Persia was then supreme at Jerusalem and throughout Asia, the Jews throughout the world must have perished; and with them the whole of the visible Church of God. Mark and admire the providence of God, using what seems the most trifling circumstance to accomplish his will (chap. 6). Mark, also, the faith of Mordecai, whose fear of the unalterable Persian decree was less than his trust in the faithfulness of God (4 : 14). Though he knew not how, he foresaw indemnity to Israel ; and he asks the aid of Esther rather for her honor than for their deliverance (see 1 John 5 : 4, 5).

For a fuller consideration of the special providence of God, as taught in this book, read the *Hand of God in History*, by Rev. H. Reade.

Biographies. The contrast throughout between the tone of Mordecai and Daniel, under similar circumstances, and the inferiority of the former to his contemporaries, Ezra and Nehemiah, is very marked. Haman was of the cursed seed of Amalek.

Connection with other parts of the Scriptures. The facts related in this book should be read between the sixth and seventh chapters of Ezra, which is their true historical position. Compare Mordecai's position under Ahasuerus (Esther 10 : 3) with that of Joseph under Pharaoh (Gen. 41 : 40) and that of Daniel at the court of Babylon (Dan. 5 : 16-29).

NEHEMIAH.

Written by Nehemiah, one of the Jewish captives, who was appointed by Artaxerxes (Ahasuerus), king of Persia, to fill the office of cup-bearer. The book of Nehemiah takes up the history of the Jews, about twelve years after the close of the book of Ezra, and it gives an account of the improvements in the city of Jerusalem, and of the reformations among the people which were carried on by Nehemiah. The rebuilding of the city wall was accomplished in fifty-two days, notwithstanding the difficulties by Sanballat and Tobiah, who were leading men in the rival colony of Samaria. They first scoffed at the attempt, then threatened to attack the workmen, and finally used various stratagems to weaken Nehemiah's authority, and even to take his life. In addition to these dangers from without, Nehemiah encountered hindrances from his own people, arising out of the general distress, which was aggravated by the cruel exactions of the nobles and rulers. These grievances were redressed on the earnest remonstrance of Nehemiah, who had himself set a striking example of economy in his office. It appears, also, that some of the chief men in Jerusalem were at that time in conspiracy with Tobiah against Nehemiah (2 : 9-20). Thus the wall was built in "troublous times" (Dan. 9 : 23), and its completion was joyously celebrated by a solemn dedication under Nehemiah's directions (12 : 27-43). With this book the history of the Old Testament closes.

Central and collateral truths in the book of Nehemiah :

REFORMATION.

Wall rebuilt and dedicated—Covenant sealed.

Key thoughts : (1) The book of civil condition upon the return from Babylon. (2) " Let us rise and build." In the ninth chapter we have an instructive summary of the history of the Jews, in its most important light, showing at once what God is and what men are. Few books, indeed, of the Bible contain a richer illustration of divine philosophy—that is, of true religion, taught by example. This work represents, in type, the restoration of civil government to the Jews, and their national supremacy in the last days.

Biography. Nehemiah—the Tirshatha—presents a noble example of true patriotism founded on the fear of God (5 : 15), and seeking the religious welfare of the state. His respect for the divine law; his reverence for the Sabbath (13 : 18);

his devout acknowledgment of God in all things (1 : 11 ; 2 : 18); his practical perception of God's character (1 : 5 ; 9 : 9-33); his union of watchfulness and prayer (4 : 9-20); his humility in ascribing all good in himself to the grace of God (2 : 12 ; 7 : 5), are all highly commendable. He was—as a reformer—very firm, a sort of second Moses.

Connection with other parts of the Scriptures. This book is a continuation of the book of Ezra. Chap. 13 : 26 sheds some light on the matter of Solomon's strange wives.

For whom is this book peculiarly suitable? All Christian workers should study well this book. In it they will find much to stimulate their faith, zeal and courage. Fainthearted ones—those who are timid and halting in the face of strong organized opposition—should read this book, especially the fourth chapter.

Miscellaneous notes. After Nehemiah, Judea became subject to the kings of Persia for nearly one hundred years. Afterwards they came under the Egyptians, then under the Syrians. To deliver the Jews from the Syrians God raised up the Asmoneans, afterwards called the Maccabees. Under the Maccabean princes Judea became a free state. The Jews afterwards came under the Romans. Under Herod the Great, in the thirty-sixth year of his reign, while Augustus was emperor of Rome, Jesus was born.

MALACHI.

Malachi—the last of inspired prophets under the Old Testament dispensation—prophesied during the time Nehemiah was governor of Judea, and about 120 years after the return of the Jews from captivity, consequently at a later period than Haggai and Zechariah, B. C. 420-397.

At this time the second temple was built, the city was in a prosperous condition, but the people, though externally religious, had become so hypocritical and wicked, that Malachi was commissioned to reprove both priests and people. He predicted the coming of the Messiah, and his harbinger, John the Baptist, the call of the Gentiles, and the extensive spread of the Gospel. God expostulates with the Israelites for their ingratitude, for offering to him useless things, and things which they would not offer their governor. The priests are reproved for corrupting his covenant, and the people for strange marriages and impiety—the very evils which Nehemiah so earnestly condemns.

Central and collateral truths in the book of the prophet Malachi:

MESSIAH.

Expostulation and reproof—Judgments and promises.

Key thought: The book of Jehovah's last pleadings with Israel. Here we learn that rebellion, sacrilege, covetousness and infidelity is "robbing God." Backsliders must take up neglected duties. "The Sun of Righteousness" to be given to the godly, but a terrible day—one that "shall burn as an oven"—await the disobedient.

"Seven times they ask the insolent question, 'Wherein hast thou loved us?' 'Wherein have we despised thy name?' 'Wherein have we polluted thee?' 'Wherein have we wearied thee?' 'Wherein shall we return?' 'Wherein have we robbed thee?' 'What have we spoken against thee?' Truly might God say, 'I am the Lord, I change not; therefore ye sons of Jacob are not consumed.' But in the midst of the empty profession there was a little remnant that feared the Lord, and spake often one to another; and the Lord hearkened, and heard with delight their prayers and conversation. Yea, their very thoughts of him he put down in his book, as he puts the tears of the saints in his bottle, and their prayers in his vial. Twenty-five times, in four short chapters, do we find 'Thus saith the Lord,' as if the people then, like many professed Christians now, were losing all faith in divine inspiration."—*Brooks.*

Connection with other parts of the Scriptures. Compare Mal. 2:11, with Neh. 13:23-31; and Mal 1:10; 3:8, with Neh. 13:10, 11. It is worthy of note that this book concludes with announcing the subject with which the New Testament commences—the ministry of John the Baptist.

Miscellaneous notes. "The last predictions of Scripture, therefore, are like the earliest. They rebuke corruption and promise deliverance. They uphold the authority of the first dispensation and reveal the second. The prophet is still the teacher; and his last words are of the law and spiritual obedience, and again of the Gospel and its healing glory (4:2)."—*Angus.*

This book is the transition link between the two great dispensations of redemption; the last note of that magnificent oratorio of revelation, whose wailing of sorrow and breathing of hope were soon to give place to that richer song, which should be not only of Moses, but of the Lamb, and tell not only of Eden and Sinai, but of Calvary and heaven.

To understand the Old Testament, consider Christ and Israel as the centre and key.

The importance of the Old Testament is seen in the number of times, proximately, in which that portion of the

Bible is quoted from, or palpably alluded to, in the New Testament books.

Matthew	100 times	Galatians	16 times
Mark	34 "	Ephesians	11 "
Luke	58 "	Philippians	3 "
John	40 "	Colossians	3 "
Acts	57 "	1 Thessalonians	2 "
Romans	74 "	2 Thessalonians	2 "
1 Corinthians	41 "	1 Timothy	6 "
2 Corinthians	13 "	2 Timothy	2 "
Hebrews	86 "	1 John	6 "
James	16 "	Revelation	245 "
1 Peter	20 "		
2 Peter	10 "	Total	855 "

Probably there is no New Testament quotation from Obadiah, Nahum, Zephaniah, or Esther.

Historical summary. "The idolatry of the Jews was punished, first by incursions of the Syrians, and afterwards by the invasion of the Assyrians, who carried the people captive, and colonized the country with a mixed idolatrous race, who mingled their native worship with that of Israel. From these sprang the 'Samaritans,' who intermarried with some of the Jews, borrowed their rites, accepted the Pentateuch, and set up a false temple at Gerizim. The two tribes, 133 years later, were carried captive by the Babylonians; but after seventy years, B. C. 536, a portion of them returned, rebuilt Jerusalem and the temple, the government being vested in a Persian Satrap, resident at Damascus. As the faith of Abraham had been rewarded by the inheritance of Canaan, the unfaithfulness of his descendants had forfeited it, and they were all sent back to the heathen 'between the rivers,' from which their progenitors were divinely called ; from which exile ten tribes never returned, but the remnant—principally of the tribe of Judah— came back, cured of idolatry, and looking hopefully for the restoration of their kingdom and the birth of the promised seed."—*Oxford Teachers' Bible.*

Preservation of the Old Testament. The "Book of the Law," placed by Moses in the side of the ark in the tabernacle (Deut. 31 : 26), with the various "annals" and prophetic books from Joshua to David, Solomon deposited in the temple, where they remained till its destruction (2 Kings 22 : 8 ; Isa. 34 : 16). Daniel had a copy of "the books" in Babylon (Dan. 9 : 2-11, and also of Jer. 9 : 2). After the temple was rebuilt, Nehemiah collected the sacred books and made "a library" of them (2 Macc. 2 : 13), to which were added the writings of Ezra and his contemporaries, Nehemiah and the later prophets.

The Apocrypha, sometimes bound with the Bible, is a collection of ancient books. They are not found in any catalogue of canonical writings made in the first four centuries after Christ. Philo never quotes them as he does the Scriptures. Josephus expressly rejects them. The Jewish Church never received them as part of the canon. Christ and the apostles never quote them ; and Malachi said no other messenger would come till the second Elijah. All external evidence is against their inspiration. As for internal evidence : 1. None of the Apocryphal writers claimed divine authority ; and some virtually disowned inspiration (see 2 Macc. 2 : 23 ; 15 : 38). 2. The books contain statements at variance with history, are self-contradictory, and opposed to the doctrines and precepts of Scripture. They never formed a part of the rule of faith ; yet the Council of Trent, A. D. 1545, gave them canonical authority. The writings are of value, however, for historical purposes, illustrating the progress of knowledge among the Jews; their tastes, manners, customs, religious character, their government; some books explain prophecies; others show the fulfilment of prophecies; and some passages express high and noble sentiments.

THE FOUR GOSPELS.

It is a remarkable fact that there are only *four* accepted Gospels, when so many pretended ones were written, and that there are as many as four recognized by the whole Church as genuine and authentic. The Divine Spirit guided in the selection as well as in the composition of the Gospels.

In the following analysis of the Gospels we have sought to avoid that fatal error of the harmonists, of attempting to secure chronological unity at the expense of the individuality of the Gospels.

MATTHEW.

That Matthew's Gospel was written by the disciple whose name it bears is proved (1) by the name; (2) by tradition; (3) by coincidences between the man and the book.

The writer, before his conversion named Levi, a publican, and collector of the tolls and customs of persons and of goods crossing the lake at Capernaum, was son of Alphæus, and a Hebrew.

Notice the variation in the accounts of his call as given in Matt. 9 : 9 ; Mark 2 : 14 ; Luke 5 : 27, 28. As illustrating his Christian modesty, Matthew omits to mention that he was Levi, the son of Alphæus, and that he left all and made a great feast for Jesus. But he mentions what the others omit--that he was a publican. His modesty is also exhibited by the difference in the order of the disciples' names in Matt. 2:4; Mark 3:16, 19: Luke 6:13, 16; in his record of the disrepute in which publicans were held (Matt. 5:46, 47; 9:11; 11:19; 18:17; 21:31); and also in his omission of all favorable to publicans, as the conversion of Zaccheus (Luke 19:2): the parable of the Pharisee and publican. Written about A. D. 37.

Character of contents. Matthew gives the human descent of our Lord from Abraham, as evidence of his being the promised seed, in whom all nations should be blessed. Thus he completes the Old Testament history and covenant. He is the one Antitype in whom all has been fulfilled; in him the Old Testament passes into the New; the prohibitions of the law into the encouragements of the Gospel ; Sinai into the Mount of Beatitudes; the prophetic into the teaching office; priesthood into redemption by suffering; kingship into the supremacy of Almighty grace restoring a fallen race.

The Gospel of the discourses and miracles, of types and fulfilment of prophecy. Christ, the true Israel, called out of Egypt; the true Solomon, to whom the East brings its treasures; the true Moses, who gives the law; the wonder-worker, teacher, high priest. Gospel of warning Prophetic warning (Matt. 24 and 25). The high priest rends his clothes (Matt. 26:65), and God rends the veil of the temple (Matt. 27:51). Pilate's wife dreams, and Pilate washes hands, and the people imprecate on themselves the blood of him whom the Gentile centurion confessed to be the Son of God (Matt. 27:19, 24, 25, 54).

It is easy to perceive also that Matthew does not observe any chronological order in his narrative, but ranges over the whole field of our Lord's ministry, in order to call out and group together the facts and incidents that illustrate the point he has before him.

For whom written ? "Matthew wrote especially for Jews in Palestine ; hence he gives no explanation of Jewish customs or topography, and shows the fulfilment of the Old Testament in the New.

"Matthew presents one continued comparison of Jesus of Nazareth with the Messiah of the Prophets, a comparison which could not fail to have marvellous convincing power with any candid Jew. His argument is nothing, and his Gospel almost unintelligible without this. Besides the capital fact, emphasized by Matthew, that Jesus changed from plain teaching to parabolic, because of the blindness and obduracy of the Jews, it may be shown that most of the long list of parables contained in the latter half of this book are especially condemnatory of the Jews. This is true of the parable of the unmerciful servant, which opposes the boundless forgiveness required in the kingdom to the teaching of the Jew, which confined the forgiveness of an offending brother to three successive offences ; that of the laborers in the vineyard, which lifts the Gentile to the same level of divine privilege with the Jew ; that of the two sons, which exalts the Gentile above the Jew ; that of the marriage of the king's son, which threatens that the kingdom shall be taken wholly from the Jewish people and given to the Gentiles ; that of the ten virgins, which contrasts true piety with Jewish formality ; that of the talents, which opposes productive spiritual activity to Jewish obduracy and barrenness.

"That this book was written for the Jews is also seen in its *omissions*. Matthew in his Gospel, in writing for the Jews, characteristically omits as useless for his purpose

whatever is distinctively Roman or Greek. The careful
reader will note the entire absence of such explanations of
Jewish customs, as that which Mark gives of the religious
washing of the hands before eating, and of the washing of
cups, pots, etc., which were *necessary for strangers of Roman
birth*. There are no explanations of Jewish topography, as
that which Luke gives of the ' village called Emmaus, which
was from Jerusalem about threescore furlongs,' which are
necessary to strangers of Greek birth.

"There is an absence of such explanations of Jewish facts
as that which John gives of the ministry of the Jews to the
Samaritans (John 4 : 4), and which were necessary for the
Christians over the world after the destruction of Jerusalem. Matthew gives none of these scenic representations
of events which are seen to abound in Mark, which were
fitted for the Roman. He also omits those eminently
human features in which Luke's Gospel abounds, and of the
facts of the ministry of Jesus in Perea. One who duly
considers this omission by Matthew will see that it constitutes the very heart of Luke. The most remarkable of all
omissions by Matthew is the absence of the ministry in
Judea, and those spiritual discourses which constitute the
greater part of the fourth Gospel; but, on more careful consideration, it will be seen that they were mainly addressed
to that small class of Jews who had adopted the Christian
faith. That this Gospel was written for the Jews is still
further seen in its *additions*. The most noted of these are :
The visit of the wise men ; our Saviour's flight into Egypt ;
the slaughter of the infants by Herod ; the parable of the
ten virgins ; the dream of Pilate's wife ; the resurrection of
many saints, and their appearing unto many immediately
after our Saviour's resurrection ; and the bribing of the

Roman guard appointed to watch the sepulchre. The sermon on the mount is peculiarly adapted to the Jew, which Mark entirely omits; also the judgment of the Scribes and Pharisees, and of Jerusalem. His description of the last judgment demands our special attention, in order that, while looking simply to his merits for the remission of sins, we may manifest our interest in those merits by active love to his people. But while we see his relations to Israel all the way through, in every miracle, in every parable, in every action, there are bright intimations of his grace flowing out to the Gentiles. Hence, in the opening chapter, there are only four women mentioned, and upon each of these there was a dark stain in the estimation of the proud Jew. There were many illustrious women in the line of his human ancestry, but only Tamar, Rahab, Ruth, belonging to the accursed race of Moab, and the wife of Uriah, are named, as if the Holy Ghost were hinting that the king knew how to go beyond Israel, in order to seek and to save that which was lost. He chooses twelve apostles and sends them forth, first to 'the lost sheep of the house of Israel,' but only one of them, Judas Iscariot, or Judas, the man of *Kerioth*, is of Judea, while all the rest are Galileans (chap. 10)."— *Why Four Gospels.*

See story of the Gentile magi, of the Gentile centurion's faith, greater than any in Israel, the parable of Christ judging the world, and the command to disciple all nations.

Peculiarities of style in this Gospel. It is in this Gospel we find the phrase, "the kingdom of heaven," or, more literally, "the kingdom of the heavens." It occurs thirty-two times, and does not occur elsewhere in the New Testament. The word *kingdom* is found fifty-six times; and although the expression, "the kingdom of God," is used three times, there is an obvious reason for the change in the language. God's king was there in Israel, but being denied and disowned, he was taken up into the heavens, and "the kingdom of the heavens" began upon his ascension to the right hand of the Father. Hence the phrase is equivalent to the present Christian dispensation, during which Christ from the heavens is exercising rule in an especial manner over that part of the earth in which his Gospel is proclaimed. The phrase, "that it might be fulfilled," occurs thirteen times. "Then" occurs ninety times (in Mark 6 and Luke 14); "Heavenly Father," six times; "Father in heaven," sixteen times; "church," two. The other evangelists never use this word.

His business habits caused his Gospel to be more systematic than the others. He groups things of the same kind— discourses, parables, miracles. As discourses, in Matt. 5-7; parables in chap. 13; and miracles in chaps. 8 and 9.

Central and collateral truths in the Gospel by Matthew:

THE LORD JESUS AS THE KING.

Righteousness—Conquests—Glory.

Key thoughts: Christ, son of Abraham, and David's son and Lord, according to promise.

Another central truth of Matthew's Gospel, one which seems to us its most striking characteristic, is its varied picturing of the final reckoning of God with men, as his stewards, a part of Christ's teaching which naturally made a deeper impression on the converted tax collector than on either of the other evangelists. No book in the Bible, not even those in the Old Testament that record God's curses and threatenings, had so much about the final reckoning of rewards and punishments as this Gospel of Matthew. The 23rd chapter contains the severest denunciations of sin that are to be found anywhere in the Scriptures. In the book, as a whole, the words, "judgment," "hell," "fire," "hypocrites," "woe," are found on almost every page.

Connection with other parts of the Scriptures. Compare the facts, discourses and incidents with those of the same character in the other Gospels. Read this Gospel in connection with the epistle to the Romans. Read Matt. 24 with the book of Revelation. Matthew makes no less than ninety allusions, references and verbal quotations from the Scriptures. Forty-three of these are verbal quotations, while Mark has only fourteen, Luke sixteen, and John fourteen. Matthew rests his Gospel entirely upon the basis of Scripture revelation.

Matthew can be read, without haste, for a comprehensive view, in two hours, and should be read continuously at some time in each Christian's life, in order to get its great leading thoughts, by taking a bird's-eye view of it as a whole.

I. THESSALONIANS.

Written by Paul from Corinth. This is the earliest written epistle. On their second missionary tour Paul and Silas visited Thessalonica, which was, and still is, an important and prosperous commercial city and seaport, after having been driven from Philippi. Great success attended the preaching of the Word; "some of the Jews believed, and of the devout Greeks a great multitude, and of the chief women not a few." The special object of the epistle was to encourage and strengthen the newly formed church, the apostle having been compelled to leave

Thessalonica on account of the persecutions from the unbelieving Jews. Timothy was sent from Athens to establish the believers, and to comfort them under afflictions, and the good tidings brought by him of their faith and love, coupled with the insuperable difficulties in the way of a personal visit, induced Paul to write this letter. It seemed to have been occasioned partly by his wish to express his earnest affection for them, and to encourage them under trials and persecutions, but it was also called for by some errors into which they had fallen. Many of the converts were uneasy about the state of their relatives or friends who had died since their conversion. They feared that these departed Christians would lose the happiness of witnessing their Lord's second coming, which they expected soon to behold. In this expectation others had given themselves up to a religious excitement, and neglected to work at the business of their calling, but might claim support from the richer members of the church. Others, again, yielded to the same temptations which afterwards influenced the Corinthian Church, and despised the gift of prophesying in comparison with those other gifts which afforded more opportunity of display. This and the second epistle are appropriately placed in the Bible as the last of the seven epistles to the Gentile churches, because they are chiefly filled with " the last things," or the coming of the Lord.

"The royal state of Christ's second advent was one chief topic which was urgently enforced and deeply impressed on the minds of the Thessalonian converts. This subject tinges the whole atmosphere through which the aspect of this church is presented to us. It may be said that in each of the primitive churches, which are depicted in the apostolic epistles, there is some peculiar feature which gives it an individual character. . . . And if we were asked for the distinguishing characteristic of the first Christians of Thessalonica, we should point to their overwhelming sense of the nearness of the second advent, accompanied with melancholy thoughts concerning those who might die before it, and with gloomy and unpractical views of the shortness of life and the vanity of the world. Each chapter in the first epistle to the Thessalonians ends with an allusion to this subject, and it was evidently the topic of frequent conversations, when the apostle was in Macedonia."—*Angus*.

Central and collateral truths in the first epistle to the Thessalonians :

THE SECOND ADVENT.

Resurrection—Translation—Eternal glory.

Key thoughts: (1) Christ coming *to* and *for* the Church, and her eternal blessedness. (2) "Comfort one another with these words." We learn, also, " The apostle's primary success and unflinching courage in preaching; not flattering, but warning ; not self-asserting, but displaying a blameless example ; entreating, exhorting, rebuking ; his self-support by manual labor. His converts were principally from idolatry (1 : 9), but partly Jewish proselyte women of rank and influence (Acts 17 : 4)."

Connection with other parts of the Scriptures. Read, in connection with this epistle, Acts 17 : 1-10, and portions of 1 Cor. 15.

II. THESSALONIANS.

Written by Paul from Corinth. Paul found it necessary to write again to the Thessalonians. The excitement which he had endeavored to allay, by his first epistle, had increased, and the fanatical portion of the church had availed themselves of the impression produced by Paul's personal teachings to *increase* it. This epistle was probably written after Paul had received an answer to the first, to correct an erroneous impression gained from the vividness of his picture of the resurrection; viz., that it was near at hand, which led to a neglect of practical duties. "Those who encouraged this delusion supported it by *imaginary revelations of the Spirit;* and they had recourse to forgery, and circulated a letter purporting to be written by Paul in confirmation of their views. To check this evil Paul wrote his second epistle, reminding them of *certain signs* which must precede the second advent."—*Conybeare and Howson*.

Central and collateral truths in the second epistle to the Thessalonians:

THE SECOND ADVENT.

Apostasy—The man of sin—Consuming destruction.

Key thoughts: (1) Christ coming with his saints. The eternal judgment of sinners. (2) "Comfort one another with these words." (3) Antichrist foretold. The difference between the two epistles may be described in a single word: "Christ coming *for* his saints" is the subject of the first; "Christ appearing *with* his saints" is the proper title of the second.

The predictions of Paul in this epistle afford another illustration how the thread of prophecy is interwoven with the whole scheme of revelation, and evidently proceed from the mind of him who alone knows the end from the beginning. For the apostle takes up a subject which Daniel, five hundred years before, had introduced, adding various particulars, but leaving it to John to perfect all that prophecy intended to communicate.

Connection with other parts of the Scriptures. Read, in connection with this epistle, Dan. 7, Joel 3, Rev. 13, 17, 19; and contrast and compare chap. 1 with Joel 3 : 9-16; Rev. 19 : 11-21; chap. 2 with 1 Tim. 4 : 1-5; Dan. 7 : 8, 11, 19-26; 9 : 26, 27; Rev. 13 : 1-8; 17 : 11-17.

GALATIANS.

Written by Paul from Corinth. We learn from the inspired history that the apostle twice visited Galatia, a central province of Asia Minor, whose inhabitants were originally Gauls. The first visit was during the progress of his second missionary tour (Acts 16 : 6); and the second was some years later, during his third missionary journey, when he "went over all the country of Galatia and Phrygia in order, strengthening all the disciples" (Acts 18 : 23).

A painful surprise awaited Paul on his arrival at Corinth. He found that intelligence had reached that place concerning the state of the Galatian churches, which excited both his astonishment and indignation. His converts there, whom he regarded with peculiar affection, whose love and zeal for him had formerly been so conspicuous, were rapidly forsaking his teachings, and falling an easy prey to the arts of Judaizing teachers from Palestine. We know how great was the difficulty which Paul had to meet with this restless party at Corinth (2 Cor. 3); and now he heard that they had been working the same mischief in Galatia, where he had least expected it. Paul, in addressing the Galatians, although he assumes that there were some who were familiar with the Mosaic law, yet evidently implies that the majority were converts from heathenism. At any cost of falsehood and detraction these false teachers resolved to loosen the hold of Paul upon the affections and respect of these converts. Thus to the Galatians they accused him of a want of uprightness in observing the law himself while among the Jews, yet persuading the Gentiles to renounce it; they declared that he was an interested flatterer, "becoming all things to all men," that he might make a party for himself; and, above all, they insisted that he falsely represented himself as an apostle of Jesus Christ, because he had not, like the twelve, been a follower of Jesus when he was on the earth, and had not received his commission; that, on the contrary, he was only a teacher sent out by the authority of the twelve; whereas his doctrine, they alleged, was now in opposition to that of Peter and James and other "pillars" of the Church. In this letter his principal object is to show that the doctrines of these *false teachers* did in fact destroy the very essence of Christianity, and reduced it from an *inward* and *spiritual life* to an *outward* and *ceremonial system*. In order to remove the seeds of distrust, which had been planted in the minds of his converts, he begins by fully contradicting the falsehoods which had been propagated against himself by his opponents, and especially by vindicating his title to the apostolic office as received directly from Christ, and exercised independently of the other apostles. Such were the circumstances and such the objects which led him to write this epistle.

Central and collateral truths in the epistle to the Galatians:

JUSTIFICATION BY FAITH.

Law and works—Grace and faith.

Key thoughts: (1) Christian blessing and liberty contrasted in the law. (2) "Stand fast in the liberty with which Christ has made you free." (3) The law *versus* Gospel. (4) The Spirit is the beginning, middle and end of Christian life and power. (5) Thou art no longer a bondservant (to law), but a son whose service is in love. The fickleness of the Galatians, as manifested in this epistle, shows how little we can depend upon warmth of feeling in religion as an evidence of the strength of religious principle. They manifest all the susceptibility of impression and fondness for change which authors, from Cæsar to Thierry, have ascribed to that race. The only epistle Paul wrote in which he did not give thanks.

Connection with other parts of the Scriptures. This epistle is one of a set on doctrinal subjects which should be read together, viz., those to Romans, Galatians and Hebrews—since they clearly define the relation of Jews and Gentiles to the Church of Christ, and form one whole treatise, each alone being incomplete. It also has affinity with those to the Corinthians, as it vindicates the writer against the defamation of Judaizers. This book and that to the Romans dwell largely on justification by faith.

I. CORINTHIANS.

Written by Paul from Ephesus, A. D. 57. Two epistles are addressed to this church, which included not only those who lived at Corinth, but in the adjacent towns of Achaia (the upper portion of the Morea, along the coast of the Gulf of Lepanto). Paul passed eighteen months at Corinth during his second missionary tour, visiting the neighboring cities, and establishing churches in them. Corinth was the great centre of commercial traffic on the overland route from Rome to the East, and also between Upper and Lower Greece. Possessing the only good harbor in that quarter, and being the shortest and safest route, small vessels were dragged across the isthmus, larger ones transhipped their cargoes, and hence all the trade of the Mediterranean flowed through it, so that "a perpetual fair was held there from year's end to year's end;" to which were added the great annual gatherings of Greeks at the "Isthmian Games" (to which Paul alludes, 1 Cor. 9 : 24-27). Hence it was proverbial for wealth, luxury and profligacy. Its population, and that of Achaia, was mainly foreign, formed of colonists from Cæsar's army, and of manumitted slaves (*e.g.*, Tertius, Quartus, Achaicus, Fortunatus, etc), settlers from Asia Minor, returned exiles from the islands, and at this time a large influx of Jews lately expelled from Rome (Acts 18 : 2).

Paul's preaching in the synagogue was acceptable till he boldly testified that Jesus is the Messiah, when persecution set in, he was rejected from the community, brought before the Roman governor, and set up a rival church. His disciples were mostly of the lower orders, partly Jews, but mainly Roman freedmen and heathen Greeks, who became enthusiastic admirers of the apostle. Here he wrote the latter or both of his two epistles to the Thessalonians, and one to the Romans ; immediately after which he returned to Ephesus, and was succeeded in his mission by Apollos, who also made many converts. The latter was imperfectly instructed in Christianity, but was well versed in the Jewish Scriptures, and very eloquent. There arose two factions— a Jewish, clinging to a Pharisaic attachment to the law ; a Gentile, prone to push evangelical freedom to license, while keeping the right faith, claiming to indulge in even heathen licentiousness. They joined freely in heathen sacrificial feasts, degraded the holy communion into a festive banquet, women threw off the usual eastern veil of modest attire, and the Greek love of intellectual speculation and discussion ran riot on sacred subjects, till appeals on Christian disputes were brought before heathen tribunals, and morality was scandalized by even incestuous intercourse.

Under such corruption, during three years, factions attained a formidable height. Paul was defamed by the Jewish party, and rumors of alarming disputes reached him, followed by a letter full of inquiries on matters of morality and doctrine, brought by a deputation of freedmen. Paul had already despatched thither Timotheus, but now writes the first epistle to the Corinthians from Ephesus (A. D. 57), instead of going to them, as he intended, because he deemed it his duty to stay for the great Pan-Ionian festival to Diana, held that year at Ephesus.

Central and collateral truths in the first epistle to the Corinthians:

THE RESURRECTION.

Purity—Consecration—Steadfastness.

Key thoughts: (1) Church order and discipline. (2) "Let all that ye do be done in love" (16:14). Secondary keys: (14:40 and 7:29-31). See double address (1:2).

A careful study of this epistle, with reference to the character of the apostle, will afford a fine illustration of the practical influence of those doctrines of grace which he taught: for instance, his awful sense of his responsibility as a minister, and his jealousy over himself; his entire dependence for success on the divine blessing, yet his diligent use of means; his prudence, fidelity and tenderness; his humility—even while asserting his apostolic authority; and his little regard for those gifts by which he was so distinguished, as compared with charity, *i.e.*, Christian love.

Such conduct is a pattern not only to ministers, but also to private Christians in every age.

For those who profess to have no sympathy with superstition, and little respect for authority, these epistles are peculiarly instructive. They combine, in the most striking way, the utterances of a liberal, manly spirit, with doctrines the most humbling. They cherish the loftiest hopes for man and for truth, and they tell us how alone these hopes may be fulfilled. Further, these epistles more than any other of Paul's writings throw light on the state of the early Christian Church, and on the evil tendencies with which the Gospel had to struggle, even among good men.

Connection with other parts of the Scriptures. Read in connection with this epistle, Acts 18 and 19 : 10.

II. CORINTHIANS.

Written from Ephesus by Paul, about the latter part of A. D. 57 or the beginning of 58.

This epistle was called for by the effect of the first. In the interval occurred the riot at Ephesus, headed by Demetrius, and Paul's expulsion. Timothy and Titus had both been sent to Corinth, and at Troas he waited their return in vain, till he was bowed down with anxiety and evil foreboding. Titus at last brought sufficiently cheering accounts: the church, as a whole, had bowed to its "father's" reproofs; the incestuous man had been expelled and brought to repentance; the Gentile license had been restrained; confidence between the church and its founder had been restored, but the Judaizers had been reinforced by some bearing "letters of commendation" from some higher authority, and now were arrogant in their supremacy. This epistle expresses two conflicting emotions: (1) Thankfulness for the removal of evils; (2) Indignation at the arrogance of his opponents. The former epistle is a careful and systematic intellectual treatise; the latter is more emotional, expressing the gushing of a warm heart.

Central and collateral truths in the second epistle to the Corinthians:

THE ETERNAL FUTURE.

Afflictions—Revelations—Glory.

Key thoughts: (1) Christian ministry and superiority over all circumstances. (2) "Our sufficiency is of God." This epistle, as well as the first, displays the character of the apostle in many interesting points of view. His intense affection for the Corinthians as his spiritual children in Christ; his joy at their return to repentance, yet anxiety that it should be perfected among those who still inclined to the false teacher; the delicacy and address with which he exhorts them to a more liberal contribution; his astonishing labors taken in connection with the deep sense he everywhere expresses of his insufficiency to think or to do anything as of himself; his humility in noticing his thorn in the flesh, and in allowing fourteen years to elapse before he mentioned the extraordinary mark he had of the divine favor, in being caught up to the third heaven, with various other topics, may be very profitably followed out by the reader; while interwoven with the whole, he will easily discover the most important doctrines of the Gospel. Thus, 3:5 shows us the inability of man; 5:21, the righteousness which God has provided for him; 5:9, 10, the diligence with which we must nevertheless labor in the great work of our salvation; 7:1 instructs us as to the proper effects of the promises of the Gospel; 5:14, what is its great motive to obedience; 13 : 14 concentrates every blessing which language can express, or the heart of man conceive, as flowing to us from that love of God which leads us to love him in return.

Further reasons for a second epistle. Of the seven Gentile churches formally addressed by the Holy Ghost, the Romans, Galatians, Ephesians, Philippians and Colossians received but one epistle each, and the moment the contents of these various epistles are clearly understood, it will be seen that nothing can be added to them. They are complete in themselves. But the reasons for second epistles to the Corinthians and Thessalonians are equally obvious. The condition of these two churches demanded second epistles; and it was not by chance, or oversight, or forgetfulness on the part of the Holy Spirit to say something in the first epistles which needed mention, that two of the seven churches are addressed a second time.

Moreover there is a profound significance in all of the second epistles, which should not escape the notice of careful students of God's Word. Besides the two to the Corinthians and Thessalonians, we have the second epistle of Timothy, the second epistle of Peter, the second and third epistles of John. In all of these much is made of the proper ministry of the Word, much is made of the truth ; and there are solemn warnings and awful denunciations against false teachers. This fact, taken in connection with repeated references to the second coming of Christ, shows that the Holy Ghost in the second epistles designs to make a special application to the last days of the truth brought out in the first epistles. Hence the peculiar value of the second epistles at the present time, when all manner of false doctrine is rapidly increasing on every hand.

Connection with other parts of the Scriptures. Study this book in connection with 1 Corinthians, Romans and Galatians.

ROMANS.

Written by Paul from Corinth. 1. Sinfulness of the human race : (*a*) of the heathen (1) ; (*b*) of the Jews (2) ; (*c*) Comparison of Jews and Gentiles. 2. The plan of salvation explained : (*a*) in theory (3) ; (*b*) by illustration (4, 5). 3. Its value : (*a*) union with Christ (6) ; (*b*) as servants of Christ (6) ; (*c*) supplying defects of the law (7). 4. Justification by faith : (*a*) Christian's duty and privilege ; (*b*) cause of rejection by some, election of others, of Abraham's seed ; (*c*) blindness and final rejection of the Jews. 5. Development of truth (12-15). 6. Personal communications (15-17).

The moral conditions of the nations to whom the Gospel came, Paul has described in his epistle to the Romans.

We find there were opponents to the Gospel at Rome, who argued against it on the ground of the immoral consequences which followed, as they thought, the doctrine of justification by faith, and even charged Paul himself with maintaining that the greater man's sin is, the greater was God's glory (3 : 8). Moreover, not all the Jewish members of the church could bring themselves to acknowledge their uncircumcised Gentile brethren as their equals in the privileges of Christ's kingdom (3 : 9, 29 ; 15 : 7-11). On the other hand, the more enlightened Gentile converts were inclined to treat the lingering Jewish prejudices with scornful contempt (14 : 3). It was the aim of Paul to win the former of these parties to *Christian truth*, and the latter to *Christian love*. Two things the Jews then stumbled at : (1) Justification by faith without the works of the Mosaic law; and (2) the admission of the Gentiles into the church. Therefore, both these, Paul in his letter to the church of Rome, studied to clear and vindicate.

For whom written? For the Christians at Rome. The name of the original founder of the Roman church has not been preserved to us by history, nor even celebrated by tradition. It is therefore probable that it was formed in the first instance by private Christians converted in Palestine, who had brought back Christianity with them from some of their periodical visits to Jerusalem, as the "strangers from Rome," from the great Pentecost in A. D. 29 (Acts 2 : 10).

Central and collateral truths in the epistle to the Romans :

JUSTIFICATION AND SANCTIFICATION.

Faith—Conflict—Peace—Consecration.

Key thoughts : (1) Christianity unfolded. (2) Condemnation in sin, and justification by faith through grace.

God is kept prominently in view throughout the epistle — his name occurring one hundred times in the book, and twenty-one times in the opening chapter, where we read of the Gospel of God, the Son of God, the beloved of God, the will of God, the power of God, the righteousness of God, and the wrath of God. In connection with this, we see in the same chapter the progress of the human race apart from God (v. 21), the results of human culture (v. 22), the achievements of the human intellect (v. 23), the manifestations of human virtue (v. 24), the end reached of human love of truth (v. 25), human religion when man is left to his own resources (v. 25), and the true picture of society, after philosophy, science and art had done their best for the Greek and Roman world (vs. 26-32).

Connection with other parts of the Scriptures. Read in connection with this epistle the Gospel by Matthew and the epistle to the Galatians. Read chapters 10, 11, with Ezek. 36, Zech. 12, 13. A knowledge of the Old Testament is requisite to an understanding of this letter of Paul, as he makes reference to it over *seventy* times, fifty of which are verbal quotations bearing directly in answer to the great question raised by Job, and which pervades the entire Old Testament ; viz., " How shall a man be just with God ? "

CATHOLIC OR GENERAL EPISTLES.

JAMES.

Written from Jerusalem by James "to the twelve tribes scattered abroad," A. D. 62.

The design of this epistle was to encourage the believing Jews under their present and approaching sufferings, and to correct several errors into which they had fallen. Amid sins and iniquities, James the apostle and Bishop of Jerusalem, wrote this epistle—an epistle of warning to Jerusalem—the last warning it received from the Holy Spirit. Alone of the twenty epistles of the New Testament, this book begins with no benediction, and ends with no message of mercy. It should be remembered that among these "twelve tribes" were some who were Christians, and some, of course, who had never advanced beyond the Jewish faith; and if this fact is remembered, every apparent difficulty can be readily explained.

Central and collateral truths in the epistle of James:

JUSTIFICATION BY WORKS.

Patience— Purity —Wisdom—Service--Benevolence— Prayer.

Key thoughts: (1) Christian morality in and out of the Church. (2) Religion justified evidentially before men by works. The words "brother" and "brethren" occur sixteen times. "Patience" is also frequent, in the sense of steadfast endurance in piety. The word "perfect" occurs five times in this epistle. The prevailing error which attended the *introduction* of the Gospel—and which Paul was appointed to meet, especially in his epistles to the Romans and Galatians—was, that "man is justified in part by works." As opposed to this, Paul shows that we are justified freely by grace through faith alone, independent of the Mosaic law. But now, where the Gospel had been for some time *established*, the tendencies of corrupt nature were to prevert it by overlooking the importance of works as a necessary evidence of saving faith. Many professing Christians, it appears, were guilty of partiality to the rich, contempt of the poor, censoriousness, envy, contention, covetousness, presumptuous disregard of God's providence, oppression and luxury; and yet, confident of salvation, because they held a speculative belief of the doctrines of the Gospel. To show them the unsoundness of such a faith is the object of the apostle's arguments; and from the very example of Abraham, by which Paul illustrates the doctrine of justification by faith alone, he proves that it is of the very nature of *saving* faith to bring forth good works; and that if good works are not the result, though a man *say* he have faith, he has none which will profit to his salvation. This epistle may be considered as of the greatest practical importance, especially as a test of character to those who have long made a profession of religion. The vigor of Abraham's faith appeared in that, more than twenty years after he was admitted into a state of justification before God, he displayed its continued practical influence in his readiness to offer up even his son Isaac at the command of God (compare Gen. 15 : 6 with chapter 22 : 9-12). This fact again is a lesson to us, and is decisive proof that justifying faith, once exercised, is to be habitual, it is not so much an *act* as a *state*.

Connection with other parts of the Scriptures. Read and compare this book with the epistles of Paul to the Romans and to the Galatians. A careful study will show that much of this book is a striking commentary upon Christ's sermon on the mount. Compare

Jas.	1 : 2,	with	Matt.	5 : 10-12
"	1 : 4,	"	"	5 : 48
"	1 : 5, }	"	"	7 : 7ff
"	5 : 15,			
"	1 : 9,	"	"	5 : 3
"	1 : 20,	"	"	5 : 22
"	2 : 13,	"	{ "	5 : 7
			{ "	6 : 14-15
"	2 : 14ff,	"	"	7 : 21ff
"	3 : 17,	"	"	5 : 9
"	4 : 4,	"	"	6 : 24
"	4 : 10,	"	"	5 : 3, 4
"	4 : 11,	"	"	7 : 1ff
"	5 : 2,	"	"	6 : 19
"	5 : 10,	"	"	5 : 12
"	5 : 12,	"	"	5 : 33

Compare this book also with Mark 13 : 7, 9, 29, 32.

For the very remarkable and close parallels to the *book of Ecclesiasticus*, compare 1 : 5, 8-12, 13, 19, 23, 25 ; 3 : 5, 6, respectively, with Eccl. 20 : 15 ; 12 : 22 ; 1 : 28 ; 15 : 11 ; 5 : 11 ; 20 : 7 ; 12 : 11 ; 14 : 23 ; 28 : 10, 19 (especially in the Greek). For parallels to the *book of Wisdom*, compare Jas. 1 : 10, 11, 17, 20 ; 2 : 21 ; 4 : 14 ; 5 : 1-6, with Wisdom 2 : 8 ; 5 : 8 ; 7 : 17-20 ; 12 : 16 ; 10 : 5 ; 5 : 9-14 ; 2 : 1-24. For parallels to the *book of Proverbs*, compare 1 : 5, 6, 12, 19, 21 ; 3 : 5 ; 4 : 6 ; 5 : 20, respectively, with Prov. 3 : 5, 6 ; 33 : 34 ; 3 : 11 ; Eccl. 5 : 2 ; Prov. 30 : 12 ; 16 : 27 ; 3 : 34 ; 10 : 12.

For whom is this book peculiarly suitable? For inconsistent, deceived professors of religion. For Antinomians, and loose-living church members, generally.

EPHESIANS.

Written by Paul from Rome. The renowned city of Ephesus was visited by Paul A. D. 54, and whose earnest proclamation of the truth resulted in the conversion of numbers to the Christian faith, many of the sorcerers burning their books, fear falling on Jew and Greek alike, the name of the Lord Jesus being magnified, and the Word of God mightily growing and prevailing. A Christian church was formed, the members of which were commended for their faith and love ; and the apostle addressed this epistle to them from Rome while a prisoner there, A. D. 62. It was not evoked by any relapse or special errors, but was written to confirm and strengthen the believers in the faith and hope of the Gospel, and to give them some most important teaching in the deepest and sublimest truths of the Christian religion.

Central and collateral truths in the epistle to the Ephesians:

SALVATION BY GRACE.

Election—Redemption—Eternal purpose of God—Union with Christ—Conflict—Victory—Rest.

Key thoughts: (1) Christ the measure of Christian standing and blessing. (2) "Be filled with the Spirit." (3) "In." Notice how frequently the Holy Spirit is presented in this epistle. "Sealed with the Holy Spirit of promise," 1:13. "The Spirit of wisdom" given, 1:17. "Access in the Spirit," 2:18. "Builded up by the Spirit," 2:22. "Strengthened through the Spirit," 3:16. Brought into the "unity of the Spirit," 4:4. "Filled with the Spirit," 5:18. "Equipped with the sword of the Spirit," 6:17. "Praying in the Spirit," 6:18. A warning. "Grieve not the Holy Spirit," 4:30. Another prominent and suggestive line of thought in this epistle is represented by the words, "No longer walk as the Gentiles also walk." "Walk as children of the light." "Walk in love."

"The style of this epistle shows remarkably the state of the apostle's mind at the time of his writing it—a mind transported with the unsearchable riches of God's wisdom and love in the redemption of man, though at the very time his body was restrained by bonds and a prison. Of this his prayer for the Ephesians is a very striking example; yet, with a heart thus filled with heavenly things, his minute attention to relative and moral duties is very observable, as also his resting the motive to every duty on the relation in which we stand to Christ and the Holy Spirit. It is sad to know that, years afterwards, a church honored with such a revelation was rebuked by our Lord, because it had left its first love (Rev. 2 : 1-7), and started that downward course of the professing Christian body that is now fast hastening to a shameful and melancholy end. The candlestick has long been removed out of its place in Ephesus; and the most advanced saint will walk in darkness, unless he keeps his eye single and steadily fixed upon the Lord Jesus Christ. This is a solemn warning to Christians in every age of the fearful consequences of forsaking their first love."—*Sel.*

Connection with other parts of the Scriptures. Read in connection with this epistle Acts 19 : 20 ; Rev. 2 : 1-7. Read and compare with the book of Joshua and the epistles to the Philippians and Colossians.

For whom is this book peculiarly suitable? For the Christian who hungers and thirsts after the deep things of God. We recommend all young converts especially to study well this book.

COLOSSIANS.

Written from Rome by Paul. The letter to the Colossians itself gives us distinct information as to the cause which induced Paul to write it. Epaphras, the founder of that church (Col. 1 : 7), was now at Rome, and he had communicated to the apostle the unwelcome tidings that the faith of the Colossians was in danger of being perverted by false teaching. Hence, the object of this epistle was to counteract their errors and to establish the believers in faith and practice. The apostle gives a solemn caution against the philosophical speculations and carnal ordinances set forth by the false teachers, who appear to have been speculatists, mere professors of Christianity, advocating angel worship, occult science, the keeping of feasts and fasts, and a false worldly humility and wisdom, thus endeavoring to combine the doctrines of oriental theosophy and carnal asceticism with those of pure Christianity. He sets before them the majesty and all-sufficiency of Christ, as the source of all spiritual blessings. The attention is fixed upon the person of Jesus Christ, whose sacrifice completes the typical offerings of Judaism, crucifies the old man with his affections and lusts, while the resurrection unfolds a new life in him, elevating the soul above earthly objects more effectually than mere mortification of the flesh to quench the emotions of the heart, according to a Stoic philosophy.

There are many points of resemblance between this epistle and that to the Ephesians, written from Rome at about the same time, and sent by the hands of the same messenger (Eph. 6 : 21, 22 ; Col. 4 : 7, 8). But there are also points of difference that will not escape the attention of the careful reader. The epistle to the Ephesians tells us that we are Christ's fulness (Eph. 1 : 23), the epistle to the Colossians that he is our fulness (Col. 2 : 10) ; the former that we are in him (1 : 3), the latter that he is in us (Col. 1 : 27) ; the former is largely occupied about the body, the Church, and the latter about the head, Christ.

Conybeare and Howson, in their valuable life of St. Paul, present two extended tables of resemblance between the epistles, and add in foot note, "From the first of the above tables, it will be seen, that there is scarcely a single topic in the Ephesian epistle which is not also to be found in the epistle to the Colossians ; but on the other hand, that there is an important section of Colossians (2 : 8-23) which has no parallel in Ephesians. From the second table it appears, that out of the 155 verses contained in the so-called epistle to the Ephesians, seventy-eight verses contain expressions identical with those in the epistle to the Colossians. The kind of resemblance here traced is not that which would be found in the work of a forger, servilely copying the epistle to Colossæ. On the contrary, it is just what we might expect to find in the work of a man whose mind was thoroughly imbued with the ideas and expressions of the epistle to the Colossians when he wrote the other epistle."

Central and collateral truths in the epistle to the Colossians :

THE DIVINE HEADSHIP OF CHRIST.

Creation—Redemption—Life—Glory.

Key thoughts : (1) The Church's glories and fulness in Christ, her head. (2) "Christ in you." This epistle is full of deep spiritual truths.

Connection with other parts of the Scriptures. Whoever would understand the epistles to the Ephesians and Colossians must read them together. The one is, in most places, a commentary on the other ; the meaning of single passages in one epistle, which, if considered alone, might be variously interpreted, being determined by the parallel passages in the other epistle. Read this book also in connection with the epistle to the Philippians.

For whom is this book peculiarly suitable? For the same class of people mentioned in analysis of the epistle to the Ephesians.

PHILEMON.

Written by Paul to Philemon, from Rome. Philemon, to whom Paul wrote this epistle was an inhabitant of

Colosse, and probably owed the means of his conversion to the apostle. His slave, Onesimus, had run away from him to Rome, having, perhaps, been guilty of misappropriation of his master's goods (verse 8). Falling into Paul's hands, he was converted to Christianity, reclaimed to his duty, and sent back to his master with this letter of reconciliation. It is remarkable for its delicacy, generosity and justice. The apostle maintains civil rights (even of slavery), maintaining that Onesimus, though under the liberty of the Gospel, is still the slave of Philemon, and justly liable to punishment for desertion. The damage caused by his absconding, Paul takes upon himself, playfully using his name, "Onesimus" (*profitable* both to thee and to me), as a means of urging his suit for pardon. As the returning slave was the bearer also of the epistle to the Colossians, it was probably written at the same time (A. D. 62), near the close of Paul's first imprisonment at Rome.

Central and collateral truths in the epistle to Philemon :

CHRISTIAN COURTESY.

Kindness—Benevolence—Wisdom—Confidence.

Key thoughts: (1) Christian love counting upon love between brother and brother. (2) "Brother." (3) Reconciliation. This little epistle is very sweet, as it shows the interest of the Holy Ghost in a poor slave. It is a significant comment upon Paul's preaching, that such a man either desired, or was induced, to hear him. Besides the somewhat new point of view in which it presents the apostle's character, the most important truths are implied in this epistle. In the conversion of a runaway slave by one himself in prison are displayed the wonders of God's providence and grace, overruling evil for good; it also affords great encouragement to us, even when our means are most limited, to attempt to reclaim the wicked. The nature of Christian liberty is also illustrated. While Onesimus, as a Christian, became the apostle's son and Philemon's brother, this in no respect interfered with the civil duties he owed Philemon as his master. Yet those of the highest rank are taught by this epistle to condescend to men of low estate, and especially to those who, however mean their station, are truly the disciples of Christ.

Connection with other parts of the Scriptures. Read this epistle in connection with Col. 4. Compare on the whole spirit of this epistle, 1 Tim. 6:1, 2; Jas. 1:9-11; Phil. 2:3-8.

For whom is this book peculiarly suitable? For servants and masters.

PHILIPPIANS.

Written from Rome by Paul. Philippi was a city of Macedonia, and the capital city of a Roman colony. It is distinguished as being the *first* place in Europe where Paul preached the Gospel, about A. D. 51 (Acts 16:12). Here Paul and Silas converted Lydia, came into contact with heathen paganism—the worship of evil spirits—were scourged and imprisoned, which led to the jailer's conversion, and the founding of a faithful Christian community. The epistle was written during Paul's first imprisonment at Rome (Acts 28).

The Philippians were greatly attached to Paul, and testified their affection by sending him supplies, even when laboring for other churches; and when they heard he was under confinement at Rome, they sent Epaphroditus, one of their pastors, to minister to his wants. On the return of Epaphroditus, Paul, by this letter, acknowledges their kindness. His leading object seems to be, while cautioning them against Judaizing teachers, to urge them to higher attainments in holiness and mutual love ; directing them to the wonderful condescension of Christ as their pattern ; his grace as their strength ; and presenting his own example to enforce his precepts. It has often been remarked that this epistle contains less censure and more praise than any other of Paul's letters. It gives us a very high idea of the Christian state of the Philippians, and the liberality which distinguished them above other churches. The only blemish recorded as existing in the church at Philippi is, certain of its members were deficient in lowliness of mind, and were thus led into disputes and altercations with their brethren.

Two women of considerable note among them—Euodias and Syntche by name—had been especially guilty of this fault; and their variance was the more to be regretted because they had labored earnestly for the propagation of the faith. Paul exhorts the church with great solemnity and earnestness to let these disgraceful bickerings cease, and to be all "of one soul and one mind."

Central and collateral truths in the epistle to the Philippians :

FRUITS OF RIGHTEOUSNESS.

Love—Service—Humility—Joy—Trust—Peace.

Key thoughts : (1) Christian experience. (2) Joy in affliction. (3) The work of God in the heart perfected. As in other places, here again, the tenderness, the dignity, the humility, the disinterestedness of the apostle, are very observable. He wrote this epistle " weeping." The following titles of the various chapters have been suggested as appropriately expressing their leading thoughts: Christ the believer's *life*, chap. 1 ; Christ the believer's *pattern*, chap. 2 ; Christ the believer's *object*, chap. 3 ; Christ the believer's *strength*, chap. 4. But perhaps a better analysis would be : The Gospel, and Christ the theme, chap. 1 ; Humility, and Christ the pattern, chap. 2 ; Earnestness, and Christ the object, chap. 3 ; Peacefulness, and Christ the strength, chap. 4.

Connection with other parts of the Scriptures. Read in connection with this epistle Acts 16, and read and compare with the epistles to the Ephesians and Colossians.

For whom is this book peculiarly suitable? For the afflicted ; the persecuted for the Gospel's sake ; for those who murmur and chafe under trials, poverty, ill treatment, etc.

HEBREWS.

Written from Rome for the Hebrew Christians by Paul. The Gospel according to Moses is explained and the " better things " of the New Testament Gospel added ; viz., The Son better than angels, 1 : 4. Christ better than Melchizedec, 7 : 7. Better hope, 7 : 19. Better covenant, 8 : 6. Better promises, 8 : 6. Better sacrifice, 9 : 23. Better substance, 10 : 34. Better country, 11 : 16. Better resurrection, 11 : 35. Better thing for us, 11 : 40. The blood of Christ better than that of Abel, 12 : 24.

This epistle was probably composed by Paul when in very strict custody, either at Cæsarea or at Rome, A. D. 62-64, just before his martyrdom (2 Tim. 4 : 6). It was addressed especially to those Aramaic Christians of Palestine who were exposed to severe persecution from their fellow-countrymen, who adhered to the expected return of visible glory to Israel. Brought up in fond reminiscence of the glories of the past, they seemed in Christianity to be receding from their peculiar privileges of intercommunion with God, as a favored people. Angels, Moses, the High Priest, were superseded by Jesus, the peasant of Nazareth; the Sabbath by the Lord's Day; the Old Covenant by the New; while the temple and sacrifices were still in vogue, but virtually obsolete. What, they asked, does Christianity give in their place? And Paul answers, CHRIST; *i.e.*, God for their Mediator and Intercessor; superior to *Angels*, because nearer to the Father; to Moses, because a Son, not a servant; more sympathizing than the high priest, and more powerful in intercession, because he pleads *his own* blood. The Sabbath is but a type of the rest in heaven, the New Covenant is but the fulfilment of the Old. Christ's atonement is perfect and eternal, and heaven itself the true Jerusalem, of which the Church is the temple, whose worshippers are all advanced into the Holy of Holies.

Thus the *exceptional* ministration of angels is superseded by the *continuous* ministration of man.

The *legislative* ministration of Moses is perfected by the Divine Lawgiver.

The *typical* sacrifice of the high priest, by a real sacrifice of a Priest of a *higher order*.

The *indirect* communion with God is supplanted by the direct union of God and man in Christ, and the communion of the Head with his body, the Church.

Central and collateral truths in the epistle to the Hebrews:

THE DIVINITY, HUMANITY AND PRIESTHOOD OF OUR LORD JESUS CHRIST.

Sacrifice — Mediation — Forgiveness — Faith — Sanctification — Rest.

Key thoughts: (1) "Better." (2) Book of contrasts. (3) Christ the Apostle, Sacrifice, Priest and Witness.

Mark in this epistle the following lessons, as derived from the different chapters: Christ, the divine and eternal Son of God, 1; Christ, the captain of our salvation, 2; Christ, the head of his house, 3; Christ, the rest of his people, 4; Christ, our great high priest, 5; Christ, our forerunner, 6; Christ, our living intercessor, 7; Christ, the mediator of the new covenant, 8; Christ, our perfect sacrifice, 9; Christ, perfecting forever them that are sanctified, 10; Christ, the only object of faith, 11; Christ, the princely leader and pattern of faith, 12; Christ, the great shepherd of his sheep, 13.

The practical lessons of this epistle are remarkable for the peculiarly appropriate motives to which the inspired writer appeals. Be thankful, steadfast and obedient, for the darkness and terror of the ancient law have ceased, and a kingdom that cannot be moved is revealed (12 : 18-29; 1 Pet. 2 : 4-10). Be content, though no earthly inheritance is set before you. There still remain Joshua's promise and the care of Joshua's God (13 : 5, 6). Note the beauty, to a Jew especially, of the reason given for exercising hospitality (13 : 2). Follow faithful teachers, hold fast the unchangeable doctrine of Christ, discountenance vain traditions and ritual observance, joining Christ without the camp, and look for the New Jerusalem, in return for what is lost (13 : 7-14). The closing benediction (vers. 20, 21) is beautifully comprehensive and rich in allusions to the chief doctrine of the epistle, the New Covenant, and the dignity and grace of the Mediator. Note the twelve "*let us*" and the seven "*once*" (9 : 10) in this glorious epistle.

Connection with other parts of the Scriptures. Read this epistle in connection with the epistle to the Romans, the book of Leviticus, and portions of the books of Exodus and Joshua. This book is a masterly supplement to the epistles to the Romans and Galatians, also a luminous commentary on them, showing that all the *legal dispensation* was originally designed to be superseded by the new and better covenant of the *Christian dispensation*, in a connected chain of argument, evincing the profoundest knowledge of both. This book is an epitome of the dispensations of God to man, from the foundation of the world to the advent of Christ. It is not only the sum of the *Gospel* but a sum of the *Law*. Without this book the law of Moses had never been fully understood, nor God's design in giving it. With this, all is clear and plain. The apostle appears to have taken for his text: " Christ is the end of the law for righteousness to them that believe."

In this book there are over ninety references to the Old Testament, forty of which are verbal quotations. The majority of them refer the reader to the book of Leviticus.

For whom is this book peculiarly appropriate ? For converted Jews.

LUKE.

Little is known of him. Said to be one of the seventy, but this is not probable, Luke 1 : 2. Tradition and Luke 1, and Acts 1, proof of his authorship. A Gentile convert, Col. 4:11; a physician, Col. 4:14; Paul's companion, Acts 16:11; 2 Tim. 4:11.

It is the unvarying testimony of the early Church, that Luke's Gospel originated in his companionship and work with Paul, and that it was moulded and inspired by that great apostle, who combined the Jewish soul with the culture of the Greek, the world citizenship of the Roman, and the undying devotion of the chief of sinners saved by grace.

Paul, who played so important a part in the preparation of the Gospel for the Gentile world, was pre-eminently fitted to furnish, with the aid of Luke, the complete instrument for that work. No more striking example of the fitness of the means devised for the accomplishment of divine ends can be found even in sacred history. Written about the year A. D. 63.

The author states at once the two main objects of the historical writer: to draw up a continuous narrative, derived from a careful scrutinizing of the testimonies of eyewitnesses and ministers of the word; and to commit it to writing in chronological order. Christ's humanity more fully delineated as a babe, child, lad, man. Only in this Gospel do we read of Christ's eating earthly food after his resurrection (Luke 24; 30, 43). Compare John 2:13, 15. His human sympathies more fully set forth. For children. Infants brought to him. The only daughter of Jairus, and only son of the father who besought him. For women, Mary and Elizabeth, and Anna, Martha and Mary, the women that ministered to him (8:2, 3). The daughters of Jerusalem (23:28). For widows (4:25; 20:47; 2:37; 7:12; 18:3,5; 21:2, 3). For the poor and outcasts, illustrated by the parable of the rich man and Lazarus,

Zaccheus, the woman who was a sinner, and the parable in Luke 15.

Here only are we told that "a certain man went down from Jerusalem to Jericho;" that "a certain man had a fig tree planted in his vineyard;" that "a certain man made a great supper;" that "this man receiveth sinners, and eateth with them;" that "a certain man had two sons;" that "there was a certain rich man, which was clothed in purple and fine linen;" that "two men went up into the temple to pray;" and that the centurion, deeply impressed by the scenes which attended the crucifixion, said, "Certainly this was a righteous man." The last statement is the more striking when compared with the testimony of Matthew, "Truly this was the son of God," and of Mark, "Truly this man was the son of God."

Here, too, the human side of his character is brought out in the frequent mention of his praying. Nowhere else do we learn that "when all the people were baptized, it came to pass, that Jesus also being baptized, and praying, the heaven was opened;" that "he withdrew himself into the wilderness and prayed;" that "he went out into a mountain to pray, and continued all night in prayer to God," before his choice of the twelve; that as he was alone praying, Peter confessed him "the Christ of God;" that "he went up into a mountain to pray; and as he prayed" the transfiguration occurred; that "as he was praying in a certain place, when he ceased" he taught the disciples the Lord's prayer; that he said to Peter, "I have prayed for thee, that thy faith fail not;" that "being in an agony, he prayed more earnestly;" that on the cross he prayed, "Father, forgive them; for they know not what they do." Surely in all this he brings himself very near to us as the pattern man.

When our Lord sent forth the twelve, according to Matthew, he commanded them, saying, "Go not into the way of the Gentiles, and into any city of the Samaritans enter ye not; but go rather to the lost sheep of the house of Israel;" because Matthew gives us the Gospel of the king of Israel. But in Luke we are told that "they departed, and went through the towns, preaching the Gospel and healing everywhere," because here we have the Gospel of the Son of man in his relations to the whole world.

As compared with the first or second Gospels, it will be found that the third gives peculiar prominence to the Holy Ghost and his gifts, operations and divine personality. See Luke 1:15, 35, 41, 44, 46, 67; 2:25-27; 3:22; 4:1; 7:11; 11:13.

For whom written. "Intended for the Greeks, and through them, Gentiles everywhere. Hence Christ is traced to Adam, Jewish customs and chronology made intelligible to a foreigner, and the parables of the good Samaritan and prodigal son and the lost piece of silver introduced.

"The Greeks required that the future destiny of man should be made clear. Accordingly, we see that Luke has taken care to record two sayings of our blessed Lord, which reflect the clearest light on this mysterious subject—the state of the soul immediately after death, and during the interval of its dissolution and the day of resurrection. He has done this in his recital of the history of the rich man and Lazarus, and in the speech of our Lord to the penitent thief on the cross, 'To-day thou shalt be with me in paradise.' He, also, alone of the evangelists, in his recital of the miracle of the raising of the daughter of Jairus, has taken care to specify the fact that her spirit came back to her again. He thus corrected the erroneous notions of popular belief and philosophical incredulity, and revealed to the Greeks the great doctrinal and practical truth, that the human soul, on its separation from the body by death, passes immediately into a place of joy or of sorrow ; and that it remains there until the last day, when it will be re-united to the body, and be admitted to the full fruition of heavenly bliss, or be consigned to the bitter pains of everlasting woe."—*Wordsworth.*

"A gospel for the Greeks must be shaped by the Greek idea—must present the character and career of Jesus of Nazareth from the Greek point of view, as answering to the conception of a perfection and divine humanity; must exhibit him as adapted, in his power and mercy, in his work and mission, to the wants of the Greek soul, and of humanity as represented in it. It must present Jesus as the perfect man to meet the Greek ideal; as the divine man to cure the wretchedness of the despairing Greek. It must bring God and the invisible world near, to meet the wants of the longing Greek soul, and elevate it above itself and into communion with God ; must open the eyes of the blind Greeks to see the sinfulness of sin, and the beauty and desirableness of virtue and holiness. It must open the way to a mission grand enough for man here, and must bring to light an immortality beyond."—*Why Four Gospels.*

Wordsworth has well said, " The universality of man's apostasy from the primeval law of God ; the universality of the guilt of mankind; the universality of the misery in which the human race lay ; the universality of their need of a Redeemer and a Saviour ; the universality of the redemption accomplished by Christ dying on the cross for the sins of the world ; the universality of the Christian Church, constituted by him to be the dispenser to all the nations of all the means of grace flowing from his sacrifice; and the preparatory and transitory character and functions of the Levitical law and priesthood—these were solemn topics on which all men needed to be instructed, particularly the Gentile world."

"To the Greek these are the credentials of Jesus, no less essential than prophecy to the Jew, or power to the Roman. The Greek soul of that age furnishes the true key to the third Gospel."—*Ibid.*

Central and collateral truths in the Gospel by Luke:

THE LORD JESUS AS THE SAVIOUR.

Compassion—Death—Resurrection and ascension.

Key thoughts: "The Son of man establishing his kingdom in all the world." Christ the Son of man in his service amongst men. The central idea of the third Gospel, in its internal aspect, appears throughout. It is this: Jesus is the perfect, divine man, the Saviour of the world. Especially does it present the universal grace of God. In the character and condition of the Greek civilization in the apostolic age is to be found the key to the third Gospel.

Peculiarities of style. Luke's favorite expression, used also by Matthew, and less frequently by Mark, is, " And it came to pass." He used the word *sinner* oftener than all the other evangelists combined. The word *people*, also, is used oftener than in either of the other Gospels. *There was*, or it *happened that*, occurs about sixty times in the two compositions of Luke. Other characteristic words: "Son of man," "heal," "compassion," "prayer," "man," "all," "Gentile," "joy," "house," "blessed," "word," "women," "children," "sat at meat," "kingdom of God," thirty times.

The word "prayer," more frequent in Luke than in any other Gospel. The style of Luke is more classical than that of the other evangelists. The Gospel more of a biography than any of the others, it and Acts alone have dedications. The *physician* shows himself in the particular details of diseases; the *artist* in the vivid pictures of life-like scenes; the companion of Paul in the extension of the Gospel to the Gentiles (4 : 16-30). His history, complete, begins earlier, ends later; gives particulars about the Saviour's youth; has more references to dates and coeval events, etc. See Luke 1 : 5 ; 2 : 1, 2 ; 3 : 1 ; 2 : 21 ; 2 : 33 ; 2 : 37 ; 3 : 42 ; 9 : 20; 9 : 28; 13 : 16. Traces of his profession ; quotation of Isa. 59 : 1 ; in Luke 4 : 18 ; also in Luke 4 : 23. Compare Matt. 8 : 14, and Luke 4 : 38 ; Matt. 8 : 15 and Luke 4 : 39 ; Matt. 8 : 2, and Luke 5 : 12; Matt. 8 : 6, and Luke 7 : 2 ; Matt. 9 : 20, and Luke 8 : 43. Influence of Paul : Compare Luke 22 : 17, 20, and 1 Cor. 9 : 23, 26. Predilection for triplets, 1 Cor. 13 : 13 ; 1 Thess. 5 : 23 ; 2 Cor. 13 : 13.

Connection with other parts of the Scriptures. Compare Luke 21 with Mark 13 and Matt. 24, and compare generally with the Gospel by Mark.

ACTS.

Written for the Church by Luke, from Rome, A. D. 64. This book forms the sequel of Luke's Gospel. It is the history of the foundation and spread of the Christian Church— the former under Peter (1-12), the latter under Paul (12-28). It was founded on the day of Pentecost; its first sons were Jews, hence it appeared only a Jewish sect in Judea. The former part of the book is occupied with its establishment there, with arguments in its favor, and with challenges to disprove the fundamental fact of Christ's resurrection. Its first development into an organized community, with official staff, provoked the first persecution and martyrdom, which precipitated its extension to Samaria and Syria, caused a new and more independent centre of operations to be planted at Antioch, whence under Paul (the first converted persecutor) it spread to Asia Minor, Greece, Rome, and various parts of the Gentile world. The motive influence was the direct impulse of the Holy Spirit, not any preconceived plan of the apostolic body (2 : 4 ; 11 : 17 ; 15 : 6, 7, 9.)

Analysis. 1. The Acts of Peter: Birth of the Christian Church and extension to Samaria, comprising (1) foundation and progress of the Church in Jerusalem and Judea (1-8) ; (2) first persecution and extension to Samaria, and to Gentile family of Cornelius (8-11 : 18) ; (3) second persecution and foundation of the Church at Antioch (11 : 19 ; 13 : 3).

2. The Acts of Paul: Extension of the Church to the Gentiles. (1) Paul's call and first apostolic journey (13 : 4-15); (2) Council of Jerusalem fixing terms of admission (15); (3) second apostolic journey (15 : 36-18 ; 22) ; (4) third apostolic journey, (18 : 23-21 ; 17) ; (5) Paul's imprisonment at Cæsarea, and voyage to Rome (21 : 18-28). So the progress is recorded from a small Jewish sect to the universal Church. In this book all the articles of the Apostles' Creed may be found, chiefly in Peter's speeches (1-5).

This book might properly be called "The Acts of the Holy Ghost," for it contains his name nearly sixty times. It comprises a history of about thirty years, from the Saviour's ascension to Paul's arrival at Rome after his appeal to Cæsar.

Central and collateral truths in the Acts of the Apostles:

THE POWER OF THE GOSPEL.

Depravity—Darkness—Conversion—Illumination—Service.

Key thoughts: (1) Christ in heaven, and the energy of the Holy Ghost on earth. (2) " By the name of Jesus does this man stand before you whole." Others give chapter 1 : 8, as the key verse. It is a most suggestive fact that prayer, and united prayer, occupies so prominent a place in this instructive book. Another striking fact is the scriptural preaching of the apostles; and further, the dependence of the apostles and early Christians upon the Spirit.

Looking at the writings of Luke, in his Gospel and the Acts, as one book, they present to us four great thoughts clustered about their key words, "The Son of man."

1. Christ is the Son of man in the sense that *he has our true humanity*, and is one of our "brethren."

2. Christ is the Son of man in the sense that *he belongs to the whole race as "the uni-national man."*

3. Christ as the Son of man sends forth every Christian to "act" in his stead, and sends the Holy Spirit to give strength for the required activity.

4. Christ as the Son of man, is come to seek and to save that which was lost. Christ as the Son of man, feeling our infirmities, grasping the whole race with his atoning love, calling the Church to noble activity, and longing to save every lost soul.

Notice the frequent words, "accused" and "accusers" in contrast with "accord" and "added." Contrast also the oft repeated words, " boldness" with " bonds," and "joy" with " prisons."

Among the doctrines prominent in this book are: The divine nature of the Son of God; also of the Holy Ghost. Jesus is the object of divine worship by Stephen. He is spoken of as Lord of all. The Holy Ghost is called God, and many instances of his personality are given (8:29; 10:19; 13:2; 16:7; 20:28).

Prophecies and promises fulfilled. The Gospels close with a prophetic allusion to several facts recorded in the Acts, a promise of the Holy Spirit, of which this book gives the fulfilment (Luke 24:47-49; Mark 16:17, 18; John 14:12-17).

Biographies. Paul. His history, as given by himself in different parts of the New Testament, is as follows: He was a Jew of Tarsus, a city of Cilicia; a freeborn Roman citizen; a Pharisee and the son of a Pharisee; circumcised the eighth day; of the tribe of Benjamin; a Hebrew of the Hebrews; brought up at the feet of Gamaliel; taught according to the perfect manner of the law of the fathers; being conversant, also, not only with Jewish but Greek literature; and thus distinguished from the rest of the apostles as a man of education and learning. None of the twelve apostles were—humanly speaking—fitted to preach the Gospel to the *cultivated Gentile* world. To be by divine grace the spiritual conqueror of Asia and Europe, God raised up another instrument, from among the highly educated and zealous Pharisees.

Connection with other parts of the Scriptures. Luke undoubtedly intended this book as an *appendix* to his Gospel, if not, indeed, the whole may be considered as one publication in two parts. The careful reader will observe that where Luke's Gospel leaves off, the latter begins after the introduction contained in the first thirteen verses. The epistles plainly suppose that those facts had actually occurred which this history relates. Hence appears the importance of the Acts, as a kind of proscript to the Gospels, and as an introduction to the epistles, in the study of which it forms a most useful guide. Read this book particularly in connection with the epistles to the Romans, Ephesians, Colossians, Philippians, and Thessalonians; also the Gospel by Luke and Joel 2.

I. PETER.

Written from Babylon by Peter. Peter wrote this letter to the Hebrew Christians of the Eastern dispersion; "strangers scattered throughout Pontus, Galatia, Capadocia, Asia (Minor) and Bithynia," to whom he is said to have preached. As this was during the reign of the emperor Nero, it is supposed to have been a time of violent persecution, hence, the general design is to comfort them under their afflictions. Two of Paul's companions were his intimate associates, and one of them the bearer of this letter. "By Sylvanius (Silas), a faithful brother unto you, as I account him, I have written briefly, exhorting and testifying that this is the true grace of God wherein ye stand" (1 Pet. 5 : 12). This distinctly Pauline phrase sums up what has been called the Pauline element, running throughout the whole epistle. The epistle may well be designed as Peter's testimony to the truth of the Gospel taught by Paul.

Central and collateral truths in the first epistle of Peter:

STRENGTH AND PATIENCE UNDER TRIAL.

Obedience—Faith—Example of Christ—Hope—Trust —Glory.

Key thoughts: (1) God's righteous government in relation

to his saints. (2) "Precious." (3) Hope. The broad subject of Christian trials is the chief burden. The second advent of Christ is frequently referred to. Frequent mention is made of the possibility of living down, or "putting to silence the ignorance of foolish men," and winning the same by "good conversation." It contains a statement that Christ, by the agency of the Holy Spirit, preached to the inhabitants of the antediluvian world, who were spiritually dead. They were limited to 120 years further probation, which is styled a "prison." The writer's honorable mention of Paul as his beloved brother—though Paul had publicly exposed him to reproof, and had recorded that reproof in his epistle to the Galatians—exhibits a fine comment on his exhortation to others: "Be clothed with humility." Mark that the incorruptible word is the appointed means of the Christian's growth in holiness (1 Pet. 2 : 3 ; Col. 1 : 5, 6 ; 2 Pet. 1 : 8 ; 3 : 18 ; John 17 : 17 ; Psa. 109).

Connection with other parts of the Scriptures. Read in connection with this book, Acts 1 to 4; 10 to 12, 15. These two epistles seem to be founded on Matt. 16th and 17th chapters.

For whom is this book peculiarly suitable? For Christians under affliction and trials.

II. PETER.

Written by Peter "to them (Gentiles) who have obtained like precious faith *with us*" (Jews).

As in the first epistle Peter exhorts to patience under the *tyranny of persecution*, so in this he exhorts to perseverance in the truths of the Gospel against the deceptions of *heretics* and the profaneness of scoffers, describing their character and the certainty of their destruction, and urges diligence in the improvement of every Christian grace.

Summary. (1) An exhortation to persevere in faith and good works, by an assurance of the reality of the glorification of Christ as the pattern man, accepted by God, and the Messiah of prophecy (I). (2) Warning of the certainty of punishment on impenitent sinners, by reference to past history, e.g., the flood, overthrow of Sodom (2 : 1-10). (3) Warning against false teachers, by the example of Balaam (2 : 11-12). (4) The certainty of the Second Advent, and its warning, (a) to the godly, (b) to the wicked (3).

This book, like the other second epistles, is largely occupied with the last days.

Central and collateral truths in the second epistle to Peter :

FAITHFULNESS TO THE DIVINE WORD.

Scoffers—False teachers—Prophecy—Inspiration— Godliness—Day of Judgment.

Key thoughts : (1) God's righteous judgment upon the public Christian profession. (2) " Putting you in remembrance."

" How prone men seem to be to pervert the truth ! The Thessalonians supposed that our Lord's coming would be immediately. But those of whom Peter writes supposed it would be indefinitely delayed. Amidst such tendencies nothing less than the Divine Spirit could have preserved apostles in a watchful, patient frame, nor could anything less than the energy of the same Spirit have taught poor fishermen to speak as they do of God, of sin and of coming judgment. The sublimity, spirituality and harmony of these revelations are among the most decisive evidences of a divine inspiration. This epistle, like the second of those from Paul to Timothy, was penned when the writer knew himself to be drawing near to martyrdom ; and it derives a solemn interest from that consideration. It may be remarked, how important holiness appears to him at the moment when he was enjoying the highest anticipation of a glorious immortality ; and with what peculiar earnestness, as in the prospect of Christ's second coming, he urges it. Peter, after a life of suffering, and with the immediate prospect of the agonies of crucifixion, rejoices in the choice he had made of the service of Christ."—*Sel.*

Connection with other parts of the Scriptures. Read in connection with this epistle Matt. 16, 17, 24, Luke 21, Rev. 20, and the epistle of Jude.

For whom is this book peculiarly suitable? For believers who are suffering for the truth's sake. For the wavering and faltering.

MARK.

According to tradition this Gospel is Peter's, Mark being only his amanuensis. Internal evidences : For instance, he mentions things he would be likely to know or observe (see Mark 1 : 29 ; Luke 4 : 38 ; Matt. 21 : 20 and Mark 11 : 13, 14, 21). He omits anything that specially honored Peter : his walking on the sea (Matt. 14 : 28, 31 ; also Matt. 16 : 13, 19 ; 19 : 28 ; John 21 : 15, 19) ; and that he was the first of the disciples to whom Jesus appeared. Inserts all discreditable to himself, as Mark 8 : 32, 33 ; compare Matt. 26 : 75, and Mark 14 : 72 ; but mentions the message sent specially to him (Mark 16 : 7).

Mark was the John Mark mentioned in Acts 12 : 12, 25 ; 13 : 5, 13 ; 15 : 39 ; Col. 4 : 10 ; 1 Pet. 5 : 13. Supposed by some to be the young man mentioned in Mark 14 : 51, 52. Referred to by Paul (Phil. 24 ; 2 Tim. 4 : 11).

Neither of these men could have accomplished this work alone; for, even if Mark was of Roman birth and nature, he had not the facts of the Gospel; and even if Peter was a man of action and training, as such, he was at the same time of Jewish birth and nature. The two were indispensable. Written about A. D. 64 or 65.

Character of contents. Mark relates the works rather than the discourses of our Lord. Jesus is presented as the faithful servant. According to the terms of the prophecy (Isa. 43 : 1-3, 19 ; 49 : 6 ; 52 : 13 ; 53 : 11). This service was undertaken in secret prayer; it was a service promptly rendered. Ten times in the opening chapter we find the words *immediately, straightway, forthwith,* as indicating the haste and energy with which the obedient servant did the bidding of him who sent him. The Greek word so translated occurs eighty times in the New Testament, and forty times it is found in the short Gospel of Mark. It was a universal service—a service that entered into minute details, a service rendered in great tenderness, a service not performed for display, but carried on unobtrusively. He himself declares, only in this Gospel, " of that day and that hour knoweth no man, no, not the angels which are in heaven, neither the Son, but the Father." This language, which has perplexed so many, becomes perfectly plain, when we remember that it is the purpose of the Holy Ghost in Mark to reveal him as the faithful servant. All the way through this Gospel it is service. It is important, too, to state that Mark observes the chronological order of events, as Matthew does not, and hence it is easy to follow him in his narrative. Rabbi, not Lord (only so addressed by the Syro-Phœnician woman).

While Mark has so much in common with Matthew that many insist that he is a mere copyist or abridger, there is yet this wide difference, that whereas Matthew rests wholly on prophecy, Mark is so entirely independent of prophecy that, after the opening verses, he never even records the words of a prophet, except as he quotes from the mouth of Jesus.

For whom written. "Mark wrote for the instruction of Roman converts. No work of old Roman was ever more Roman in its rhetorical movement than the Gospel by Mark. This is further seen in its omissions and additions. Mark omits the parables of special Jewish significance and condemnatory of the Jews. The omission of the merely Greek features is equally apparent. He takes pleasure in giving the identical Aramean words used by Jesus. Note the employment by Mark of Latin words in Greek form, a thing which is nowhere else found in the New Testament, and which would have been unintelligible to readers of a purely Greek culture. The portions usually reckoned additions to this Gospel are the following: the parable of the seed corn; the healing of the blind man of Bethsaida; the healing of the deaf man of Decapolis; and the form of the last commission."—*Why Four Gospels*.

"Mark has altogether only four parables; viz., the sower, the seed corn, the mustard seed, and the wicked husbandman. The first three can best be understood together; these are employed in unfolding the growth of the kingdom as an *outward objective thing*. The first—the sower—contradicts the false Roman idea, by putting the invisible, spiritual power of truth in the place of the visible, material power of the Cæsars; the second—the seed corn—presents a development as independent of human will and as inevitable as that of Rome herself, according to the most Roman conception; the third—the mustard seed—completes the sketch of the development of the kingdom, showing the rapid growth into that universality which Rome alone, of all the worldly empires, had even imperfectly realized."—*Ibid.*

Central and collateral truths in the Gospel by Mark:

THE LORD JESUS AS THE DIVINE MAN.

Ministering service—Compassionate sympathy—Alleviated misery—Salvation.

Key thoughts: Christ the servant of his Father, and the meeter of man's need. The book of miracles wrought immediately by Christ as the Divine Servant, for the sake of those who believe, being astonished.

If the Roman was, as can be shown, the man of action, of state worship, of universal empire, these characteristics must furnish the key to the Gospel intended for him.

Peculiarities of style in this Gospel. Personal traits of Christ are recorded in this Gospel, not found elsewhere, as in Mark 11:11 and 10:32; and also mention in several places of Christ's being moved, grieved, loving, sighing. Only in Mark do we find the words in Mark 2:27 and 4:39.

In Mark, "straightway" or "immediately" occurs forty-one times. Vividness of description, as in Mark 1:13; 1:33. Compare Matt. 9:2, and Mark 2:3, 4; Matt. 8:23, 25, and Mark 4:36, 38.

The words " ran," " much," " many," " multitude," " all," " great," " forthwith," " amazed," " marvelled," " noised," "ablaze," "astonished," "great things," and "mighty works," abound in this intense Gospel.

Connection with other parts of the Scriptures. Compare Mark 13 with Matt. 24 and Luke 21; Mark 5 : 22-43 and Matt. 9 : 18-26 ; Mark 9 : 14-29 and Matt. 17 : 14-21, and compare generally with the Gospels by Matthew and Luke.

PASTORAL EPISTLES.

I. TIMOTHY.

Written by Paul from Macedonia to Timothy at Ephesus. Paul finding that his sad prophecy to the Ephesian elders (Acts 20 : 29-30) was already fulfilled, he left Timothy with this church to strengthen the things that remained. The church at Ephesus was in much confusion when the apostle was led by the Spirit to address his son Timothy. Ceremonialism, foolish questions, vain jangling, legalism, and even the putting away of faith and a good conscience on the part of some, had taken the place of the sublime doctrines set forth in the epistle they had previously received. This called for the exercise of discipline, and it was administered by one who speaks of himself as the chief of sinners (chap. 1). He also wrote to guide and encourage Timothy in the duties of his office, laying down rules of church organization for all times.

Central and collateral truths in the first epistle to Timothy:

MINISTERIAL FAITHFULNESS.

Mediation— Watchfulness—Purity—Meekness—Earnestness —Love.

Key thoughts : (1) "The doctrine which is according to godliness." (2) Church order, according to God.

"It is a remarkable fact that the inspired writer turns in his last epistles from addressing churches to individuals, as if in the last days only one here and another there will be found to receive the messages of the Holy Ghost. It is also remarkable that in the epistles to Timothy and Titus, he invokes 'grace, mercy and peace from God our Father and Jesus Christ our Lord,' whereas in the epistles to the seven churches previously addressed, he leaves out the word *mercy* in his invocation."—*Brooks.*

It is a striking fact that the epistle closes with a solemn and tender warning against the "oppositions of science falsely so-called," which some professing erred concerning the faith in that day, as they do in this (chap. 6).

Connection with other parts of the Scriptures. Read this epistle and compare with the second epistle to Timothy and the epistle to Titus. Also compare it with those portions of Ezekiel that speak of false prophets.

For whom is this book peculiarly suitable? For ministers of the Gospel.

TITUS.

Written by Paul to Titus, from Ephesus.

The name of this servant of the Lord is not mentioned in the Acts of the Apostles, and all that we know of him is gathered from the inspired epistles. He is referred to, however, in terms of warm commendation in 2 Cor. 2 : 13 ; 7 : 6, 7, 13-15 ; 8 : 6, 16-23 ; 12 : 18. In another place we learn that he was for a time at least the apostle's travelling companion, and that, being a Greek, Paul refused to have him circumcised, in order that the freedom of Gentile believers from the law might be vindicated and maintained at all hazards (Gal. 2 : 1-15).

The commission intrusted to Titus in Crete appears to have been peculiarly difficult. Although nature had endowed this island with all that could tend to make man happy, and the inhabitants had formerly been renowned for the wisdom of their constitution and their laws, long before this time the state of law and of morals had sunk very low. The character of the people was unsteady, insincere and quarrelsome: they were notoriously given to licentiousness and intemperance. This may in part account for the very severe remarks against the Cretans which occur in this epistle. We know nothing of the first introduction of the Gospel into Crete, but as there were Jews from that island among Peter's audience on the day of Pentecost (Acts 2 : 11), and they were numerous there, it is probable that the Christian faith was carried thither by converts from among them. It appears, also, from this epistle, that Paul had labored there, and with success, but that, by some means, he had been hurried thence, before he could order the state of the churches in a regular manner. Titus was left in Crete, in the same position which Timothy had occupied at Ephesus during Paul's absence, "to set in order the things that are wanting, and to ordain elders in every city."

Central and collateral truths in the epistle to Titus :

CHURCH ORDER AND DISCIPLINE.

Counsels—Cautions—Obedience—Doctrines—The Church's hope.

Key thoughts : (1) Christian qualifications for ministry and godly conduct. (2) " Shewing all good fidelity ; that they may adorn the doctrine of God our Saviour in all things." The words "Saviour" and "good works" are the most prominent expressions in this epistle. This book is remarkable, as compressing into a very short compass a very large amount of instruction, embracing doctrine, morals and discipline. It is very observable in this epistle, that those of the *humblest* rank are exhorted to *adorn* the Gospel (2 : 10), and that while our salvation is ascribed exclusively to grace (2 : 11), this fact is made the ground of the most urgent exhortations to holiness (2 : 14 ; 3 : 8).

Connection with other parts of the Scriptures. There is a striking resemblance between this epistle and the first to Timothy, both of which should be studied together.

For whom is this book peculiarly suitable ? For ministers of the Gospel.

II. TIMOTHY.

Written by Paul to Timothy during his second imprisonment at Rome, A. D. 68.

This epistle is the last written by the beloved apostle, and it possesses all the interest which gathers about the farewell message of a dying father to his son. He viewed his case as desperate (4 : 16), and his martyrdom as imminent (4 : 6-8), and he entreats Timothy to come to him at once (5 : 9-21), to be with him at his last trial.

This book obviously reaches on, not only to the latter times, as in the former epistle, but to the last days, when something worse than the Romish apostasy will come ; for apostate Christendom will get back to ancient heathenism, as may be seen by comparing 2 Tim. 3 : 1-8, with Rom. 1 : 21-32. Hence the apostle seeks to stir up Timothy, who seems to have been alarmed and discouraged by the turning away of all Asia from the servant of the Lord, even then awaiting death (chap. 1).

Central and collateral truths in the second epistle to Timothy:

DYING COUNSELS.

Endurance—Purity—Perilous times—Faithfulness—Crown of rewards.

Key thoughts : (1) "The doctrine that is according to godliness." (2) Church disorder, and the individual pathway. (3) Personal holiness.

"This epistle contains a noble view of the consolation which Christians enjoy in the midst of suffering, and in the prospect of death (1 : 9-18 ; 2 : 9-13 ; 4 : 6-8, 16-18). The holiest spiritual affection to God and Christ is not only consistent with human friendships, but productive of them (1 : 2-5 ; 4 : 9-21). Nowhere are privilege and duty, grace and holiness more closely combined (2 : 19). In the approaching corruption of Christianity Paul directs Timothy to the true conservative principle of its purity ; not miracles, nor a fresh revelation, but the doctrine in which Timothy had been instructed, and those Scriptures which make the man of God perfect, thoroughly furnished unto all good works (3 : 14-17 ; 2 Thess. 2 ; 2 Pet. 1 : 15-21 ; 3 : 1-4, 14-17). How instructive that in the last writings of both Peter and Paul, nor less in the writings of John (Rev. 22), and in the prospect of the heresies that were to prevail in the Church, we should be directed to the study of the Bible, and that we are thus led to expect no additional disclosure of the divine will. THE CROSS—our hope, our model, our motive : THE CROWN—its purity, certainty, blessedness : THE WORD— promise, precept, doctrine, all complete—are among the last words of the sacred page. Only let these continue to be set forth, and the Church need not fear."—*Angus.*

Paul the prisoner, and Timothy aroused, chap. 1. Paul the soldier, and Timothy encouraged, chap. 2. Paul the witness, and Timothy warned, chap. 3. Paul the martyr, and Timothy charged, chap. 4

Connection with other parts of the Scriptures. Read this epistle, and compare with the first epistle to Timothy and the epistle to Titus. Compare chap. 3 with Rev. 3 : 14-22.

For whom is this book peculiarly suitable? For ministers of the Gospel.

JUDE.

Written by Jude—called Lebbeus and Thaddeus.—A. D. 67.

"The design of this epistle is clearly to guard the Christian Church against those false teachers who resolved all religion into speculative belief and outward profession, and sought to allure the disciples into insubordination and licentiousness. Apart from the fact that both Peter and Jude wrote under the direction of the Holy Ghost, any attentive reader can readily perceive that Peter wrote in his second epistle of sin, while Jude advances the thought of apostasy. A comparison of 2 Peter 2 : 4 with Jude 6 will illustrate the difference."

Central and collateral truths in the epistle of Jude :

EVILS OF APOSTASY.

Ungodliness—Lasciviousness—Denial of Christ—Lawlessness—Judgment—Darkness forever.

Key thoughts : (1) Apostasy traced down to the last days. (2) " Ungodly."

One of the perverse things which these corrupt teachers

spoke, for the purpose of alluring the wicked, was that *God was so good that he would not punish men* for indulging those natural appetites which he has himself implanted in them, nor be displeased with them for committing a *few sins*, which can do him no harm, but which are necessary to their present happiness. Wherefore, to show the impiety and falsehood of that doctrine, and to secure the disciples from being seduced by it, the apostle, by facts recorded in Scripture, proved that, as God had already punished the angels who sinned, notwithstanding their *dignity*, and the antediluvians, notwithstanding their *number*, so will he at length most assuredly punish all obstinate sinners in the severest manner.

Connection with other parts of the Scriptures. Read in connection with this epistle 1 Tim. 4 ; 2 Tim. 3, and compare with 2 Peter generally.

For whom is this book peculiarly suitable? For the careless professor and trifler with sin. It, however, contains suitable warnings for the most advanced saint.

I. JOHN.

Written from Ephesus by the apostle John.

Most expositors tell us that this epistle was addressed wholly to genuine believers. That the most of it is we will admit, but not entirely so. There was living in John's day a class of religionists who styled themselves *Gnostics*, or, those who know everything. They were the antipodes of the *Agnostics* of the present day, who claim to know nothing. These Gnostics claimed that they were part of Deity, and consequently they not only knew everything as God knows everything, but they were also as pure and holy as God, and always had been. Consequently they had no need of the Gospel, no need of the cleansing blood of Jesus Christ. They claimed to have fellowship with God, and yet their lives, as everybody could see, were full of sin, and they were living in moral darkness and condemnation. It was evidently one object of this epistle to counteract errors already prevalent. Some questioned the *divine dignity* of our Lord and denied him to be the Son of God. These the apostle calls deceivers and Antichrist (2 : 22 ; 4 : 15 ; 5 : 1). Others denied his *humanity*, thus contradicting the real fellowship of Christ with men (Heb. 2 : 16 ; 4 : 15), and the reality of his death and propitiation. His incarnation was, as they held, but an appearance, and the story of his life, a myth. This delusion the apostle strongly denounces (4 : 3), and declares that he had himself felt with his hand the body of his Lord (1 : 1). A third party seems to have held that it was enough to worship God with the spirit, and that the body might have all possible indulgence. This immoral creed the apostle refutes by showing that every sin is real transgression (3 : 4) ; that fellowship with God purifies the Christian, and that by this purity only can we be recognized as his (3 : 8-10 ; 2 : 5 ; 4 : 13 ; 5 : 11).

But the special object of this epistle was to confirm believers in the doctrines of Christianity, and to promote brotherly love, and is addressed to Christians everywhere. While the Gospel of John is about the Son of God, this beautiful epistle is about the sons of God.

Central and collateral truths in the first epistle of John :

LIGHT AND LOVE.

Propitiation — Sonship — Obedience — Fellowship — Victory.

Key thoughts : (1) Christ the eternal life and power of communion with God. (2) "These words have I written

unto you, that ye may KNOW that ye have eternal life."
(3) Christ our advocate. The word "know" as an expression of Christian assurance is very frequent in this epistle. The truth most largely insisted upon in this epistle is the necessity of *holiness*, as the evidence and fruit of faith. Note the contrast drawn between hatred and love.

HATRED.	LOVE.
He that saith he is in the light, and hateth his brother, is in *darkness* even until now (2 : 9). But he that hateth his brother, is in darkness, and *walketh in darkness*, and knoweth not whither he goeth, because that darkness hath blinded his eyes (2 : 9). Whosoever doeth not righteousness *is not of God*, neither he that loveth not his brother (3 : 10). He that loveth not his brother *abideth in death* (3 : 14). Whosoever hateth his brother *is a murderer* (3 : 15). He that loveth not *knoweth not God* (4 : 8). If a man say I love God and hateth his brother, *he is a liar* (2 : 20).	He that loveth his brother, *abideth in the light*, and there is none occasion of stumbling in him (3 : 10). If we love one another God dwelleth in us, and his love is perfected in us (4 : 12). Every one that loveth *is born of God and knoweth God* (4 : 7). He that abideth in love *abideth in God* and God abideth in him (4 : 16).

The epistle is throughout especially useful, as it presents many *tests* by which to try the sincerity of our Christian profession.

The writer of this book was noted for a peculiarly affectionate disposition. So that he obtained the title of "the loving disciple," yet none has spoken of false doctrines more sharply. The gentlest Christian may be a son of thunder (Luke 3 : 13-19) when Christ's honor is at stake, and charity may be exercised in denouncing sin, as well as in loving the brethren.

Connection with other parts of the Scriptures. Study this book in connection with the Gospel and the two following epistles by the same writer.

For whom is this book peculiarly suitable ? For Unitarians, Socinians, and for believers generally.

II. JOHN.

Written from Ephesus, by the apostle John. The object of this letter—addressed to the elect lady, or the elect *Kyria* and her children—was to congratulate this lady on the piety of her children, exhorting her to continue in the truth and in love, cautioning her against the deceiver and Antichrist, and urging the importance of abiding in the doctrine of Christ.

Central and collateral truths in the second epistle of John:

FAMILY RELIGION.

Truth—Love—Obedience—Steadfastness.

Key thoughts: (1) Christ and the truth, the safeguard against heresy. (2) "Truth." The word "truth" rings out five times—the Jewish number—in this little epistle. An apostolic epistle so addressed, shows with what vigilant affection the ministers of the Gospel ought to cherish the piety of those whom they have gained, and it shows no less *the importance in the sight of God* of the station of a *Christian mother*, the earnestness with which she should interest herself in the religious welfare of her children, and the encouragement which by so doing, she will give to Christian mothers and to the progress of truth.

Connection with other parts of the Scriptures. Should be read in connection with the other epistles and the Gospel by this apostle. Also with certain portions of the book of Proverbs which treat on the government of children.

For whom is this book peculiarly suitable? For Christian mothers.

III. JOHN.

Written from Ephesus, by the apostle John. Gaius of Corinth, to whom this epistle is addressed, and who is probably the person mentioned (1 Cor. 1 : 14 and Rom. 16 : 23), was an eminent Christian, particularly distinguished for his hospitality to those who went about preaching the Gospel. The apostle expresses his affectionate joy at this other evidence of his piety, cautions him against one Diatrephes, noted for his ambition and turbulence, and strongly recommends Demetrius to his friendship; deferring other things to a personal conversation.

This brief epistle, reaching on to the very last days, is also addressed to an individual, and seven times—the church or Jewish number of completeness—does the word *truth* sound forth. The first epistle, like the first epistle of Peter, comforts believers amid trials arising from the world; but the second and third epistles, like the second of Peter, seek to confirm them against far greater trial arising from within the Church.

Central and collateral truths in the third epistle of John :

CHRISTIAN HOSPITALITY.

Soul prosperity—Brotherly love—Truth—Helping—Sincere friendship.

Key thoughts : (1) Christian hospitality to the saints, especially to laborers. (2) "Truth."

Peter, says one, wrote about hope, " when the chief Shepherd shall appear." The key-note of Paul's writing appears to be of faith, and John's of love. Faith, Hope and Charity; these were the three characteristics of three men—the key-note of the whole of their teachings.

"As in the second epistle of Peter *knowledge* is mentioned seven times, so in the third epistle of John, brief as it is, *truth* is mentioned seven times, showing to what manifold and dangerous errors and lies believers will be exposed in the last days or Christian age. As the second epistle of John tells us whom to reject, the third epistle tells us whom to receive, not merely as an act of charity, not simply as an expression of Christian courtesy, but 'that we might be fellow-helpers to the truth.' It is the most significant that in this last of the inspired epistles, touching the condition of things in the last days, so much is made of the truth, and that the Church is mentioned three times, though existing amid surrounding ruins. But the dear old apostle could lift up his eyes above earth's gloom to look for the ' Bright and Morning Star,' and in the expectation of soon beholding its golden light he could say, ' I trust I shall shortly (immediately) see thee, and we shall speak face to face.' There will not be many left, however, and hence he closes with the sweet and solemn words, 'Greet the friends by name.'"— *Brooks*.

This epistle should be studied with the other writings of the apostle John, and is suitable for all Christians to profit by. The word Antichrist occurs only in these epistles. It means either one who claims to be Christ, or one opposed to him; and such are all who deny that Jesus is Messiah (or Christ) or that the Messiah has come in the flesh. When the word is applied to the great apostasy (2 Thess. 2 : 3-10), as it is in modern discussion, it means that that apostasy is supremely opposed to our Lord in his teaching and office.

REVELATION.

Written by the apostle John when "in the isle that is called Patmos."

John was banished by Domitian to Patmos, after a vain attempt to martyr him; but on the emperor's death he may have returned, under a general amnesty, to Ephesus, and resumed the supervision of that church. While in exile he saw and recorded these visions. The book consists of matters partly historical, but chiefly prophetical, revealed to the apostle by the Lord Jesus. The special object of it is to make known the things that are, and the things which shall be hereafter; and in this way to exhibit the prophetic history of the Church of Christ down to the end of the age; at the same time to comfort the early Church under impending persecutions.

The Message to the Seven Churches (2, 3): viz., (1) EPHESUS: reproof for forsaking its first love and first works. (2) SMYRNA: commendation of works, poverty, endurance of persecution. (3) PERGAMOS: reproof for false doctrine, immoral conduct, idolatrous pollution. (4) THYATIRA: reproof to one party for similiar corruptions; commendation to the other for their fidelity. (5) SARDIS: reproof for spiritual deadness with mere nominal life. (6) PHILADELPHIA: approval of its steadfastness and patience. (7) LAODICEA: rebuke for lukewarmness. These predictions have long been fulfilled, but the remainder of the book is still a mystery, though generally regarded as prophetic of the history of the Church from the close of the first century to the end of time. By some, the major part is considered to have had its fulfilment in the early ages of the Church; by others, to have been gradually realized by successive religious revivals and persecutions; by others, it is regarded as a picture of the historical epochs of the world and the Church.

The interpretation of this book. "The Apocalypse had its immediate origin in two events which happened at this period of the life of St. John. One was the Neronian persecution. The other was the outbreak of the Jewish war. It was not until these events were over, it was not until their divine teaching had done its work, that a third and more gradual event—the development of gnostic teaching in the form of new Christologies—called forth in its turn the Gospel and the epistles of 'St. John as the final utterance of Christian revelation. Unless we study these events, there is no chance of our understanding the writings of John.

"It is true that our want of familiarity with Apocalyptic symbols which were familiar to the Jewish Christians of that epoch, seems at first to give to many of the apostle's thoughts an unwonted obscurity. But on the other hand, the obscurity does not affect those elements of the book which we at once feel to be of the most eternal import; and on the other, we are only left in the dark about minor details which have found no distinct record in history. Let any student compare the symbols of the Apocalypse with those of Joel, Isaiah, Ezekiel, Zechariah and Daniel; let him then see how those symbols are applied by the almost contemporary writers of such Jewish Apocalypses as the book of Enoch, the fourth book of Esdras, and the vision of Baruch; let him meditate on the conditions of the age in the particulars which we have just been passing in review;

lastly, let him bear in mind the luminous principle that the Apocalypse is a stormy comment on the great discourse of our Lord on Olivet, as it was being interpreted by the signs of the times, and he will read the vision of the apostle with a freshness of interest and a clearness of apprehension such as he may never previously have enjoyed."—*Sel.*

It is " The Revelation of Jesus Christ—not of St. John the Divine, as the uninspired title falsely asserts—which God gave unto him to show unto his servants things which must shortly come to pass." As he gave it, therefore, to show his servants what is certainly coming to pass, it cannot be his will to have them turn from its solemn testimony in utter unconcern.

"The plea that is constantly urged as an excuse for indifference to this portion of the inspired Word, is our inability to understand it. But, as if God foresaw the excuse, and determined to sweep it out of the way of obedience to his command, says, 'Blessed is he that readeth, and they that hear the words of this prophecy, and keep those things which are written therein.' There is a blessing for him that readeth, and for them that hear. Any child of God can get this blessing, and every one should desire it. '*He* that readeth' implies that it should be read personally, and '*they* that hear' indicates that the people should have an opportunity of listening to it, and of understanding it. Even if they cannot read, it is blessed to hear and to keep the words of the prophecy."—*Ibid.*

"To those who would trifle with the prophetic parts of this book because of their mystery, the following considerations may not be without value: No prophecies in the Revelation can be more clouded with obscurity than that a child should be born of a pure virgin—that a mortal should not see corruption—that a person despised and numbered among malefactors should be established forever on the throne of David. Yet still the pious Jew preserved his faith entire, amidst all these wonderful, and, in appearance, contradictory intimations. He looked into the holy books in which they were contained with reverence, and, with an eye of patient expectation, 'waited for the consolation of Israel.' We in the same manner look up to these prophecies of the Apocalypse for the full consummation of the great scheme of the Gospel, when Christianity shall finally prevail over all the corruptions of the world and be universally established in its utmost purity."—*Ibid.*

Central and collateral truths in the book of Revelation:

THE ADVENT OF OUR LORD IN GLORY.

Antichrist— Warfare—Destruction—Resurrection— Judgment— Victory.

Key thoughts: (1) Christ assuming the government of the world. (2) Things to come. (3) "Overcome." The word "overcome" is used twenty-two times by John—sixteen in Revelation; and only three by all other New Testament writers.

Among the prophetic visions of the Apocalypse, there is one which appears peculiarly prominent (17, 18); and which acquires the greater importance, as well as clearness, from other prophetic intimations evidently referring to the subject (2 Thess. 2 : 3-12 ; 1 Tim. 4 : 1-5). There is an unusual agreement among the greater number of the best expositors, in explaining these combined prophecies ; although some consider them to refer to events still future. They are regarded as predicting the rise and temporary ascendancy of a great apostate power, in the midst of the Christian Church, which should be distinguished by the following characteristics : (1) Eminent corruption of religion, which corruption, by fraud as well as force, it spreads and maintains throughout the world (2 Thess. 2 : 3, 8-10 ; 1 Tim. 4 : 1, 2 ; Rev. 17 : 2-5 ; 18 : 3-5 ; 19 : 2). (2) Gross immorality and licentiousness, combined with hypocritical and self-righteous asceticism (1 Tim. 4 : 2, 3). (3) Arrogant and blasphemous pretensions, usurpation of divine prerogatives, opposition against God, and persecution of his people (2 Thess. 2 : 4, 5 ; Rev. 17 : 6-14 ; 18 : 6-20 ; 19 : 2). (4) Great wealth, magnificence and luxury (Rev. 17 : 4 ; 18 : 7, 8, 11-19). (5) Reliance upon the support and aid of worldly powers, whose tyranny it sanctions and upholds (Rev. 17 : 1, 2, 15, 17 ; 18 : 3, 9).

Connection with other parts of the Scriptures. Read in connection with this book Dan. 7, 8, 11, 12 ; Isa. 10 ; Matt. 24 ; 2 Thess. 2. Compare Rev. 19 with Ezek. 39, Joel 3, Zech. 14. Compare the pouring out of the vials with the description of the plagues inflicted on Egypt. Ezekiel is almost repeated in various parts of Revelation. There is this difference between Daniel and Revelation, that what the former is told to shut up and seal to the time of the end, the last is told to reveal. Revelation has 250 allusions to the Old Testament, as if to sum up all before it. The reader will notice many contrasts between this last book and Genesis, the first—paradise—tree of life, etc.

For whom is this book peculiarly suitable? For the diligent, prayerful student of the Word of God.

JOHN.

Written from Ephesus by John, about A. D. 97. It is clearly a fact of history that the fourth Gospel was prepared and given to the Church long after the other three had been completed. If, as is generally supposed, his Gospel was not written till near the close of the first century, he was ripened for it by an experience of nearly seventy years.

John was not what the painters have represented him, an effeminate man, but with much of force and fire in his nature, yet a reverent, loving man, with special gifts of insight. These points are illustrated by his never giving the name of John to any one but the Baptist. His delineation of his character in John 3 : 25, 36 ; also in his record of the mingled familiarity and reverence marking the intercourse between Christ and his disciples (John 4 : 27 ; 13 : 23, 36). His love is shown in Mary being committed to his care ; in his full account of Peter's restoration (John 21 : 15, 19) ; and in his making a companion of Peter (John 21 : 7 ; Acts 3 : 1).

John is said to have remained at Jerusalem till the death of Mary, about the year A. D. 48. After Paul had left Asia Minor, John went to labor there, residing chiefly at Ephesus, and founding several churches in that country. Shortly afterwards, during the persecution under Domitian —or, according to others, toward the end of the reign of Nero—he was banished to Patmos, an island in the Ægean Sea, where he received the visions of the Apocalypse. On the accession of Nerva he was liberated and returned to Ephesus, where he continued to labor during the rest of his life. He died in the hundredth year of his age, about A. D. 100.

Character of contents. This Gospel was intended to correct what was false in the Jewish and heathen systems of religious philosophy.

Tradition says he wrote this Gospel to present an aspect of Christ's nature apt to be too little regarded by readers of the other Gospels—the divinity of Christ. His Gospel was written after the destruction of Jerusalem (see John 11 : 18 and 18 : 1—hence safe to relate the resurrection of Lazarus—and John 18 : 10, and 18 : 26, which compare with 18 : 16).

Generally, his Gospel is rather a compilation of distinct dissertations than a continuous narrative. It connects the redemption of mankind with the creation by the same source of life. Its subject is: " The Eternal Word made Flesh." 1. As pre-existent. 2. As incarnate. 3. As revealing the Father. 4. As connecting humanity with divinity through his own incarnation by means of spiritual agency. Hence, the transmission of this spiritual influence through material substances is *evidenced* by the first miracle, 2 ; *expounded* to *Nicodemus*, 3 ; *allegorized* to the Samaritan woman, 4 ; *exemplified* in the impotent man, 5 ; *symbolized* and emphasized in the feeding of 5,000 and subsequent discourse. The revelation of the Father is developed by miracle and parable in 7 : 10. His life-giving power communicated to human nature temporarily and eternally by spiritual agency in 11-13 ; the perpetual transmission of that power from himself to mankind through his apostles, and their commission to execute their functions, in 14 : 21. This Gospel was probably *the last written* of all the books of the Bible ; and while proving the divine nature of Christ, it corrected several of the heresies—Gnosticism, etc.—which sprang up in
19

the first age of Christianity, and it supplies an answer to some that prevail in our own.

For whom written. John's Gospel was written for mankind. In it Christ is the light of the world, and in it no knowledge of Jewish custom or topography is assumed.

"The fact that the first three Gospels were missionary Gospels, originally preached to unspiritual men with the view of bringing them to Christ, accounts for their so marked variation from John, the Christian Gospel, originally preached to spiritual men already brought to faith in Christ by the Gospel in its first three forms, and preached for the purpose of aiding them in making progress in the divine life. The impossibility of only one Gospel, the absurdity of four Gospels of precisely similar character, and the completeness of the four Gospels as they are, all appear manifest from this point of view.

"In the *I ams* which fell from the lips of Jesus himself, as given by John, is summed up the fullest possible exhibition of his person and work, and of that perfect satisfaction for the spiritual wants of all men which is to be found only in him.

"The Christian aim of the fourth Gospel appears especially in its *omission* of facts and truths made prominent in the other Gospels. He omits parables, with the partial exceptions of John 10 : 1, 16, and 15 : 1, 5 ; because he does not record Christ's popular discourses, but his private conversations with his disciples, and theological discussions with the highly educated Pharisees and Sadducees. He repeats only two of the miracles recorded by the other evangelists—the feeding of the five thousand and the walking on the sea. The explanation of the first of these, in John 6 : 35, 51, makes known to us that miracles are parables, and form a complete system illustrated by the miracles of resurrection, of which the first was that of an only daughter, the second that of an only son, and the third that of an only brother. The first, that of one just dead; the second, dead one being carried to the grave; the third, that of one buried four days. The culminating miracle of resurrection is that of him who was the only begotten Son of God. No human genealogy, no divine origin of the Messiah, no early experience and preparation for his work, no sermon on the mount, no apprehensions of the cross, no delivering to the Gentiles and mocked and spitefully treated and spitted upon, no prayer in the garden or agony, no angel strengthening him, not a word of sweating as if it were great drops of blood; no weakness, but power; no darkness, no commending himself to God. The divine beams though the human everywhere.

"Still more clearly does the Christian aim of John's Gospel appear from the *additions* which he makes to the material furnished by the other evangelists. These additions are: John the Baptist directing his disciples to Christ; Christ turning water into wine; his healing the nobleman's son; the infirm man at the pool of Bethesda, and the blind man at the pool of Siloam; and his raising Lazarus from the dead; to which may be added his discourses with Nicodemus, with the Samaritan woman, with the Pharisees concerning his divinity at Capernaum, concerning himself as the bread of life, and with his disciples on various occasions, particularly on the night preceding his crucifixion; his intercessory prayer; and after his resurrection his appearence to his disciples at the sea of Tiberias, and the restoration of Peter to the apostolic office."—*Why Four Gospels*,

Central and collateral truths in the Gospel by John:

THE LORD JESUS AS GOD.

Light—Life—Salvation—Union—Power—Glory.

Key thoughts: (1) Christ the Son of God in the moral glory of his person and ways. (2) Believe on the Son of God, who is before all and above all. The character and needs of the Christian furnish the key to John's Gospel. The first eighteen verses of the first chapter will give a clue to the intention of the whole Gospel.

Peculiarities of style. John's favorite expression is "After," and "After these things." John's Gospel is remarkable for peculiar terms applied to Christ: "The Word," "Only begotten," "Life," "Light," "Lamb"—all designed to set him forth as the Divine Saviour of men. The words "love," "truth" and "faith," are of frequent occurrence—the latter especially is used one hundred times, or almost as many times as all the other New Testament writers—Paul included—taken together. No other evangelist uses the expression, *Verily, verily,* even once, but John uses it twenty-five times. Other characteristic words: "Him that sent me," "Father," "Holy Spirit," "disciples," "believe," "love," "abide." He alone of the evangelists indulges in comment, as John 7 : 39 ; 11 : 51 ; 11 : 13. His style is simple, vivid, earnest, reverential, often full of pathos.

CHAPTER VII.—MISCELLANEOUS HELPS.

A MODEL BIBLE-SCHOOL.

Neh. 8.

BY REV. R. CRITTENDEN.

ABBREVIATIONS: f. c., first clause; m. c., middle clause; l. c., last clause.

1. The inspired writer describes here (Neh. 8 : 1-12) what may be properly termed a Bible-school. The object of their meeting was to read and learn the law of God.

Proof.—And they spake unto Ezra the scribe to bring the book of the law of Moses, which the Lord had commanded to Israel (v. 1, l. c.).

And Ezra opened the book in the sight of all the people (v. 5, f. c.).

2. They took the morning, the best part of the day, for this important service.

Proof.—And Ezra read therein before the street that was before the water-gate, from the morning until midday (v. 3, f. c.).

3. The school was composed of men and women, as well as young people and children.

Proof.—And Ezra the priest brought the law before the congregation both of men and women, and all that could hear with understanding (v. 2, f. c.).

4. Officers, teachers, and scholars were punctual. There is no record of any one being late.

Proof.—And all the people gathered themselves together as one man (v. 1, f. c.).

5. Their lessons were uniform. Old and young had the same lesson.

Proof.—And the ears of all the people were attentive unto the book of the law (v. 3, l. c.).

6. The pastor (Ezra the priest), the governor (Nehemiah), and other leaders in religious service (the Levites), were present, and took part in the exercises.

Proof.—And Nehemiah, which is the Tirshatha, and Ezra the priest the scribe, and the Levites that taught the people (v. 9, f. c.).

7. The school was opened with prayer by the pastor (Ezra the priest).

Proof.—And Ezra blessed the Lord, the great God (v. 6, f. c.).

8. The whole school joined in the opening exercises.

Proof.—And all the people answered, Amen, Amen, with lifting up their hands (v. 6, m. c.).

9. The exercises were performed in a reverent manner, consistent with the worship of God.

Proof.—And they bowed their heads, and worshipped the Lord with their faces to the ground (v. 6, l. c.).

10. More than fourteen of the best men were teachers in this school.

Proof.—Also Jesh'-u-a, Ba'-ni, Sher-e-bi'-ah, Ja'-min, Ak'-kub, Shab-beth'-a-i, Ho-di'-jah, Ma-as-ei'-ah, Kel'-i-ta, Az-a-ri'-ah, Joz'-a-bad, Ha'-nan, Pel-a-i'-ah, and the Levites caused the people to understand the law (v. 7, f. c.).

11. Instead of giving their own opinions, the teachers endeavored to explain the meaning of the Scripture lesson.

Proof.—They gave the sense, and caused them to understand the reading (v. 8, l. c.).

12. The exercises were so conducted as to secure the attention of both old and young.

Proof.—And the ears of all the people were attentive unto the book of the law (v. 3, l. c.).

13. All remained until the close of the school. There were none going out or coming in during the session.

Proof.—And the people stood in their place (v. 7, l. c.).

14. The members of this Bible-school were encouraged to make contributions to benevolent objects.

Proof.—He said unto them, ... send portions unto them for whom nothing is prepared (v. 10, f. c.).

15. The lesson was so taught as to make a deep impression upon the entire school.

Proof.—For all the people wept when they heard the words of the law (v. 9, l. c.).

16. At the close of the school, the lesson was summed up and applied in a few encouraging words.

Proof.—He said unto all the people, This day is holy unto the Lord your God (v. 9, m. c.).

Neither be ye sorry; for the joy of the Lord is your strength (v. 10, l. c.).

17. The object of their meeting was accomplished.

Proof.—And all the people . . . made great mirth because they had understood the words that were declared unto them (v. 12).

THE SEVEN BIBLES OF THE WORLD.

The seven Bibles of the world are the Koran of the Mohammedans, the Eddas of the Scandinavians, the Try Pitikes of the Buddhists, the Five Kings of the Chinese, the Three Vedas of the Hindoos, the Zendavesta, and the Scriptures of the Christians. The Koran is the most recent of these seven Bibles, and not older than the seventh century of our era. It is a compound of quotations from the Old and New Testaments, the Talmud, and the Gospel of St. Barnabas. The Eddas of the Scandinavians were first published in the fourteenth century. The Pitikes of the

Buddhists contain sublime morals and pure aspirations, but their author lived and died in the sixth century before Christ. There is nothing of excellence in these sacred books not found in the Bible. The sacred writings of the Chinese are called the Five Kings—king meaning web of cloth, or the warp that keeps the threads in their places. They contain the best sayings of the best sages on the ethico-political duties of life. These sayings cannot be traced to a period higher than the eleventh century B. C. The three Vedas are the most ancient books of the Hindoos, and it is the opinion of Max Müller, Wilson, Johnson and Whitney that they are not older than eleven centuries B. C. The Zendavesta of the Persians is the grandest of all the sacred books next our Bible. Zoroaster, whose sayings it contains, was born in the twelfth century B. C. Moses lived and wrote his Pentateuch fifteen centuries B. C., and therefore has a clear margin of 300 years older than the most ancient of the sacred writings.—*Sel.*

THE LIFE-GIVING WORD.

What encouragement, what hope may be drawn from seeing how precisely the words of one part of Scripture meet and supplement words of other parts, promise meeting supplication, encouragement meeting despondency, light driving away darkness, love casting out fear. Let us take, for instance, that most heart-broken of utterances, that "prayer of the afflicted when he *is overwhelmed*," the first twelve verses of the one hundred and second Psalm, and hear how God answers from his Holy Word:

HELPS TO BIBLE STUDY.

PSALM CII.	ANSWER OF THE HOLY SPIRIT THROUGH THE WORD OF GOD.
(A prayer of the afflicted, when he is overwhelmed and poureth out his complaint before the Lord.)	
1. Hear my prayer, O Lord, and let my cry come unto thee.	He will fulfil the desire of them that fear him, he also will hear their cry and will save them (Psa. 145 : 19).
2. Hide not thy face from me in the day when I am in trouble; incline thine ear unto me; in the day when I call answer me speedily.	He shall call upon me and I will answer him : I will be with him in trouble; I will deliver him and honor him (Psa. 91 : 15).
3. For my days are consumed like smoke, and my bones are burned as a hearth.	A bruised reed shall he not break and the smoking flax shall he not quench (Isa. 42 : 3).
4. My heart is smitten and withered like grass ; so that I forget to eat my bread.	Thy words were found and I did eat them ; and thy word was unto me the joy and rejoicing of my heart (Jer. 15 : 6).
5. By reason of the voice of my groaning my bones cleave to my skin.	And the Lord shall guide thee continually and satisfy thy soul in drought and make fat thy bones : and thou shalt be like a watered garden, and like a spring of water, whose waters fail not (Isa. 58 : 11).
6. I am like a pelican of the wilderness ; I am like an owl of the desert.	I give waters in the wilderness and rivers in the desert to give drink to my people, my chosen (Isa. 43 : 20).
7. I watch and am as a sparrow alone upon the housetop.	Are not five sparrows sold for two farthings? and not one of them is forgotten before God (Luke 12 : 6).
8. Mine enemies reproach me all the day ; and they that are mad against me are sworn against me.	Blessed are ye, when men shall revile you, and persecute you, and shall say all manner of evil against you falsely, for my sake (Matt. 5 : 11).
9. For I have eaten ashes like bread, and mingled my drink with weeping.	To give unto them beauty for ashes, the oil of joy for mourning (Isa. 61 : 3).
10. Because of thine indignation and thy wrath : for thou hast lifted me up and cast me down.	For yet a very little while and the indignation shall cease (Isa. 10 : 25). Cast down, but not destroyed (2 Cor. 4 : 9).

11. My days are like a shadow that declineth ; and I am withered like grass.

12. But thou, O Lord, shalt endure for ever, and thy remembrance unto all generations.

The grass withereth, and the flower fadeth, but the word of our God shall stand forever (Isa. 40 : 8).

And a book of remembrance was written before him for them that feared the Lord and that thought upon his name. And they shall be mine, saith the Lord of Hosts, in that day when I make up my jewels (Mal. 3 : 16, 17).

"Observe how, as the soul, like an overtired child, utters all its complaint, going on from grief to grief, each one more hopeless than the former, the Spirit gently, tenderly, encouragingly replies, giving back word of cheer for word of woe, until finally, in spite of herself, the soul breaks forth into exultation, 'But thou, O Lord, shalt endure forever, and thy remembrance unto all generations,' and then goes on to anticipate the mercy and the glory that shall be revealed. It is 'the prayer of the afflicted' still, through the remainder of the chapter, but it is no longer 'complaint ;' it is what true prayer should always be, the open communion of the soul with the Friend in whom she has all confidence, the God of all comfort."—*Am. Messenger.*

GREAT CHAPTERS OF THE BIBLE.

"There are chapters, like books and verses, in the Bible that stand out like bright stars in a deep blue sky. Some of them we name: The Bottomless chapter is Ephesians 3 ; the Character chapter is Job 29, while Wisdom is the name of the 28th of the same book. The Rest chapter is Hebrews 4 ; Resurrection chapter is 1 Corinthians 15, and Victory is well described in Romans 8. For Duty, read

Ezekiel 33, and Work in James 2. Courage is in Joshua 1, which, with the Convert's chapter, Isaiah 12, forms a harmonious duet. Psalm 121 is for the Traveller, while 51 is for the Prodigal. Luke 15 is the Lost and Found chapter. The Minister's chapter is Ezekiel 34, while Charity is the beginning and end of 1 Corinthians 13. For Atonement read Hebrews 9, and then Leviticus 16. None will know how to Fast until they read Isaiah 58, nor can Promises be found that reach higher up or go further down than in John 14. The Blessing chapter is Deuteronomy 28 ; and where is heaven spoken of so beautifully as in Revelation 21 ? When one feels his feet slipping he should go to the Rock chapter, Deuteronomy 32. Hypocrites should read their chapter, Matthew 23. 'Come' is the key-word of Isaiah 54, and 'Gifts' of 1 Corinthians 12."—*Watchman.*

PAUL'S MISSIONARY JOURNEYS.
From the Oxford Teachers' Bible.

1. WITH BARNABAS AND JOHN MARK (Acts 13 : 14).

ANTIOCH (*in Syria*), the centre of Gentile evangelization. Barnabas and Saul, specially called by the Holy Ghost to mission work, and taking with them John Mark, go to

SELEUCIA (*port of Antioch*), whence they sail to the island of

CYPRUS (the native place of Barnabas), landing at the eastern extremity.

SALAMIS, a populous mercantile port. The apostles preached in the synagogues there ; then traversed the isle (100 miles) to

PAPHOS, its western extremity, the capital city. Here

Elymas was struck blind, and the Roman proconsul, Sergius Paulus, converted. They crossed to the southern shore of Asia Minor, landing at

PERGA, the ancient port of Pamphylia, whence goods from the interior were exported. Here John Mark returned home. The apostles went up into the mountains, on which journey they are supposed to have suffered the trials enumerated in 2 Cor. 11 : 26, 27, till they reached

ANTIOCH (*in Pisidia*), a central resting-place, just over "the pass," where the great road from Ephesus into Asia intersected the southern road. It was a Roman colony. They preached in the synagogue, one Sabbath to Jews (Paul's *first recorded sermon*), and the next to Greeks. Ejected by the rulers, they followed the great road to

ICONIUM, (*capital of Lycaonia*, a dreary plateau). They stayed "a long time," making many converts, till, a factious mob trying to stone them, they fled to

LYSTRA, a small rural town of simple heathens. Paul healing a cripple, they were treated as gods (Jupiter and Mercury), till Jews from Iconium followed, declaring them to be impostors, and had them stoned. They fled to

DERBE, a small town away from the high-road, where they rested awhile, returning by the same route through Lystra, Iconium, Antioch, to

PERGA, where they taught with no great success : so sailed back to

ANTIOCH, where they reported their work to a full assembly of the congregation, and abode there a long time (probably six or seven years).

2. WITH SILAS (Acts 15 : 36 ; 18 : 22).

ANTIOCH (*in Syria*), the starting point, whence they went by land through

SYRIA and CILICIA, confirming the churches, and delivering the decrees of the Council of Jerusalem. Thence across the mountains to

DERBE and LYSTRA, where Paul circumcised Timothy, and took him with him through

PHYRGIA and GALATIA, where Paul fell sick (Gal. 4 : 13), and being forbidden by the Spirit to go into the province of Asia, went into

MYSIA ; but again being forbidden to pursue his intended journey to Bithynia, he was divinely guided to

TROAS, where he met with Luke ; had a vision of a Macedonian inviting him to Greece ; embarked, touched at SAMOTHRACIA, and landed at

NEAPOLIS (*Kavala*), the seaport ; whence he went up by land, across the Pharsalian plain, to

PHILIPPI (*in Macedonia*), a Roman "colony," *i.e.*, having the same laws and rights as Rome itself. Lydia was converted ; the sorceress exorcised, her masters charged the apostles before the magistrates, who scourged and imprisoned them. They were miraculously released by night ; converted and baptized the jailer and his household. Paul left here Luke and Timothy, passed through AMPHIPOLIS and APPOLLONIA to

THESSALONICA (metropolis of Macedonia), where he stayed three Sabbaths. Assailed by a Jewish mob, Jason, his host, being bound over to keep the peace, Paul escaped to

BEREA, where he was well received till persecutors followed him ; then he was sent to

ATHENS, probably by sea, leaving Silas, for whom he waited; conversing with the philosophers, till forced to address them on Mars' hill, but with little success; so he retired to

CORINTH, a great mercantile centre, which for one and a half years he made the head-quarters of the evangelizing efforts on Achaia. Here he was joined by Silas and Timothy, and wrote the two epistles to the Thessalonians. He was driven from the synagogue, and brought before Gallio; was received by Aquila and Priscilla, whom he converted, and with whom he sailed from

CENCHREA, the eastern port of Corinth, to

EPHESUS; where he left Aquila and Priscilla, going on himself to

CÆSAREA; whence it is supposed he went by land to Jerusalem, to keep the Feast of Pentecost (18:21), and then returned to

ANTIOCH, where he remained "some time" (probably less than a year).

3. WITH TIMOTHY (Acts 18:23; 21:33).

ANTIOCH (*Syria* starting point); thence through

GALATIA and PHYRGIA, of which no incidents are recorded, to

EPHESUS, where Apollos had baptized converts only to repentance, and with an imperfect form, whom Paul rebaptized; staying there three years, refuting false philosophy and imposture of sorcerers, who publicly burnt their books, confessing their imposture. He retired from the synagogue; taught in the school of Tyrannus; wrote one epistle to Corinthians, and to Galatians; remained over the great annual Pan-Ionic festival of Diana, when Demetrius roused the craftsmen, and Paul was sent away by his friends to

MACEDONIA, where he visited and encouraged his converts in the various places visited in the former journey; passing on into

GREECE, where he stayed three months, probably visiting the churches established at Corinth and in Achaia. He intended to sail from Cenchrea to Syria, but was waylaid by the Jews, so he sent the main body of his companions on in advance to Troas; viz., Sopater (of Berea), Aristarchus and Secundus (of Thessalonica), Gaius (of Derbe), Timotheus (of Iconium), Tychicus and Trophimus (of the province of Asia).

PHILIPPI was reached by some secret and unrecorded route by Paul, who was there joined by Luke. They sailed thence together, and in five days reached

TROAS, where they remained seven days. Paul preached in an upper room; Eutychus fell from the window, but was healed by Paul, who "broke bread" in the congregation, and departed by land to meet his companions at Assos, who had gone round the coast on board the ship. At

Assos Paul embarked, and they touched at

MITYLENE; the next day anchoring off Chios, and the day following put in at

TROGYLLIUM, a promontory on the coast opposite the island of Samos. The next day they touched at

MILETUS, where they probably remained two days, as Paul sent a messenger by land to the presbyters of Ephesus to come to him, when he took a solemn farewell of them. Launching thence, they sailed with a fair wind past Coos and Rhodes to

PATARA, where they changed vessels, embarking on one

sailing direct to Syria; sighting Cyprus, but leaving it to the left (*i.e.*, sailing south of it), landed at

TYRE, where the vessel discharged her cargo, remaining seven days, and where the disciples warned Paul not to go to Jerusalem. The Christians accompanied him to the ship, knelt on the shore, and prayed; thence to

PTOLEMAIS (*Acre*), remaining one day; from whence they went to

CÆSAREA, staying many days with Philip, the deacon, where Agabus bound his hands and feet with Paul's girdle, signifying his approaching imprisonment. From thence, Paul's party, accompanied by Mnason (of Cyprus), went up by land to

JERUSALEM, where they were received by a full assembly of the apostles and elders, who advised Paul to purify himself from his contact with Gentiles by joining four men in the completion of a vow, defraying their expenses. While engaged in these religious exercises, he was seized by a tumultuous mob, from whom the Roman chief captain extricated him, put him in prison, and sent him to Cæsarea, to the governor Felix.

PAUL'S VOYAGE TO ROME, WITH ARISTARCHUS AND CERTAIN
PRISONERS UNDER CHARGE OF JULIUS, A CENTURION
OF THE AUGUSTAN COHORT.

CÆSAREA. Paul sailed thence on a vessel bound for Adramyttium, touching at

SIDON, where he visited his friends. Thence to leeward of

CYPRUS (*i.e.*, on the north side), under the shores of Cilicia and Pamyhylia, to

MYRA (a city of Lycia), where they were transhipped to an Alexandrian corn vessel bound for Italy, which coasted along the southern shore of Asia Minor (130 miles in "many days") to

CNIDUS, the extreme south-west promontory; where the wind and current from the archipelago caught and drove the ship southward to

CRETE, where they rounded Cape Salmone, and got under the shelter of its southern coast, and sailed along it to

FAIR HAVENS, near which, inland, was Lasea, and where Paul advised them to winter; but the harbor being incommodious they tried to reach

PHENICE, which had a harbor, sheltered toward the northwest and south-west; but they were caught by the wind Euroclydon from the north-west; but under shelter of

CLAUDA (an island to the south of Crete) they prepared for a tempest by striking sail, undergirding the ship, turning her head to the wind, and lying to, so as to avoid being driven on the "Syrtes" to the north of Libya. So they drifted slowly west by north at the rate of thirty-six miles in twenty-four hours, till the fourteenth day, *i.e.*, thirteen and a half days, till midnight—486 miles; and St. Paul's Bay is 480 miles from Claudia in an exact line west by north. *Second day*, "they lightened the ship"; *third day*, they "cast out the tackling"; *fourteenth night*, they drew near to land in the neighborhood of rocks; *fourteenth day*, they ran the ship aground in a creek of

MELITA (*Malta*), where they landed by swimming, or on portions of wreck. Here the viper fastened on Paul's hand; and he healed Publius (the chief man of the island) of fever and dysentery. *After three months*, they sailed in an Alexandrian corn ship by

SYRACUSE (*Sicily*), where they stayed three days ; and, making a circuit, they came to

RHEGIUM (*Italy*), and after one day they reached

PUTEOLI (*Pozzuoli*), in the Bay of Naples, where they rested *seven days;* thence they went by the Appian Way to

APPII FORUM, where brethren from Rome met him, with whom they came to

ROME, and Paul remained in custody of a soldier for two full years in his own hired house.

HARMONY OF THE GOSPELS.

From the Oxford Teacher's Bible, slightly changed.

B.C.	EVENTS.	LOCALITY.	MATT.	MARK.	LUKE.	JOHN.
	The DIVINITY OF CHRIST					1:1-5
	Preface to Luke's Gospel				1:1-4	
5	Annunciation of the birth of John the Baptist	Jerusalem (Temple)			1:5-25	
	Espousal of the Virgin Mary	Nazareth	1:18		1:27	
	The annunciation of the birth of Jesus	"			1:26-38	
	The visitation of Mary to Elisabeth	Hebron or Juttah			1:39-55	
	Her return to Nazareth	"			1:56	
	Joseph's vision	Nazareth	1:20-25			
	Birth and infancy of John the Baptist	Hebron			1:57-80	
4	Birth of Jesus	Bethlehem			2:1-7	
	Adoration by Shepherds	"			2:8-16	
	Circumcision	"			2:21	
	Presentation and purification	Jerusalem			2:22-29	
	Genealogies				3:23-38	
3	Adoration by the wise men	Bethlehem	1:17			
A.D.	Flight into Egypt	Egypt	2:1-12			
	Massacre of the Innocents	Bethlehem	2:13-15			
1	Return to Nazareth	"	2:16-18			
	Childhood of Jesus	"	2:19-23		2:39	
7	With the doctors in the temple	Jerusalem			2:40	
7-26	Youth of Jesus	Nazareth			2:46-50	
					2:51	

HARMONY OF THE GOSPELS—(Continued).

A.D.	Events.	Locality.	Matt.	Mark.	Luke.	John.
	Mission of John the Baptist.					
26	Ministry of John the Baptist	Bethabara	3:1-4	1:1-8	3:1-6	1:6-15
	Baptisms by "	"	3:5	1:5	3:7	
	Witness to Christ by John the Baptist	"	3:11,12	1:7, 8	3:15-18	
	Baptism of Jesus by "	"	3:13-17	1:9-11	3:21-22	
	Temptation of Jesus	Wilderness of Judea	4:1-11	1:12,13	4:1-13	
	John the Baptist's second testimony	Bethabara				1:19-35
	Call of first disciples (five)	"				1:35-51
	Christ's First Appearance.					
27	First Miracle, at Cana	Cana				2:1-11
	Visit to Capernaum	Capernaum				2:12
	First Passover; first cleansing of temple	Jerusalem				2:13-23
	Discourse with Nicodemus	"				3:1-21
	John the Baptist's last testimony	Ænon				3:25-36
	Christ's visit to Samaria	Sychar				4:1-42
	" return to Cana	Cana				4:43-46
	" healing of nobleman's son	"				4:46-54
	First Public Preaching.					
27	Imprisonment of John the Baptist	Machærus	4:12	1:14		
	Christ's preaching in Galilee:—					
	At Nazareth	Nazareth			4:15-30	
	At Capernaum	Capernaum	4:13	6:1	4:31	

HELPS TO BIBLE STUDY.   301

Event	Place	Matt.	Mark	Luke
Call of Andrew, Peter, James and John	Capernaum	4:18-22	1:16	
Miracles:—				
Casting out a devil	"		1:23	4:33
Healing Peter's mother-in-law	"		1:29	4:38
Healing many sick and diseased	"		1:32	4:40
FIRST GENERAL CIRCUIT.				
Preparatory Prayer.				
Circuit through Galilee		4:23-25	1:35	4:42
SERMON ON THE MOUNT	Hill above Gennesaret	5-7:27	1:39	4:44
Sermon in the boat; miraculous draught of fishes	Gennesaret			5:1
Healing of a leper		8:2-4	1:40	5:12
Retirement for Prayer.			1:45	5:16
Healing of palsied man	Capernaum	9:2	2:1	5:17
Call of Matthew (Levi), supper and discourse	"	9:9	2:13-18	5:27-33
Second Year's Ministry.				
Second PASSOVER	Jerusalem			5:1
Miracle at Bethesda, and discourse on it	"			5:2-47
The Sabbath: plucking corn	Galilee	12:1	2:23	6:1
The miracle of the withered hand	Capernaum	12:10	3:1	6:6
Opposition of Herodians	"	12:14	3:6	6:11
Retirement for Prayer.	"		3:13	6:12
Ordination of Twelve Apostles	"		3:14	6:13
SERMON IN THE PLAIN (of Gennesaret)	"			6:17-49
Healing centurion's servant	near "	8:5-13		7:1
" son of widow of Nain	Nain			7:11

HARMONY OF THE GOSPELS—(Continued).

A.D.	EVENTS.	LOCALITY.	MATT.	MARK.	LUKE.	JOHN.
	Message from John the Baptist; Christ's testimony	Capernaum	11:2-7		7:17-24	
	Warning to Chorazin, etc.	"	11:20-28			
	The sinful woman forgiven	Capernaum (?)			7:36-50	
	SECOND GENERAL CIRCUIT.					
	Through Galilee	Galilee			8:1-3	
	Healing a demoniac	Capernaum	12:22	3:19		
	Blasphemy against the Holy Ghost	"	12:24	3:22		
	The unclean spirit	"	12:43			
	The interruption of his relatives	"	12:46	3:31		
	Parables:—					
	The sower	Plain of Gennesaret.	13:1-9, 18-23	4:1-14-20	8:4, 11-15	
28	The tares	"	13:24			
	The mustard seed	"	13:31	4:30		
	The leaven	"	13:33			
	The candle	"		4:21	8:16	
	The treasure	"	1:44			
	The pearl	"	13:45			
	The net	"	13:47			
	Christ calms the storm	Sea of Gennesaret.	8:24	4:37	8:23	
	" suffers devils to enter the swine	Gadara	8:28	5:1	8:27	
	Parables:—					
	Bridegroom	Capernaum	9:15			

HELPS TO BIBLE STUDY. 303

New cloth and new wine	Capernaum	9:16,17		
Miracles:—				
Issue of blood	Gennesaret	9:18	5:22	8:41
Jairus' daughter	Capernaum	9:27		
Two blind men	"	9:32		
Dumb spirit	"			

THIRD GENERAL CIRCUIT.

Mission of the Twelve Apostles		10:1	6:6-11	9:1-3
Death of John the Baptist	Machaerus	14:1	6:14	9:7
Feeding five thousand	Bethsaida	14:13	6:30	9:12
Walking on the water	Lake	14:25	6:48	
Discourse on the plain and in the synagogue	Capernaum	14:34		6:1
				6:19
				6:22-70

Third Year's Ministry.

28 Discourse on pollution	Capernaum	15:1-20	7:1-23	
Syrophœnician woman	Phœnicia	15:21	7:24	
Miracles:—				
Healing of the deaf and dumb man	Decapolis		7:32	
Healing of many sick	"	15:29		
Feeding four thousand	Gennesaret	15:32	8:1	
Parable of leaven	"	16:5	8:14	
Healing blind man	Bethsaida		8:22	
Peter's confession of Christ's divinity		16:13	8:27	9:18
TRANSFIGURATION	Mt Tabor or Hermon	17:1	9:2	9:28
Healing demoniac child		17:14	9:14	9:37
Predictions of his passion		17:22	9:30	9:43
The silver in the fish's mouth	Galilee	17:27		
Lesson on docility	Capernaum	18:1	9:33	9:46
" on forgiveness		18:15	9:43	

HARMONY OF THE GOSPELS—(Continued).

A.D.	EVENTS.	LOCALITY.	MATT.	MARK.	LUKE.	JOHN.
	Lesson on self-denial					7:2-10
	Parable of the unmerciful servant		18:18			7:10-46
	The FEAST OF TABERNACLES	Jerusalem	18:23			7:30-46
	Discourses	"				8:3
	Officers sent to arrest him	"				8:12
	The adulteress	"				8:59
	Discourses	"				9:1
	Threatened with stoning	"				10:1
	Healing of blind man, and discourses	"				10:11
	Christ the DOOR	"				10:22
	" GOOD SHEPHERD	"				10:30
	FEAST OF DEDICATION	"				10:40
	Christ's oneness with the Father	"				11:1
	Christ's retreat across the Jordan	Perea				11:54
	raising of Lazarus	Bethany				
	" retreat to Ephraim	Ephraim				
	" repulse by the Samaritans	Samaria				
28	*Mission of the Seventy	Galilee			9:53	
	*Parable of the Good Samaritan	Jerusalem			10:1-17	
	*Visit to Martha and Mary	Bethany			10:30	
	*The Lord's Prayer	Mount of Olives			10:38	
	Parable of the importunity of a friend	Jerusalem	6:9-13		11:2-4	
	The dumb spirit	"			11:5	
	The rich fool	"			11:14†	
	God's providence to birds and flowers				12:16	
					12:22-30	

HELPS TO BIBLE STUDY.

The barren fig tree	Jerusalem			13:6
The woman with an infirmity	"			13:11
*The mustard seed	"			13:18
*Healing the man with dropsy	"			14:1-4
*Lesson on humility	"			14:7
Parables:—				
The great supper	"			14:12
The lost sheep and piece of silver	"			15:1
The prodigal son	"			15:11
The unjust steward	"			16:1
Dives and Lazarus	"			16:19
*The ten lepers	Samaria			17:11
Parables:—				
The importunate widow	Jerusalem			18:1
The Pharisee and Publican	"			18:9
The rich young man	"	19:16		18:18
The laborers in the vineyard	"	20:1		
The ten pounds				19:12
*Healing Blind Bartimæus	Jericho	20:29	10:46	
THE LAST PASSOVER.				
29 The supper in Simon's house	Bethany	26:6-13	14:3-9	12:1
20 Mary anoints Jesus	Bethany	26:7	14:3	12:3

* As an interval of nearly three months occurred between the Feasts of Tabernacles and Dedication, some place the events marked * in that interval, and vary their order, putting the "healing of ten lepers" immediately after the "repulse by the Samaritans."

† An English clergyman, Rev. J. J. Halcombe, has published a book maintaining that a section of the Gospel of Luke, extending from chapter 11:14 to chapter 13:21, has been misplaced from its proper position, and should be inserted before chapter 8:22. He claims, beside other strong arguments, that this rearrangement would bring the four Gospels into perfect harmony with one another. We advise the reader to try this rearranzement.

HARMONY OF THE GOSPELS—(Continued).

A.D.	EVENTS.	LOCALITY.	MATT.	MARK.	LUKE.	JOHN.
	Triumphal entry into the temple	Jerusalem	21:1-17	11:1-11	19:29-41	12:12-20
	Retirement to Bethany	Bethany	21:17	11:11		
	Cursing the fig tree	Mount of Olives	21:18	11:12		
	Cleansing the temple	Jerusalem	21:12	11:15		
	Retirement to Bethany	Bethany		11:19	10:45	
	The withered fig tree and its lesson	Mount of Olives		11:20		
	Discourses in the temple:—	Jerusalem				
	The father and two sons	"	21:28			
	The wicked husbandmen	"	21:33	12:1	20:9	
	The wedding garment	"	22:1	—		
	Tribute money	"	22:15	12:13	20:20	
	The Sadducees and resurrection	"	22:23	12:18	20:27	
	The great commandment	"	22:34	12:28		
	The widow's mite	"		12:41	21:1	
	The eight woes	"	23:13-33			
	Destruction of Jerusalem and of the world	"	24:1	13:1	21:5	
	Parables:—					
	The ten virgins	Mount of Olives	25:1			
	The talents	"	25:14			
	The sheep and goats	"	25:31			
	Warning of the betrayal	Bethany	26:1			
	The counsel of the Sanhedrim	Jerusalem	26:3	14:1	22:1	
	Judas' betrayal	"	26:14	14:10	22:3	
	Preparation of the Passover	"	26:17	14:12	22:7	
	Washing the disciples' feet					13:1-17

HELPS TO BIBLE STUDY.   307

Event	Location	Matt.	Mark	Luke	John
The breaking of bread	Jerusalem	26:26	14:22	22:19	
"One of you shall betray me"	"			22:21	13:18
"Is it I?"	"	26:22-25	14:19		
The giving of the sop, "That thou doest, do quickly"	"				13:26,27
Departure of Judas	"				13:30
Peter warned	"				13:36
The blessing the cup	"	26:34	14:30	22:34	14:16
The discourses after supper	"	26:28	14:24		17
Christ's prayer for his apostles	"				
The hymn	"	26:30	14:26		16:1
The agony	Gethsemane	26:37	14:33	22:39	
His prayer (repeated thrice)	"	26:39-44	14:36-39	22:42	
His sweat, and the angel's comfort	"		14:37-41	22:43,44	
The sleep of the apostles	"	26:40-45	14:43,44	22:47	18:2-4
Betrayal by Judas	"	26:47-50	14:47	22:50	18:10
Peter smites Malchus	"	26:51		22:51	
Christ heals the ear of Malchus	"				
" forsaken by his disciples	"	26:56	14:50		
" led to Annas	Jerusalem				18:12
" tried by Caiaphas	"	26:57	14:53	22:54	18:15
Peter follows Christ	"	26:58	14:54	22:55	18:15
The high priest's adjuration	"	26:63	14:61		
Christ condemned, buffeted, mocked	"	26:66,67	14:64,65	24:63-65	18:17-27
Peter's denial of Christ	"	26:69	14:66	22:55-59	18:28
Christ before Pilate	"	27:1	15:1	23:1	
Repentance of Judas	"	27:3			
Pilate comes out to the people	"				18:28
" speaks to Jesus privately	"				18:33
" orders him to be scourged	"	27:26	15:15		19:1
Jesus crowned with thorns	"	27:29	15:17		19:2

HARMONY OF THE GOSPELS—(Continued).

A.D.	EVENTS	LOCALITY.	MATT.	MARK.	LUKE.	JOHN.
	Jesus exhibited by Pilate: "Ecce Homo!"	Jerusalem				19:5
	" accused formally	"	27:11	15:2	23:2	
	" sent by Pilate to Herod, mocked, arrayed in purple	"			23:6-11	
	"Behold your King!"	"				19:14
	Pilate desires to release him	"	27:15	15:6	23:17	
	" receives a message from his wife	"	27:19			
	" washes his hands	"	27:24			
	" releases Barabbas	"	27:26			
	" delivers Jesus to be crucified	"		15:15	23:25	19:16
	Simon of Cyrene carries the cross	"	27:32	15:21	23:26	
	They give him vinegar and gall		27:34	15:23	23:36	
	Nail him to the cross	Golgotha	27:35		23:33	19:18
	The superscription	"	27:37	15:26	23:38	19:19
	THE SEVEN WORDS.					
	1. *Father, forgive them*	"			23:34	
	His garments parted, and vesture allotted	"	27:35	15:24	23:23-34	19:23
	Passers-by rail, the two thieves revile	"	27:39-44	15:29-32	23:35	
	The penitent thief	"			23:40	
	2. *To-day shalt thou be with me in Paradise.*	"			23:43	
	3. *Woman, behold thy son, etc.*	"				19:26, 27
	The darkness	"	27:45	15:33	23:44	
	4. *My God, my God, why hast thou forsaken me?*	"	27:46	15:34		

Event	Location	Matt	Mark	Luke	John
5. *I thirst*	Golgotha				19:28
The vinegar	"				19:29
6. *It is finished*	"				19:30
7. *Father, into thy hands I commend my spirit*	Jerusalem				
Rending of the veil	"	27:51	15:38		
Opening of graves, and resurrection of saints	"	27:52			
Testimony of centurion	Golgotha	27:54	15:39	23:47	
Watching of the women	"	27:55	15:40	23:49	
Piercing his side	"				19:34
Taking down from the cross, and burial by Joseph of Arimathea and Nicodemus	"	27:57-60	15:46	23:53	19:38
A guard placed at the door, which was sealed	Jerusalem	27:62-66			19:39-42
THE GREAT FORTY DAYS.					
Women carry spices to the tomb	"	28:1	16:2		
An angel had rolled away the stone	"	28:2			
Women announce the resurrection	"	28:8			
Peter and John run to the tomb	The garden			24:12	20:1,2
The women return to the tomb	"			24:1	20:3
The guards report it to the chief priests	Jerusalem	28:11-15			
APPEARANCES OF CHRIST AFTER HIS RESURRECTION.					
1. To Mary Magdalene	The garden				20:14
"*All hail! fear not. Touch me not.*"	"	28:9	16:9,10		20:17
2. To the women returning home	"	28:9			
"*Go, tell my brethren that they go into Galilee; there shall they see me.*"					

HARMONY OF THE GOSPELS—(Continued).

A.D.	EVENTS.	LOCALITY.	MATT.	MARK.	LUKE.	JOHN.
	3. To two disciples going to Emmaus...... (*Exposition of prophecies on the Passion.*)	Emmaus		16:12	24:13	
	4. To Peter......(1 Cor. 15:5)	Jerusalem			24:34	
	5. To ten apostles in the upper room...... "*Peace be unto you. As my Father hath sent me, even so send I you.*" "*Receive ye the Holy Ghost. Whosoever sins ye remit,*" etc.	"			24:36	20:19
	6. To the eleven apostles in the upper room "*Peace be unto you.*" To Thomas. "*Reach hither thy finger,*" etc. "*Blessed are they that have not seen, and yet have believed.*"	Jerusalem		16:14		20:26
	7. To seven apostles at the sea of Tiberias. To Peter. "*Feed my sheep. Feed my lambs.*"	Tiberias				21:1-24
	8. To eleven apostles on a mountain in Galilee (1 Cor. 15:5) "*All power is given unto me in heaven and in earth.*" "*Go ye and teach all nations, baptizing them,*" etc. "*Lo, I am with you alway, even to the end of the world. Amen.*"	Galilee.	18:16			
	9. To five hundred brethren at once (1 Cor. 15:6)......		28:16-20			
	10. To James....(1 Cor. 15:7; Acts 1:3-8).					
	11. Ascension... " 1:9-12)	Galilee, or Bethany		16:19		
	12. To Paul......(1 Cor. 15:8)	Bethany			24:50,51	
	Conclusion of John's Gospel	Damascus (?)				

BIBLE QUESTIONS AND ANSWERS.

BY HARRIS KNIGHT.

1. What four cities were destroyed with fire and brimstone, and what was the reason there were not more than four destroyed?
Ans. Sodom, Gomorrah, Admah and Zeboim, Gen. 19 : 24 ; Deut. 29 : 23 ; Zoar (which was confederate with them, Gen. 14 : 2, 3), was spared on the intercession of Lot.

2. Who was king of Israel before Saul?
Ans. Abimelech, Jud. 9 : 6, 22; also Moses, see Deut. 33 : 5.

3. What three queens were severely punished for their wickedness?
Ans. Jezebel, 2 Kings 9 : 33-37; Maachah, 2 Chron. 15 : 16; Athaliah, 2 Chron. 23 : 15.

4. Which of the Patriarchs died in the same year that the flood occurred, and may (for anything mentioned to the contrary) have been then drowned?
Ans. Methuselah, Gen. 5 : 25-28 and 7 : 11.

5. Show the connection by which our Saviour was descended from Absalom and a heathen king?
Ans. 2 Chron. 11 : 20 ; Matt. 1 : 7 ; 2 Sam. 3 : 3.

6. Show the connection by which our Saviour was descended from another heathen king?
Ans. 1 Kings 16 : 31 ; 2 Kings 8 : 18 ; Matt. 1 : 8.

7. Which Church had an epistle addressed to it by Paul that has not been preserved in the Testament; and one from another apostle which has been preserved there?
Ans. Col. 4 : 16; Rev. 3 : 14.

8. Where is the tenth commandment said to be similar to the second?
Ans. Col. 3 : 5; Eph. 5 : 5.

9. When did some of the Israelites ask counsel of the Lord through an idolatrous priest?
Ans. Judges, 17 : 4-10 and 18 : 5, 6.

10. What heathen king spoke to another king by commandment of the Lord?
Ans. 2 Chron. 35 : 21, 22.

11. From whom did our Saviour's birthplace derive its name?
Ans. From Ephrath, or Ephratah, the second wife of Caleb and her descendant, Bethlehem, 1 Chron. 2 : 19, 51 and 4 : 4.

12. Who gave a name to the place where Isaac first saw Rebekah?
Ans. Gen. 16 : 13, 14 and 24 : 62.

13. Where do we find the fullest description of the severity of Joseph's imprisonment?
Ans. Psa. 105 : 18.

14. Where do we find an account of the religion of Abraham's father?
Ans. Josh. 24 : 2.

15. What was the name of Barnabas' sister?
Ans. Mary, Acts, 12 : 12; Col. 4 : 10.

16. When did the "father of the faithful" show a lack of faith?
Ans. Gen. 12 : 11-13 and 17 : 17, 18.

17. Which of David's counsellors had a son who was a chief man in the army?
Ans. 2 Sam. 16 : 23 and 23 : 34.

18. What descendant of Moses held an office under David?
Ans. 1 Chron. 26 : 24.

19. Which of Absalom's daughters became a queen, and why was she afterwards deprived of her rank?
Ans. 2 Chron. 11 : 20 and 15 : 16.

20. Where was Jonah's native place, and what victory was prophesied by him?
Ans. 2 Kings 14 : 25-28.

21. What war did Solomon engage in?
Ans. 2 Chron. 8 : 3.

HELPS TO BIBLE STUDY. 313

22. What act of disobedience was Solomon guilty of before he began to reign?
Ans. Deut. 7 : 3 and 23 : 3-6; 1 Kings 11 : 42 and 14 : 21.

23. When Saul's body was taken by the Philistines and fastened to the wall, why did the men of Jabesh-gilead feel more interest in recovering the body for decent burial than the other Israelites?
Ans. 1 Sam. 11 : 1-11.

24. When David was persecuted by Saul, and wished to find a place of safety for his parents, what reason can we find in Scripture for his selection of the land of Moab?
Ans. It was the native land of Ruth (his great grandmother).

25. How often was David annointed, and by whom?
Ans. 1 Sam. 16 : 13; 2 Sam. 2 : 4; 1 Chron. 11 : 3.

26. What man was intrusted by three different persons with the whole management of their affairs?
Ans. Gen. 39 : 4, 22, and 41 : 38-44.

27. What person took a prominent part in the government of three successive dynasties?
Ans. Dan. 2 : 48 ; 6 : 1, 2 and 6 : 28.

28. Give five instances where a Hebrew was superior to all the heathen magicians who could be found.
Ans. Gen. 41 : 8-37; Ex. 8 : 17-19; Dan. 2 : 10-47; 4 : 18-26 and 5 : 8-29.

29. What two persons objected to living in a better house than the Ark of the Lord was in, and what prophet reproved those who acted otherwise?
Ans. 2 Sam. 7 : 2 and 11 : 11; Hag. 1 : 4.

30. Give five instances where a person received a promise that a certain disaster should not occur till after his death ; and another instance where a person died so near the time of a great disaster that we may suppose it probable that he received a similar promise.
Ans. (1) Gen. 15 : 13-15; 1 Kings 11 : 11, 12 and 21 : 29; 2 Kings 20 : 17-19 and 22 : 20. (2) Gen. 5 : 25-29 and 7 : 11.

31. Where is Moses called a king?

Ans. Deut. 33 : 5.

32. What action did Moses perform in disobedience to the Lord which he had previously done in obedience to him?

Ans. Ex. 17 : 6; Num. 20 : 8-12.

33. In what particulars had Balaam disobeyed the Lord when the angel was sent to oppose him?

Ans. When the Lord had given him a positive command not to go, he yet gave an uncertain answer to the second messengers, in hopes he might still get leave to go ; and when the Lord said, "If the men come to call thee rise up and go with them," he "rose up in the morning and saddled his ass and went" without (it appears) waiting for any call.

34. How long after the flood was the tower of Babel built?

Ans. About 100 years. The building ceased in the life of Peleg (who was born 101 years after), and as he was named from this circumstance, it probably happened soon after his birth ; Gen. 10 : 25 ; 1 Chron. 1 : 19.

35. In whose dominion was it built?

Ans. Nimrod's ; Gen. 10 : 8-10 and 11 : 2, 3.

36. Who is the next king of the place that we hear of?

Ans. Amraphel ; Gen. 14 : 1.

37. Where was the second Passover held?

Ans. Num. 9 : 1-5.

38. What complaint was then made of the rules for keeping it?

Ans. Num. 9 : 6, 7.

39. What permission was granted for a change of the rules in case of this difficulty happening?

Ans. Num. 9 : 10-12.

40. What punishment was threatened to any who deviated from the rules, beyond this permission?

Ans. Num. 9 : 13.

41. When did the Israelites take advantage of this permission and go so far beyond it as to make themselves liable to the threatened punishment?

Ans. 2 Chron. 30 : 1, 2.

HELPS TO BIBLE STUDY. 315

42. Why was the punishment not inflicted ?
Ans. 2 Chron. 30 : 18-20.

43. Why did they deviate from the set time for the feast on this occasion ?
Ans. 2 Chron. 29 : 17 and 30 : 3.

44. How long was it since a passover like it had been held before ?
Ans. 2 Chron. 30 : 26.

45. From how many of the tribes of Israel did persons attend this Passover ?
Ans. 2 Chron. 30 : 11, 18.

46. What descendant from one of these tribes was still living in Jerusalem when our Saviour was there ?
Ans. Luke 2 : 36.

47. What did the king do for the benefit of these people when they came, and who joined him in the action ?
Ans. 2 Chron. 30 : 24.

48. In what respect did they exceed the usual custom at the feast ?
Ans. 2 Chron. 30 : 23.

49. What did he do for the future instruction of his people ?
Ans. Prov. 25 : 1.

50. What miracle was wrought on behalf of him and his people ?
Ans. 2 Kings 19 : 35.

51. What miracle was wrought for his individual benefit ?
Ans. 2 Kings 20 : 1-6.

52. What important event happened in his house three years after this last miracle ?
Ans. 2 Kings 20 : 6 and 21 : 1.

53. What reason may be seen in this event for his prayer at the time of his sickness ?
Ans. If his prayer had not been granted he would have had no son to succeed him on the throne (unless he had other children that are not mentioned) in which he would have been unlike any

of his predecessors, and he would not have been an ancestor of the Messiah.

54. In what way did he err when the Lord "tried him?"
Ans. 2 Kings 20 : 12-18; 2 Chron. 32 : 31.

55. What king held a still greater passover than this one of Hezekiah's?
Ans. 2 Chron. 35 : 18.

56. In what other respect does his record surpass Hezekiah's?
Ans. His cleansing of the house must have been more thorough, as it revealed the book of the law that had been hidden so long. He destroyed several idolatrous objects which Hezekiah had spared, 2 Kings 23 : 11-20. The lamentation at his death was more deep and lasting.

57. What important article did he restore to its rightful place?
Ans. 2 Chron. 35 : 3.

58. What prophecy did he fulfil?
Ans. 1 Kings 13 : 2.

59. Which of the latter prophets refers to the mourning at his death?
Ans. Zech. 12 : 11.

60. What difference was to be made by the Israelites in fighting with those seven nations whose land was originally given them, and with other enemies?
Ans. Deut. 20 : 10-16.

61. In what cases did a small number of Israelites conquer a much larger number of their enemies, and when did they receive the promise that they should do so?
Ans. (1) Jud. 3 : 31; 7 : 7 to 8 : 10; 15 : 15 and 16 : 30; 1 Sam. 14 : 1-16; 2 Sam. 23 : 8, 18. (2) Lev. 26 : 8; Josh. 23 : 10.

62. When Reuben, Gad and Manasseh left their wives and children behind them to help their brethren in Canaan, what means did they take for their protection besides building cities for them?
Ans. Num. 26 : 7, 18, 34 ; Josh. 4 : 12, 13 and 22 : 8.

63. What nation granted the Israelites a passage through their country at one time and refused it at another?

Ans. Num. 20 : 20 ; Deut. 2 : 27-29.

64. Of the people surrounding the Israelites which five nations were most nearly related to them?

Ans. Gen. 16 : 15; 19 : 37, 38 ; 25 : 2 and 36 : 1-8.

65. What people did these kindred nations drive out in making a settlement?

Ans. Deut. 2 : 9-23.

66. Who is the earliest occupant of Mount Seir that is mentioned in Scripture, and from whom did the place receive its two names?

Ans. The first occupant mentioned is Hori, and it received its names from Seir the Horite, and Edom or Esau, Gen. 14 : 6 and 36 : 1-30; Deut 2 : 12.

67. What king dispossessed one of these kindred nations of part of their land, and was afterwards himself dispossessed by the Israelites?

Ans. Num. 21 : 26.

68. What two rulers disputed about the rightfulness of this conquest and occupation some hundred years afterwards?

Ans. Jud. 11 : 12-28.

69. What was the result of the dispute?

Ans. Jud. 11 : 32, 33.

70. When were the Israelites forbidden to disturb three of these kindred nations?

Ans Deut. 2 : 5, 9, 19.

71. When did all these three become subject to Israel?

Ans. 2 Sam. 8 : 2-14.

72. What prophecy was then fulfilled?

Ans. Gen. 27 : 29.

73. What tribute was paid by one of them?

Ans. 2 Kings 3 : 4.

74. When did one of them regain its independence?

Ans. 2 Chron. 21 : 10.

75. What prophecy was fulfilled in this proceeding?

Ans. Gen. 27 : 40.

76. When did either of them rule over the Israelites?

Ans. Jud. 3 : 14.

77. Which of them made a wicked return to a kind action of the king of Israel and suffered severely in consequence ?
Ans. 1 Chron. 19.

78. What individual in one of these nations is included in the line from Abraham to our Saviour?
Ans. Matt. 1 : 5.

79. When did all these nations unite in an attempt to dispossess the Israelites ?
Ans. 2 Chron. 20 : 10, 11.

80. What punishment did they receive for it ?
Ans. 2 Chron. 20 : 22-25.

81. When did a king of one of these nations endeavor to injure the Israelites by sorcery ?
Ans. Num. 52 : 5-6.

82. What more effectual plan did he afterwards adopt for injuring them ?
Ans. Num. 25 : 1-9 and 31 : 16.

83. What condemnation was pronounced against this people for these wrong actions ?
Ans. Deut. 23 : 3-6.

84. What condemnation was pronounced against these three nations for improper conduct to their " brethren " (the Israelites) at a later time ?
Ans. Jer. 49 : 1-6 ; Ezek. 25 : 1-14; Amos 1 : 11-15 and 2 : 1-3; Oba. 9-16; Joel 3 : 19; Zeph. 11 : 8-11.

85. What instances are mentioned where those who were in want of room (instead of driving away other persons, as was so generally done) peaceably removed to another place ?
Ans. Gen. 13 : 6-12 ; 26 : 19-22 and 36 : 6-7 ; 2 Kings 6 : 1, 2.

86. What expedients are mentioned for dealing with the opposite difficulty, a lack of inhabitants ?
Ans. Neh. 11 : 1, 2; Jer. 52 : 28-30; 2 Kings 17 : 6, 24.

87. How many instances are mentioned of different sections of the Israelites quarrelling with each other before they finally separated into two kingdoms ?

Ans. Josh. 22; Jud. 9; 12 : 1-6; 20; 1 Sam. 23 : 13 to 26 : 25; 2 Sam. 2 : 12-32; and 15 to 18 ; 20 : 1-22.

88. What reason had Ephraim for assuming the lead among the Israelites?

Ans. 1 Chron. 5 : 1; Deut. 21 : 17; Gen. 48 : 19, 22. *

89. On what occasion did they take offence because they thought themselves slighted?

Ans. Jud. 8 : 1 and 12 : 1; 2 Sam. 19 : 41-43; 2 Chron. 25 : 10, 13.

90. What prophet foretells a reconciliation and casting away of these hard fellings?

Ans. Isa. 11 : 13; Ezek. 37 : 15-28; Hos. 1 : 11.

91. Where are nine tribes mentioned by name as having contributed to the population of the kingdom of Judah?

Ans. 2 Chron. 11 : 12, 13; 15 : 9 and 30 : 11, 18.

92. What city was miraculously taken by the Israelites? What curses were pronounced at the time it was taken? Who incurred those curses? By what other name is the city called?

Ans. (1st) Josh. 6 : 20. (2nd) Josh 6 : 18, 26. (3rd) Josh. 7 ; 1 Kings 16 : 34. (4th) Deut. 34 : 3.

93. What honors and rewards did Caleb and Joshua receive for their faithfulness?

Ans. Num. 14 : 30, 27 : 18-23 and 34 : 17-19 ; Josh. 14 : 6-14 and 19 : 49, 50.

94. Where is the first mention of the possession of slaves or servants?

Ans. Gen. 12 : 5.

95. Where is the first mention of the purchase of servants?

Ans. Gen. 17 : 12.

96. Where is the first mention of a free person being reduced to slavery?

---

* The high estimation in which the tribe of Ephraim was held is shown by the manner in which it is spoken of; as at Psa. 78 : 9; Jer. 31 : 9, 18-20; Hos. 7 : 8-11 and 9 : 11-13; also by the frequent use of the name Ephraim, to denote the ten tribes that separated from Judah; as at Isa. 7 : 2-17; Jer. 7 : 15; Hos. 5 : 12-14; 6 : 4; 10 : 11 and 11 : 8-12; Zech. 9 : 10, 13. It was under a man of Ephraim that Israel conquered Canaan, and under another that they cast off Rehoboam's yoke and set up a separate kingdom.

Ans. Gen. 37 : 28.

97. What punishment was afterwards prescribed for such an action?

Ans. Ex. 21 : 16.

98. What mention is made of a servant inheriting his master's property?

Ans. Gen. 15 : 2-4; Prov. 30 : 23.

99. What servant do we hear of who himself possessed a large number of servants?

Ans. 2 Sam. 9 : 2-10.

100. What difference was commanded to be made between a male and female Hebrew servant?

Ans. Ex. 21 : 2-11.

101. What conditions were recognized as placing a person in a condition of servitude?

Ans. (1) Bondage of the mother, Ex. 21 : 4. (2) Sale by the father, Ex. 21 : 7. (3) Voluntary declaration before the judges, Ex. 21 : 5, 6. (4) Voluntary sale from poverty, Lev. 25 : 47. (5) Compulsory sale for debt, Neh. 5 : 5; 2 Kings 4 : 1; Lev. 25 : 39. (6) Restitution for theft, Ex. 22 : 3. (7) Being taken in war, Deut. 20 : 14.

102. On what conditions were they to be freed?

Ans. (1) Purchasing their freedom, Lev. 25 : 48, 49. (2) Ill-treatment by the master, Ex 21 : 26, 27. (3) Expiration of six years' service, Ex. 21 : 2. (4) The year of jubilee, Lev. 25 : 10.

103. What was the law with regard to a servant escaping from his master?

Ans. The master might fetch him back, but the neighbors must not do it for him, Deut. 23 : 15, 16.

104. When did a master lose his life through the operation of this law?

Ans. 1 Kings 2 : 36-46.

105. What were the rules by which an Israelite's property had to be divided at his death?

Ans. Deut. 21, 17; Num. 27 : 8-11.

106. Give an instance of the son of a wife receiving far more than the sons of the concubines.
Ans. Gen. 25 : 6.

107. Give an instance where they were treated as equals.
Ans. The handmaids Jacob married were considered to be concubines (Gen. 35 : 22), and their sons were treated as equals.

108. Give two instances of a concubine's son being chief of the family.
Ans. Jud. 8 : 30, 31; 9 : 1-6 and 11 : 1-11.

109. When a person stole an animal what difference did it make in his punishment if he killed or sold it?
Ans. Ex. 22 : 1-4.

110. How many persons necessarily became unclean in the preparation that was required for cleansing an unclean person?
Ans. Four, Num. 19 : 7, 8, 10, 21.

111. How many other things were there which made a person unclean?
Ans. Touching human excrement, an unclean animal, a corpse, a human bone, a grave, a person with a running issue or anything which he sits or lies on or wears. Carrying part of even a clean animal that dies itself. Taking the scape-goat to the wilderness or burning the accompanying sacrifices. Leprosy, childbirth, or a running issue. Being in a tent in which a man has died within seven days previously. Lev. 11 to 17; Num. 19; Deut. 23. The objections mentioned at Mark 7 : 4; John 18 : 28 and Acts 10 : 28 may have arisen from the fear of inadvertently "touching" some of the above.

112. Mention four occasions in which it was commanded to take an animal that had never been yoked.
Ans. Num. 19 : 2; Deut. 15 : 19 and 21 : 3; 1 Sam. 6 : 7.

113. When David unintentionally passed sentence on himself (at 2 Sam. 12 : 5, 6) which part of the sentence was founded upon the Mosiac law? Where is it to be found, and how was it executed on him?
Ans. Ex. 22 : 1. He lost four sons by untimely deaths—Bathsheba's child, Amnon, Absalom and Adonijah.

114. What vices or sins are there which, while they are not in direct terms condemned or punished by either the Mosiac law or by most modern laws, are still strictly prohibited in the New Testament, and are classed with murder and other heinous crimes in the condemnation they receive?
(1) Malice, anger, Matt. 5 : 22-24, 38-47 ; Rom. 1 : 29, 12 : 19; 1 Cor. 14 : 20; 2 Cor. 12 : 20; Gal. 5 : 20; Eph. 4 : 26-31 and 6 : 4 ; Col. 3 : 8; 1 Tim. 2 : 8; Titus 1 : 7 ; James 1 : 19, 20; 3 John 10. (2) Evil thoughts, "evil eyes," envy, etc., Matt. 15 : 19; Mark 7 : 21; Acts 13 : 45 and 17 : 5; Rom. 1 : 29 and 13 : 13; Gal. 5 : 21; 1 Tim. 6 : 4; James 4 : 5; 1 Peter 2 : 1. (3) Talebearing, Rom. 1 : 29; 2 Cor. 12 : 20. (4) Pride, Mark 7 : 22; Rom. 1 : 30; 1 Tim. 3 : 6 and 6 : 4; 2 Tim. 3 : 2; James 4 : 6. (5) Lasciviousness, Matt. 5 : 28; Mark 7 : 22; Gal. 5 : 19. (6) Filthy conversation, 2 Cor. 7 : 1; Eph. 5 : 4; Col. 3 : 8; James 1 : 21; 2 Peter 2 : 7. (7) Foolishness, jesting, Mark 7 : 22; Eph. 5 : 4.

115. What sins are prominently held up to condemnation in both the Old and New Testaments, and yet are not generally recognized by modern laws?
Ans. (1) Blasphemy, Lev. 24 : 10-23; 2 Sam. 12 : 14; 1 Kings 21 : 10; 2 Kings 19 : 6, 7; Psa. 74 : 10, 18; Isa. 52 : 5 and 65 : 7; Matt. 15 : 19; Mark 3 : 29 and 7 : 22; Col. 3 : 8; James 2 : 7. (2) Fornication, Lev. 19 : 29 and 21 : 9; Deut. 22 : 20, 21 and 23 : 17; Matt. 15 : 19; Mark 7 : 21; Acts 15 : 20; Rom. 1 : 29 ; 1 Cor. 5 : 1; 6 : 13-18 and 7 : 2; 2 Cor. 12 : 21; Gal. 5 : 19; Eph. 5 : 3; Col. 3 : 5; 1 Thess. 4 : 3; Rev. 9 : 21. (3) Disobedience to parents, Ex. 20 : 12 and 21 : 15-17; Lev. 19 : 3; Deut. 21 : 18-21 and 27 : 16; Prov. 1 : 8, 9 ; 20 : 20; 23 : 22 and 30 : 17; Mark 7 : 9-13; Rom. 1 : 30; Eph. 6 : 1 ; Col. 3 : 20; 2 Tim. 3 : 2. (4) Lying and Deceit, Lev. 6 : 2, 3 and 19 : 11; Psa. 5 : 6; 63 : 11; 78 : 36 and 101 : 7 ; Prov. 6 : 17, 19; 12 : 22 ; 14 : 5; 17 : 4; 19 : 5, 9, 22 ; 20 : 17 and 26 : 19; Isa. 63 : 8; Micah 2 : 11; Mark 7 : 22; Acts 5 : 3-5; Rom. 1 : 29; Eph. 4 : 25; Col. 3 : 9; 1 Tim. 1 : 10; 2 Tim. 3 : 13; 1 John 2 : 21; Rev. 21 : 8, 27 and 22 : 15. (5) Covetousness, Ex. 18 :

21 and 20 : 17 ; Psa 10 : 3 and 119 : 36 ; Prov. 28 : 16 ; Hab. 2 : 9 ; Mark 7 : 22 ; Luke 12 : 15-21 and 16 : 13, 14 ; Rom. 1 : 29 ; 1 Cor. 5 : 11 and 6 : 10 ; Eph. 5 : 3-5 ; Col. 3 : 5 ; 1 Tim. 3 : 3 and 6 : 10 ; 2 Tim. 3 : 2 ; Heb. 13 : 5 ; 2 Peter 11 : 14.

116. What crimes were allowed to be punished with death under the Mosaic law?

Ans. (1) Murder, Ex. 21 : 12. (2) Smiting or cursing a parent, Ex. 21 : 15, 17. (3) Stealing a man, Ex. 21 : 16. (4) Loss of life from an ox known to be dangerous, Ex. 21 : 29. (5) Stealing at night, Ex. 22 : 2, 3. (6) Witchcraft, Lev. 20 : 6 ; Ex. 22 : 18. (7) Idolatry, Lev. 20 : 2-5 ; Ex. 22 : 20. (8) Adultery and other unclean crimes, Lev. 18 : 29 and 20 : 10-18. (9) Accusing another falsely of a capital crime, Deut. 19 : 16-21. (10) Refusal to abide by the decision of the priest, Deut. 17 : 12. (11) Sabbath breaking, Ex. 31 : 15 ; Num. 15 : 32-36.

117. In what cases is death threatened for a breach of the law, but without a command for its judicial execution?

Ans. (1) High priests entering oracle without bells, Ex. 28 : 35. (2) High priests entering oracle without sacrifice and other preparation, Lev. 16 : 2-13. (3) Priest entering tabernacle without breeches, Ex. 28 : 43. (4) Priest sacrificing without washing, Ex. 30 : 20, 21. (5) Priest eating holy things while he is unclean, Lev. 22 : 3, 9. (6) Priest leaving the tabernacle during his consecration, Lev. 8 : 35. (7) Unclean persons entering the tabernacle, Lev. 15 : 31. (8) Laymen touching or looking at holy things, Num. 4 : 15-20. (9) Priest allowing them to do so, Num. 18 : 3. (10) Laymen doing any of the work of the tabernacle, Num. 18 : 22. (11) Laymen aspiring to the priesthood, Num. 17 : 10. (12) Imitating the holy oil or perfume, Ex. 30 : 33, 38. (13) Neglecting circumcision, Gen. 17 : 14. (14) Neglecting purification, Num. 19 : 13, 20. (15) Neglecting passover, Num. 9 : 13. (16) Neglecting day of atonement, Lev. 23 : 29. (17) Eating leavened bread during the feast of unleavened bread, Ex. 12 : 15. (18) Eating fat or blood, Lev. 7 : 25-27. (19) Eating peace offering when unclean, Lev. 7 : 20, 21. (20) Eating peace offering more than one day after it is offered, Lev,

19 : 8. (21) Slaughtering or sacrificing away from tabernacle, Lev. 17 : 3-9. (22) "Presumptuous" sins, Num. 15 : 30, 31.

118. Give seven instances of sinners suffering death by fire.

Ans. Gen. 19 : 24; Lev. 10 : 2; Num. 11 : 1 and 16 : 35; 2 Kings 1 : 10, 12 ; Dan. 3 : 22.

119. Give five instances of wild animals slaying persons for their sins.

Ans. Num. 21 : 6; 1 Kings 13 : 24 and 20 : 36; 2 Kings 2 : 24 and 17 : 25.

120. What instances are mentioned of the miraculous infliction of bodily punishment short of death ?

Ans. Gen. 19 : 11 and 20 : 18; Ex. 8 to 10; Num. 12 : 10; 1 Sam. 5 : 12; 2 Kings 5 : 27 ; 6 : 18 and 15 : 5; Job 2 : 7; Acts 13 : 11.

121. How many cases of suicide are mentioned ?

Ans. 1 Sam. 31 : 4, 5; 2 Sam. 17 : 23 ; Matt. 27 : 5.

122. How many cases are there of persons being killed by women ?

Ans. Jud. 4 : 21 and 9 : 53; 1 Kings 18 : 4 ; 2 Kings 11 : 1.

123.' How many cases of lives being saved by women ?

Ans. Ex. 1 : 17 and 2 : 1-10; Josh. 2 : 1-16 ; 1 Sam. 19 : 11-17 ; 2 Sam. 4 : 4 and 17 : 18-20 ; 2 Kings 11 : 2.

124. What two women took a principal part in delivering the Israelites from one of their oppressors ?

Ans. Jud. 4 : 4-21.

125. How many Christian martyrs are mentioned ?

Ans. Acts 7 : 59 and 12 : 2; Rev. 2 : 13.

126. What cases are mentioned in the Old Testament of ill-treating a good man for doing his duty ?

Ans. Gen. 4 : 8 and 39 : 20; 2 Chron. 16 : 10 ; 18 : 26 and 24 : 21; Jer. 20 : 2 ; 32 : 3 and 38 : 6.

127. In how many places does the Scripture say that the Lord considers the reception or rejection of his servants as done to himself ?

Ans. Ex. 16 : 2, 7, 9 ; Num. 14 : 2, 11, 27 and 16 : 3, 11, 21 ;

1 Sam. 8 : 7 ; Matt. 10 : 14, 15, 42 and 18 : 5, 6; Mark 9 : 41 ; Luke 9 : 48 and 10 : 16 ; John 13 : 20 ; 1 Thess. 4 : 8.

128. What chapter records the death of two women ?
Ans. Gen. 35.

129. What chapter records the death of a celebrated man and his sister ?
Ans. Num. 20.

130. What three persons died at the age of 137 ?
Ans. Gen. 25 : 17 ; Ex. 6 : 16, 20.

131. What man outlived all his descendants who are mentioned in Scripture for six generations ?
Ans. Gen. 11 : 16-32 and 25 : 7.

132. What man outlived all his descendants who are mentioned in Scripture for nine generations except one person ?
Ans. Gen. 11 : 10-32 and 25 : 7.

133. When Esau and Jacob (probably accompanied by their families) met together to attend the burial of their father (Gen. 35 : 29), what member of one of the families was absent ? where was he ? and how long did he stay there ?
Ans. Gen. 25 : 26 ; 35 : 28, 29 ; 41 : 1, 29, 30, 46 ; 45 : 6 and 47 : 9.

134. How many cases of seven days' mourning are mentioned ?
Ans. Gen. 50 : 10 ; 1 Chron. 10 : 11, 12 ; Job. 2 : 13 ; Ezek. 3 : 15.

135. How many cases of thirty days' mourning are mentioned ?
Ans. Num. 20 : 29 ; Deut. 34 : 8.

136. How many cases of embalming are mentioned ?
Ans. Gen. 50 : 2, 26 ; 2 Chron. 16 : 14 ; John 19 : 39, 40.

137. What persons had been buried in Caleb's land before he took possession of it ?
Ans. Gen. 23 : 19 ; 49 : 29-31 and 50 : 13 ; Josh. 14 : 13.

138. How old was Abraham when Isaac was married ?
Ans. 140, Gen. 21 : 5 and 25 : 20.

139. How old was Isaac when his mother died ?
Ans. 37, Gen. 17 : 17 and 23 : 1.

140. How old was Jacob when Joseph was born ?

Ans. 91, Gen. 41 : 46 ; 45 : 6 and 47 : 9.

141. How long had Abram been in Canaan when Ishmael was born ?

Ans. 11 years, Gen. 12 : 4 and 17 : 24-25.

142. How long did Jacob live at Hebron after the death of his father ?

Ans. 10 years, Gen. 25 : 26 ; 35 : 28 and 47 : 9.

143. How long was Joseph in Egypt before his promotion, and how long afterwards ?

Ans. (1) 13 years, Gen 37 : 2 and 41 : 46. (2) 80 years, Gen. 41 : 46 and 50 : 26.

144. How long were Moses and the Israelites at Mount Sinai ?

Ans. About 11 months, Ex. 19 : 1; Num. 10 : 11.

145. How long did the tabernacle stand in the first place that it was set up ?

Ans. 7 weeks, Ex. 40 : 2; Num 10 : 11.

146. How long had Saul been king when David was born ?

Ans. 10 years, 2 Sam. 5 : 4; Acts 13 : 21.

147. How long after the crucifixion was the Holy Spirit given ?

Ans. 50 days (the space between the Passover and the Feast of Weeks or Pentecost), Lev. 23 : 15, 16 ; Deut. 16 : 9 ; Luke 22 : 15; Acts 2 : 1.

148. Who was the father of the Philistines ? and which of Noah's sons was he a descendant from ?

Ans. Gen. 10 : 14 ; 1 Chron. 1 : 8-12.

149. What is the first sacrifice we read of in the place where the temple was built ? and the last one previous to the erection of the temple ?

Ans. Gen. 22 : 2, 13 ; 1 Chron. 21 : 18-30 and 22 : 1 ; 2 Chron. 3 : 1.

150. Where is the first passage showing a fulfilment of the prophecy (at Gen. 16 : 12) that Ishmael should dwell in the presence of all his brethren ?

Ans. Gen. 25 : 18.

151. What two instances are mentioned of persons who were

put into a pit by those who wished to injure them, and afterwards fared better than those who put them there?
Ans. Gen. 37 : 24 ; Jer. 38 : 6 and 40 : 4, 5.

152. What three apostles are mentioned in connection (and apart from the others) on three different occasions?
Ans. Mark 5 : 37 ; 9 : 2 and 14 : 33.

153. What two apostles are similarly mentioned on four occasions?
Ans. Matt. 4 : 21 and 20 : 20 ; Mark 3 : 17 ; Luke 9 : 54.

154. How many instances are given of a person commencing the work of his life at the age specified for a Levite to commence his? (namely 30 years, Num. 4 : 3.)
Ans. Gen. 41 : 46 ; 2 Sam. 5 : 4 ; Luke 3 : 23 and probably John ; Luke 1 : 36 and 3 : 1-23.

155. How many sons had Benjamin when he was spoken of as a "lad" and a "little one" whom his father was not willing to trust with his brothers?
Ans. Gen 46 : 21.

156. How many sons of Saul are mentioned?
Ans. 1 Sam. 31 : 2 ; 2 Sam. 2 : 8.

157. How many grandsons had Mephibosheth?
Ans. 2 Sam. 9 : 12 ; 1 Chron. 8 : 34, 35.

158. When did David and Jonathan last see each other, and what incorrect expectation did one of them entertain at the time?
Ans. 1 Sam. 23 : 16, 17.

159. What two instances are mentioned, where messengers were sent on errands of such importance, that they were forbidden to salute those they met on the way?
Ans. 2 Kings 4 : 29 ; Luke 10 : 4.

160. By whom is our Saviour called the Son of Man, except by himself?
Ans. Acts 7 : 56 ; Rev. 1 : 13 and 14 : 14.

161. What "words of the Lord Jesus" do we read of, that are not mentioned by either of the four evangelists?
Ans. Acts 20 : 35.

162. Which of the apostles was previously a disciple of John?
Ans. 1 : 35-40.

163. How many of the apostles had surnames?
Ans. (1) Simon, Peter, Cephas, Barjona, Matt. 16 : 17, 18; John 1 : 42. (2) Simon, Zelotes, Luke 6 : 15. (3) James and John, Boanerges, Mark 3 : 17   (4) Judas, or Lebbæus, Thaddæus, Matt. 10 : 3; Luke 6 : 16. (5) Judas Iscariot, Matt. 10 : 4. (6) Thomas Didymus, John 11 : 16.

164. How many had the same name?
Ans. (1) Simon Peter and Simon Zelotes. (2) James, son of Zebedee, and James, son of Alphæus. (3) Judas, son of Alphæus, and Judas Iscariot.

165. How many are mentioned in the different Gospels by different names?
Ans. Simon Zelotes, or Simon the Canaanite, Matt. 10 : 4; Luke 6 : 15; Judas, or Lebbæus Thaddæus, Matt. 10 : 3; Luke 6 : 16.

166. How many other cases are there of new names being given?
Ans. Gen. 17 : 5, 15 ; 32 : 28 and 41 : 45; 2 Kings 23 : 34 and 24 : 17; Est. 2 : 7; Dan. 1 : 7.

167. What person is mentioned in the Bible by five different names?
Ans. Matt. 16 : 17, 18; John 1 : 42; Acts 15 : 14.

168. What person is mentioned in the Bible by six different names?
Ans. Ex. 17 : 9; Num. 13 : 8, 16; Deut. 32 : 44; Neh. 8 : 17; Acts 7 : 45.

169. Where do we read of a father, son, grandson and great grandson whose names are the same as four of Jacob's sons?
Ans. Luke 3 : 29, 30.

170. What person was struck with leprosy for intermeddling in the priests' business, and by what three names is he mentioned in Scripture?
Ans. 2 Kings 15 : 1-5; 2 Chron. 26 : 19; Matt. 1, 8.

171. By what two names is the father-in-law of Uriah called?
Ans. 2 Sam. 11 : 3 ; 1 Chron. 3 : 5.

172. Who attempted to do an improper action, and was severely rebuked by a man of his own name?
Ans. Acts 8 : 9-24.

173. What man of the same name invited the Lord to his house?
Ans. Luke 7 : 36-50.

174. What man of the same name was nearly related to the Lord?
Ans. Matt. 13 : 55.

175. What man of the same name assisted the Lord when he was receiving ill-treatment?
Ans. Matt. 27 : 32.

176. What man of the same name was nearly related to a very ungrateful man?
Ans. John 6 : 71.

177. What man of the same name had one of his namesakes lodging in his house?
Ans. Acts 9 : 43.

178. Which of Paul's epistles was written to a place where the Lord appeared to him in a vision?
Ans. Acts 18 : 9.

179. Which of Paul's epistles was written to a man whom he had previously circumcised?
Ans. Acts 16 : 3.

180. Which of Paul's epistles was written to a place to which he was first sent by seeing a vision?
Ans. Acts 16 : 9-12.

181. Which of Paul's epistles was written to a place where his preaching caused them to burn a great number of wicked books?
Ans. Acts 19 : 19.

182. Which of Paul's epistles was written to a place where he worked at his trade for a year and a half?
Ans. Acts 18 : 1-11.

183. Which of Paul's epistles was written to a place where he preached and worked for three years?

Ans. Acts 19 : 8-10 and 20 : 31-34.

184. Which of Paul's epistles was written to a man who accompanied him and Barnabas to Jerusalem?

Ans. Gal. 2 : 1.

185. Which of Paul's epistles was written to a place from which he escaped by night on account of a mob attempting to molest him?

Ans. Acts 17 : 1-10.

186. Which of Paul's epistles was written to a place where he preached for two years, living in his own hired house?

Ans. Acts 28 : 30, 31.

187. Which of Paul's epistles was written to a place where they worshipped an image, which they said fell down from Jupiter?

Ans. Acts 19 : 35.

188. Which of Paul's epistles was written to a place where he was imprisoned and miraculously released?

Ans. Acts 16 : 23-26.

189. Which of Paul's epistles was written to a place where the people endeavored unsuccessfully to have him punished?

Ans. Acts 18 : 12-16.

190. Which of Paul's epistles was written to a people who were addressed by our Saviour in the Revelation?

Ans. Rev. 2 : 1.

191. (1) Where is the Lord's name repeated 38 times in 31 consecutive verses? (2) Where is the Lord's name repeated 10 times in 4 consecutive verses? (3) Where is the Lord's name repeated 4 times in 1 verse? (4) Where is the Lord's name repeated 5 times in one verse? (5) Where is the name of Christ repeated 10 times in 10 consecutive verses? (6) Where is "The Lord thy God" repeated 12 times in ten consecutive verses? (7) Where is "Thus saith the Lord God" repeated 6 times in 6 consecutive verses? (8) Where is "Thus saith the Lord of Hosts the God of Israel" repeated 3 times in 3 consecutive

verses? (9) Where is "Saith the Lord" repeated 10 times in 11 consecutive verses? (10) Where is "Saith the Lord of Hosts" repeated 5 times in 4 consecutive verses? (11) Where is "Saith the Lord of Hosts" repeated 3 times in 1 verse? (12) Where is "The children of Israel" repeated 5 times in 1 verse? (13) Where is "with" repeated 12 times in 1 verse? (14) Where are 6 different names for the Lord used in 1 verse? (15) Where are seven different names for the Lord used in 1 verse?

Ans. (1) 1 Cor. 1 : 1-31. (2) 1 Cor. 1 : 1-4. (3) 2 Cor. 2 : 17; 2 Thess. 2 : 4; 1 John 4 : 16; Rev. 3 : 12. (4) Ezek. 28 : 2; Matt. 22 : 32. (5) 1 Cor. 1 : 1-10. (6) Deut 30 : 1-10. (7) Ezek. 36 : 2-7. (8) Jer. 35 : 17-19. (9) Jer. 23 : 23-33. (10) Hag. 2 : 6-9. (11) Zech. 1 : 3. (12) Num. 8 : 19. (13) Isa. 24 : 2. (14) Isa. 54 : 5. (15) Isa. 44 : 6.

192. What four chapters are to a great extent repeated in other parts of the Bible?

Ans. 2 Kings 18 at Isa. 36; Psa. 14 at Psa. 53; 2 Kings 19 at Isa. 37; 2 Kings 20 at Isa. 38.

193. Where are two verses repeated almost *verbatim* in the next following verses?

Ans. 2 Chron. 36 : 22, 23; Ezra 1 : 1-3.

194. Where is an historical account given in four verses which in a later portion of the Bible occupies three chapters?

Ans. 2 Kings 25 : 23-26; Jer. 40 : 7 to 43 : 7.

195. Find three passages in the Old Testament which are each quoted four times in the New Testament.

Ans. Gen. 2 : 24; Matt. 19 : 5; Mark 10 : 7; 1 Cor. 6 : 16; Eph. 5 : 31. Isa. 40 : 3; Matt. 3 : 3; Mark 1 : 3; Luke 3 : 4; John 1 : 23. Mal. 3 : 1; Matt. 11 : 10; Mark 1 : 2; Luke 1 : 76 and 7 : 27.

196. Find two passages in the Old Testament which are each quoted five times in the New Testament?

Ans. Lev. 19 : 18; Matt. 22 : 39; Mark 12 : 31; Rom. 13 : 9; Gal. 5 : 14; James 2 : 8. Psa. 118 : 22; Matt. 21 : 42; Mark 12 : 10; Luke 20 : 17; Acts 4 : 11; 1 Pet. 2 : 6, 7.

332 HELPS TO BIBLE STUDY.

197. Find one passage in the Old Testament which is quoted six times in the New Testament.
Ans. Isa. 6 : 9, 10 ; Matt. 13 : 14 ; Mark 4 : 12 ; Luke 8 : 10 ; John 12 : 40 ; Acts 28 : 26 ; Rom. 11 : 8.

198. What writings are mentioned in the Bible beside the books therein contained ?
Ans. (1) Book of the wars of the Lord, Num. 21 : 14. (2) Book of Jasher, Josh. 10 : 13 ; 1 Sam. 1 : 18. (3) Book of the Acts of Solomon, 1 Kings 11 : 41. (4) Book of the Chronicles of the Kings of Israel (the Chronicles that we have are only of David's life), 1 Kings 14 : 19. (5) Book of Gad, the Seer, 1 Chron. 29 : 29. (6) Book of Nathan the prophet, 1 Chron 29 : 29 ; 2 Chron. 9 : 29. (7) Prophecy of Ahijah, 2 Chron. 9 : 29. (8) Vision of Iddo, 2 Chron. 9 : 29 and 12 : 15. (9) Book of Shemaiah, 2 Chron. 12 : 15. (10) Book of Jehu, 2 Chron. 20 : 34. (11) Acts of Uzziah, 2 Chron. 26 : 22. (12) Book of the kings of Israel, 2 Chron. 33 : 18. (13) Sayings of the Seers, 2 Chron. 33 : 19. (14) Chronicles of the kings of Media and Persia, Esther 10 : 2. (15) A former epistle to the Corinthians, 1 Cor. 5 : 9. (16) Epistle from the Corinthians to Paul, 1 Cor. 7 : 1. (17) Epistle to the Laodiceans, Col. 4 : 16. (18) Prophecy of Enoch, Jude 14.

199. What texts are there to show that the bottles mentioned in Scripture were sometimes made of leather or skins ?
Ans. Gen. 21 : 14 ; Josh. 9 : 4 ; Psa. 119 : 83 ; Matt. 9 : 17.

200. What three fables do we find in the Old Testament ?
Ans. Jud. 9 : 8-15 ; 2 Kings 14 : 9 ; Ezek. 17 : 3-10.

201. How many times did Pharaoh contradict himself in his dealings with Moses ?
Ans. Ex. 8 : 8, 15 ; 8 : 28, 32 ; 9 : 28, 35 and 10 : 16, 20.

202. How many cases are mentioned of supernatural beings appearing at our Saviour's sepulchre, and in what order of time did they appear ?
Ans. (1) The angel rolling back the stone at or before the approach of the women, Matt. 28 : 2-7. (2) A young man sitting in the sepulchre when they first entered, Mark 16 : 5. (3) Two

HELPS TO BIBLE STUDY. 333

men standing by them after they had entered the sepulchre and before they had gone to tell the disciples, Luke 24 : 4. (4) Two angels in the sepulchre after the disciples had come and returned, John 20 : 12.

203. How many other cases of angels apppearing on earth (exclusive of dreams and visions?)

Ans. Gen. 16 : 7; 19 : 1; 22 : 11 and 32 : 1; Ex. 3 : 2 and 14 : 19; Num. 22 : 31; Josh. 5 : 13; Jud. 2 : 1; 6 : 11 and 13 : 3, 11; 2 Sam. 24 : 16; 1 Kings 19 : 5; Dan. 3 : 25 and 6 : 22; Zech. 1 to 6; Matt. 4 : 11; Luke 1 : 11, 26; 2 : 9 and 22 : 43; Acts 5 : 19; 10 : 3; 12 : 7 and 27 : 23.

204. How many cases of the Lord appearing on earth before the coming of our Saviour?

Ans. Gen. 3 : 8; 12 : 7 17 : 1; 18 : 1; 26 : 2 and 48 : 3; Ex. 24 : 10 and 33 : 23; 1 Kings 3 : 5 and 9 : 2; Job 42 : 5; Amos 9 : 1; Dan. 3 : 25; Acts 7 : 2.

205. In how many instances is the Divine presence indicated by a cloud?

Ans. (1) In the pillar of cloud, Ex. 13 : 21, 22 and 33 : 9. (2) On Mount Sinai, Ex. 19 : 16-18 and 24 : 15-18. (3) In the tabernacle, Ex. 40 : 34. (4) Twice to Moses, Ex. 34 : 5; Num. 11 : 25. (5) In the temple, 1 Kings 8 : 10. (6) At the transfiguration, Matt. 17 : 5. (7) Second coming of Christ, Dan. 7 : 13; Matt. 24 : 30 and 26 : 64; Rev. 1 : 7.

206. On how many occasions did Jesus appear on earth after his resurrection?

Ans. (1) To Mary Magdalene, Mark 16 : 9; John 20 : 15. (2) To the women coming from the tomb, Matt. 28 : 9. (3) To the two disciples going to Emmaus, Mark 16 : 12, 13; Luke 24 : 13-31. (4) To Peter, Luke 24 : 34; 1 Cor. 15 : 5. (5) To the ten without Thomas, John 20 : 19. (6) To the eleven, John 20 : 26; 1 Cor. 15 : 5. (7) To seven disciples, John 21. (8) On a mountain in Galilee, Matt. 28 : 16; 1 Cor. 15 : 6. (9) To James, 1 Cor. 15 : 7. (10) To the eleven (at his visible ascension), Mark 16 : 19: Luke 24 : 50; Acts 1 : 9; 1 Cor. 15 : 7. (11) To Paul,

Acts 9 : 4-17 ; 22 : 7 ; 23 : 11 and 26 : 14 ; 1 Cor. 15 : 8. (12) To John at Patmos, Rev. 1 : 13-17.

207. What instances are given of an objection or fear at the presence of the Lord or his representatives ?

Ans. Gen. 32 : 30 ; Ex. 20 : 19 ; Jud. 6 : 22, 23 and 13 : 22 ; 2 Sam. 6 : 9 ; 1 Kings 17 : 18 ; Luke 5 : 8.

208. What passages of Scripture show a cause for such objection ?

Ans. Ex. 24 : 10, 11 and 33 : 20 ; Deut. 5 : 26 ; 2 Sam. 6 : 7 ; Lev. 10 : 2 ; Num. 16 : 35 ; 2 Kings 1 : 10.

209. Find six cases of a sacrifice being burnt by a miracle ?

Ans. Gen. 15 : 17 ; Lev. 9 : 24 ; Jud. 6 : 21 ; 1 Kings 18 : 38 ; 1 Chron. 21 : 26 ; 2 Chron. 7 : 1.

210. In how many cases were idols miraculously destroyed ?

Ans. Ex. 12 : 12 ; 1 Sam. 5 : 4.

211. In how many cases was a son miraculously bestowed ?

Ans. Gen. 17 : 16 ; 25 : 21 ; 29 : 31 and 30 : 22 ; Jud. 13 : 3 ; 1 Sam. 1 : 11-20 ; 2 Kings 4 : 16 ; 1 Chron. 22 : 9 ; Luke 1 : 13, 31.

212. How many persons received the promise that the Messiah should be descended from them ?

Ans. Eve, Gen. 3 : 15 ; Abraham, Gen. 12 : 3 ; Isaac, Gen. 26 : 4 ; Jacob, Gen. 28 : 4 ; Judah, Gen. 49 : 8-10 ; David, 2 Sam. 7 : 16 ; Psa. 16 : 10 ; Acts 2 : 30 and 13 : 23 ; Mary, Luke 1 : 31.

213. How many nations were descended from Abraham ?

Ans. Five ; Israel, Judah, Ishmael, Edom, Midian.

214. When was the ark finally taken out of the tabernacle, and where do we hear of the tabernacle being kept afterwards ?

Ans. (1) 1 Sam. 4 : 3. (2) Shiloh, 1 Sam. 4 : 3 ; Gibeon, 1 Chron. 21 : 29 ; 2 Chron. 1 : 3-13.

215. In what places do we hear of the ark after it left the tabernacle ?

Ans. 1 Sam. 4 : 1-3 ; 5 : 1, 8, 10 ; 6 : 12 ; 7 : 1, 2 ; 14 : 2, 18 and 21 : 1 ; 2 Sam. 6 : 3, 11, 12 ; 2 Chron. 5 : 2 and 35 : 3.

216. How many prophecies are recorded of the destruction of the temple ?

HELPS TO BIBLE STUDY. 335

Ans. 1 Kings 9 : 7 ; Jer. 26 : 6, 18, 20 and 38 : 18 ; Mic. 3 : 12 ; Matt. 24 : 2.

217. What eight prophets do we hear of before the Israelites left Egypt?

Ans. Enoch, Jude 14; Noah, Gen. 9 : 25-27 ; Abraham, Gen. 20 : 7 ; Isaac, Gen. 27 : 28, 29 ; Jacob, Gen. 49 ; Joseph, Gen. 40 : 12 ; Aaron, Ex. 7 : 1 ; Moses, Ex. 10 : 4.

218. How many things is the olive tree figuratively compared to?

Ans. (1) King of trees, Jud. 9 : 8. (2) A good man, Psa. 52 : 8. (3) Children, Psa. 128 : 3. (4) A prosperous nation, Jer. 11 : 16. (5) The Church of Christ, Rom. 11 : 17-24. (6) Prophets, Rev. 11 : 4.

219. By how many names is manna called?

Ans. Bread from heaven, Ex. 16 : 4; Angels' food, Psa. 78 : 25 ; Spiritual meat, 1 Cor. 10 : 3 ; Corn of heaven, Psa. 78 : 24.

220. How many methods of separating the grain from the straw are mentioned?

Ans. Deut. 23 : 25 and 25 : 4 ; Ruth 2 : 17 ; Isa. 28 : 27, 28 and 41 : 15 ; Amos 1 : 3.

221. What uses were made of house-tops?

Ans. (1) Drying flax, etc., Josh. 2 : 6. (2) Sleeping, recreation, consultation, etc., 1 Sam. 9 : 25-26 ; 2 Sam. 11 : 2. (3) Devotions, 2 Kings 23 : 12 ; Jer. 19 : 13 ; Zeph. 1 : 5 ; Acts 10 : 9. (4) Erection of booths at the feast of tabernacles, Neh. 8 : 16. (5) Safety from danger, Isa. 15 : 3 and 22 : 1. (6) Speaking to the multitude below, Matt. 10 : 27.

222. How many different materials are spoken of for making altars?

Ans. (1) Stone, Gen. 28 : 18 ; Ex. 20 : 25 ; 1 Kings 18 : 31, 32. (2) Earth, Ex. 20 : 24. (3) Shittim wood covered with brass, Ex. 27 : 1-2. (4) Shittim wood covered with gold, Ex. 30 : 1-3. (5) Cedar wood covered with gold, 1 Kings 6 : 20. (6) Gold, 1 Kings 7 : 48. (7) Brass, 2 Chron. 4 : 1.

223. Find five instances in which an "east wind" is mentioned as being used to perform the Lord's purposes?

Ans. Ex. 10 : 13 and 14 : 21 ; Psa. 48 : 7 ; Hos. 13 : 15 ; Jonah 4 : 8.

224. How many of the ten plagues of Egypt are subsequently mentioned, and what additional one is mentioned ?
Ans. Psa. 105 : 28-36.

225. How many remarkable interviews took place at a well or other water ?
Ans. Gen. 21 : 17-19 ; 24 : 11, 62 and 29 : 9, 10 ; Ex. 2 : 15 ; Isa. 7 : 3 ; John 4 : 6.

226. By how many names is Satan called in Scripture ?
Ans. Psa. 91 : 3 ; Isa. 27 : 1 ; Matt. 4 : 3 ; 12 : 24 and 18 : 34 ; John 8 : 44 and 12 : 31 ; 2 Cor. 4 : 4 and 6 : 15 ; Eph. 2 : 2 and 6 : 12 ; 1 Pet. 5 : 8 ; Rev. 9 : 11 ; 12 : 10 and 20 : 2, 10.

227. What precepts do we read of before the time of Moses ?
Ans. (1) Vegetable diet prescribed, Gen. 2 : 16. (2) Marriage relation, Gen. 2 : 24. (3) Skins of animals are here used although the animals might not be eaten, so it is probable sacrifices were then instituted, Gen. 3 : 21. (4) Sacrifices offered and accepted, but no command mentioned, Gen. 4 : 3-5 and 8 : 20. (5) Animal diet allowed, but blood forbidden, Gen. 9 : 3, 4. (6) Death to all who kill mankind, whether man or beast, Gen. 9 : 5, 6. (7) Melchizedek was "Priest of the most high God" and received "tithes" (no command, and no description of his office), Gen. 14 : 18. (8) First mention of a command to sacrifice, Gen. 15 : 9, 10. (9) Circumcision instituted, Gen. 17 : 9-14. (10) Tithes promised (but not commanded), Gen. 28 : 20-22. (11) Reason for not eating a certain sinew (no command), Gen. 32 : 32. (12) Command to build an altar, changing garments and hiding (instead of destroying) strange gods in preparation therefor, Gen. 35 : 1-4. (13) Terah served strange gods and Rachel stole her father's gods, Gen. 31: 19, 30 ; Josh. 24 : 2. (14) Drink offering and oil (no command), Gen. 35 : 14.

228. What cases are mentioned of our Saviour declaring plainly who he was ?
Ans. Matt. 16 : 15-17 ; Mark 14 : 62 ; John 4 : 26 ; 9 : 37 and 10 : 36.

229. What cases of his refusing to declare it when requested to do so, and otherwise seeking to keep it secret?

Ans. Matt. 11 : 3-6; 16 : 20; 17 : 9 and 21 : 23; Luke 4 : 41; John 8 : 25, 53-54; 10 : 24, 25 and 12 : 34, 35.

230. Which of the prophets foretold that he would act in this manner?

Ans. Isa. 42 : 1-4; Matt. 12 : 15-21.

231. Find 8 points in which Isaac typified or resembled Jesus.

Ans. (1) He was a prophet, Gen. 28-29. (2) His birth was predicted. (3) His birth was contrary to the usual course of nature. (4) He is called the father's *only son*, Gen. 22 : 2, for although he had other children who were receiving his love and his favors, yet this was above all the rest the father's *well beloved son*. (5) He was given up to die as a sacrifice by the free will of this loving father. (6) He was submissive to his father in this hard trial, Gen. 22 : 6-9; Luke 22 : 42. (7) He carried that which was intended to cause him to suffer. (8) He was bound in preparation for taking his life.

232. Find 7 points in which Joseph typified or resembled Jesus.

Ans. (1) He was a shepherd (this point applies also to Moses and David). (2) He was a prophet (this applies to all). (3) He left his home on a visit of love to his brethren, but his endeavor to serve them was repaid with ill-treatment. (4) He was sold. (5) He passes through a season of adversity, but afterwards attained to great power and honor (applies to Moses and David). (6) He freely forgave those who had ill-treated him and saved them from great suffering (applies also to Moses). (7) He prophesied that they would attain a more favored condition than they were in when he was personally with them (also Moses).

233. Find 16 points in which Moses typified or resembled Jesus.

Ans. Moses. (1-5) previously mentioned. (6) He was included with a number of other male children in a sentence of death pronounced by a king, but escaped by remarkable means. (7) He voluntarily gave up a happy condition to mingle with a degraded people. (8) He was rejected by them while endeavoring to serve them. (9) He delivered them from bondage and gave laws for their guidance, which are still highly prized. (10) He interceded with the Lord for a sinful people and "stood before him in the breach to turn away his wrath lest he should destroy them," Psa. 106 : 23. (11) The great object he was making preparation for was not accomplished till after his death. (12) His face shone on an occasion of going on to a mountain to commune with God, Ex. 34 : 29; Matt. 17 : 2. (13) The divine authority of his mission was attested by an audible voice from the Lord. (14) It was also attested by miracles that had been previously foretold, Ex. 4 : 1-9. (15) He fasted forty days. (16) He was faithful and fearless in speaking unwelcome truths to persons in high authority.

234. Find 5 points in which Aaron and his successors typified or resembled Jesus.

Ans. Aaron and his successors. (1) He was a prophet, Ex. 7 : 1. (2) He inquired of the Lord and communicated his will to the people, interceded for them, blessed them and offered their sacrifices to the Lord. (3) He entered *once* a year into the "most holy place" and made atonement for the people. (4) He put off his usual clothing of "glory and beauty" and put on plain linen garments to do this. (5) He went outside the camp to meet the leper, to prove to him his pollution and eventually to cleanse him and restore him to the position he had lost if he faithfully followed his orders. (6) His death freed from their bondage the sinners who had fled to the city of refuge.

235. Find 6 points in which David typified or resembled Jesus.

Ans. David. (1-3) above mentioned. (4) His life was threatened by a king because it had been prophesied that he would be himself king of the same nation. (5) He was king of Israel, John 1 : 49. (6) He was born in Bethlehem.

236. Find 3 points in which Zechariah typified or resembled Jesus.

Ans. (Zechariah) 2 Chron. 24 : 20-27. (1) He was killed for calling the people to righteousness and warning them of their danger. (2) One who should from gratitude have endeavored to serve him took a prominent part in causing his death. (3) This ungrateful man met with a violent death, and the people who had encouraged the murder received a severe punishment from a hostile nation. (A very marked point of difference occurs in the words spoken at their death, "The Lord look upon it and require it," and " Father forgive them, for they know not what they do."

237. How many cases are mentioned of the Hebrews offending in their connection with the Hittites?

Ans. Gen. 26 : 34, 35; Jud. 3 : 5, 6; 2 Sam. 12 : 9; 1 Kings 11 : 1, 2; Ezra 9 : 1, 2.

238. What man lived 350 years longer than any of his descendants?

Ans. Gen. 9 : 29.

239. What man lived 225 years longer than any of his descendants?

Ans. Gen. 11 : 16, 17.

240. What man lived 136 years longer than any of his descendants?

Ans. Gen. 11 : 10, 11.

241. What mention is made of any one being delivered from intemperance by embracing religion?

Ans. 1 Cor. 6 : 10, 11.

DESCRIPTION OF SCRIPTURE CHARACTERS, WITH KEY.

BY HARRIS KNIGHT.

I.

(1) A son of a wicked man had his life threatened by a wicked woman. (2) He was saved from death by a pious Jewish woman and was afterwards (3) killed by the sons of two heathen women. Before his death he (4) killed one of his first cousins, whose (5) father and (6) mother had both been instrumental in saving his own life.

KEY. (1) 2 Chron. 22 : 10. (2) 2 Chron. 22 : 11. (3) 2 Chron. 24 : 25, 26. (4) 2 Chron. 24 : 21. (5) 2 Chron. 23 : 1-15. (6) 2 Chron. 22 : 11.

II.

(1) Condemned to death by one royal person; (2) saved by another; (3) threatened or attacked by six others, but unharmed by any of them; (4) he conquered nine kings, caused the total overthrow of eight, and was a source of uneasiness to several others. (5) He is called a king, but we have no record in Scripture of his ever having been one, (6) though scores of kings had to submit to his commands. (7) One of his descendants held an office of honor under one of the most famous kings of Israel. The greatest disappointment he experienced in his life was caused by his (8) doing an action in rebellion against the Lord which he had (9) previously done in obedience to him.

KEY. (1) Ex. 1 : 22. (2) Ex. 2 : 5, 6. (3) Ex. 2 : 15; 10 : 28 and 17 : 8; Num. 20 : 20 and 21 : 1, 23, 33. (4) Ex. 14 : 27, 28 and 17 : 8-13; Num. 21 : 3, 24, 35; 22 : 2-4 and 31 : 8. (5) Deut. 33 : 5. (6) The above mentioned kings had to submit

HELPS TO BIBLE STUDY. 341

to him personally. Thirty-one kings (Josh. 12 : 9-24) had to submit to the commands he had given for their destruction, and the kings of Israel and Judah had to govern according to the rules he had left for their guidance. (7) 1 Chron. 26 : 24. (8) Num. 20 : 8-12 and 27 : 12-14. (9) Ex. 17 : 6.

III.

(1) Connected by marriage with some of the most celebrated persons in history, an (2) alien and yet more honored than most of the Israelites; (3) betrayed by two men whom he had ably served, and killed without knowing the cause of his death. Although we know very little of what he did, we still know that he (4) did worthy deeds of which no mention is made, and (5) his name appears in both the Old and New Testaments, among a list of famous persons. (6) He, his wife and his father-in-law are each called by more than one name in Scripture.

KEY. (1) Matt. 1 : 6. (2) 2 Sam. 23 : 39; 1 Chron. 11 : 41. (3) 2 Sam. 11 : 15-17. (4) If he had not done more worthy deeds than any mention is made of he would not have been counted among the 37 most valiant men in David's army. (5) 2 Sam. 23 : 39; 1 Chron. 11 : 41; Matt. 1 : 6. (6) 2 Sam. 11 : 3; 1 Chron. 3 : 5; Matt. 1 : 6.

IV.

Never a king himself, but (1) dreaded by some and talked of by many of them; remembered and honored for centuries, but no record kept of either his birth, death or parentage; (2) condemning numbers to death, but escaping all the attempts that were made against his own life; he wandered over the country with no settled home that we hear of, and was probably more famous in his day than any other inhabitant of the country. (3) A great leader of the Israelites lived in the same part of the country that he originally came from, and a great battle was fought there at a later period that caused the death of a king of Israel. (4) He received a command from the Lord to perform a certain service; but instead of doing it himself or sending his servant to do it, his servant sent a third party to do it long after the person who first received the command had been called away from the world.

KEY. (1) 1 Kings 18 : 10, 17 and 21 : 20; 2 Kings 1 : 6-17. (2) 1 Kings 18 : 40 and 19 : 1-4; 2 Kings 1 : 9-12. (3) Jud. 11 : 1-33; 1 Kings 17 : 1; 2 Sam. 17 : 26 and 18 : 15. (4) 1 Kings 19 : 16; 2 Kings 19 : 1-3.

V.

A man of great influence received a command from the Lord which, after (1) four proposals of compromise, he obeyed. (2) He did good to the people of the Lord at one time and (3) harm at another time, the same may be said of both his (4) ancestors and his (5) descendants; (6) one of his descendants by command of the Lord tendered a favor to a celebrated Jew, who neglected the opportunity presented to him, and lost his life in consequence.

KEY. (1) Ex. 8 : 25, 28 and 10 : 11, 24. (2) Ex. 12 : 31-35. (3) Ex. 5 : 6-18. (4) Gen. 12 : 16-20 and 47 : 5, 6; Ex. 1 : 8-14. (5) Jer. 37 : 5; Ezek. 29 : 6, 7; 2 Kings 23 : 29-35. (6) 2 Chron. 35 : 20-24.

VI.

A man whose usual conduct appears to have been quite exemplary (1) caused several of his step-sons to be killed without even an accusation of any crime being laid against them, and he (2) twice by deceitful conduct caused the death of innocent persons. (3) He received two promises from the Lord of a more important character than almost any other promise mentioned in Scripture. (4) He was threatened with death by a king, but (5) four other royal persons befriended him so effectually that neither he nor his people appear to have received any injury. He filled an important station among the Israelites to which he was appointed on (6) three different occasions, and while holding this station he (7) fulfilled two prophecies that had been made some hundred years before. (8) The fulfilment of another prophecy, made about one hundred years before, was brought about by his falsehood and dissimulation.

HELPS TO BIBLE STUDY. 343

KEY. (1) 2 Sam. 21 : 8, 9. (2) 1 Sam. 21 : 1-7 and 22 : 9-22; 2 Sam. 11 : 14-17. (3) 2 Sam. 7 : 11-16; 1 Kings 11 : 36; Acts 2 : 29, 30. (4) 1 Sam. 19 : 1. (5) 1 Sam. 19 : 12; 20 : 1-42; 22 : 3, 4 and 27 : 1-4. (6) 1 Sam. 16 : 13; 2 Sam. 2 : 4 and 5 : 3. (7) Gen. 15 : 18-21 and 27 : 29, 37, 40; 2 Sam. 5 : 6-25; 8 : 1-14 and 10 : 6-19. (8) 1 Sam. 2 : 30-33; 21 : 1-7 and 22 : 9-23.

VII.

(1) A man who was in much distress received a command from the Lord at a time that he was endeavoring to deceive some persons who had ill-used him, but he did not obey the command until its genuineness had been (2) four times confirmed to him. He did an important service to the Israelites, but eventually he (3) caused them a great deal of harm. (4) One of his ancestors saved the lives of a large number of persons by his discretion and ability.

KEY. (1) Jud. 6 : 11-14. (2) Jud. 6 : 21, 38, 40 and 7 : 9-15. (3) Jud. 8 : 27. (4) Jud. 6 : 15; Gen. 41.

VIII.

A man who had (1) recently escaped from a position of much danger (2) was tendered a favor from the Lord which he had not asked for, and he received it with great reluctance, although the want of it would have been a great disadvantage to him. (3) On receiving this favor he asked for another, which was immediately granted; but his confidence in the Lord's faithfulness was so weak that he (4) rejected this second favor after asking for it. (5) He was twice saved from a serious disaster through the good offices of a benevolent person, and (6) his descendants on several occasions behaved in a very improper manner to the descendants of this benevolent person.

KEY. (1) Gen. 19 : 9, 10. (2) Gen. 19 : 15, 16. (3) Gen. 19 : 17-22. (4) Gen. 19 : 30. (5) Gen. 14 : 12-16; 18 : 23-33 and 19 : 29. (6) Num. 22 : 1-9 and 25 : 1, 2; Deut. 23 : 3, 4; 2 Chron. 20 : 10, 11; Rev. 2 : 14.

IX.

(1) He is called by the same title that is elsewhere used to designate the Lord, and (2) he was engaged in the punishment of some persons whom the Lord afterwards punished still more severely. We have accounts of both success and disappointment in his career, but the latter rather preponderates, and the last we hear of him is the frustration of an enterprise in which at first he appeared likely to have complete success.

KEY. (1) Gen. 14 : 1 ; Jer. 10 : 7. (2) Gen. 14 : 10, 11 and 19 : 24, 25.

X.

(1) He committed a crime which is incidentally mentioned several times in the Bible, but is passed over in silence at the part of the history where it occurred. He received a command from the Lord, which he (2) four times sought to evade, he finally gave an unwilling compliance with the command so far as concerned his public actions, but (3) made an attempt by dishonorable stratagem to undo the effects of his obedience. He was severely punished for his disobedience and dissimulation, and is frequently held up to reprobation in subsequent parts of the Scripture.

KEY. (1) Num. 31 : 16; 2 Pet. 2 : 15; Jude 11; Rev. 2 : 14. (2) Num. 22 : 12-22 and 23 : 1, 14, 29. With the desire of obtaining the reward he gave an undecided answer to the second messengers (though the Lord had given a decided one to him), and three times afterwards he went through the forms for obtaining a curse upon the Israelites. (3) Num. 31 : 16 ; 2 Pet. 2 : 15; Jude 11; Rev. 2 : 14.

XI.

Exemplary in both words and actions, and yet subject to tyranny with no power of escape or redress. Died without hope, and yet was spoken of with approbation in both the Old and New Testaments.

KEY. Num. 22 : 23-33 ; 2 Pet. 2 : 16.

HELPS TO BIBLE STUDY. 345

XII.

Although we hear a great deal of him in Scripture, there is no sin recorded of him, yet he did not escape (1) severe trouble of mind from the sins of others. (2) He pronounced two curses on the same occasion against any one who should attempt to frustrate the full effect of a work in which he was engaged, (3) one of these threats was executed upon the offender shortly afterwards, and (4) the other some hundred years later. (5) In different parts of the Scripture he is called by six different names.

KEY. (1) Josh. 7 : 6-9. (2) Josh. 6 : 18-26. (3) Josh. 7 : 24-26. (4) 1 Kings 16 : 34. (5) Ex. 17 : 9; Num. 13 : 8, 16; Deut. 32 : 44; Neh. 8 : 17; Acts 7 : 45.

XIII.

Two first cousins were very friendly for a time, but eventually (1) the elder killed the younger, and afterwards (2) he was himself put to death by a brother of the person he had killed. At one time the younger wished to obtain a favor from the elder, and as a means of procuring it (3) he did him a great injury, which caused the desired favor to be immediately granted.

KEY. (1) 2 Sam. 18 : 14. (2) 1 Kings 2 : 29-34. (3) 2 Sam. 14 : 29-33.

XIV.

During the most brilliant portion of his career he (1) uttered a prophecy which is referred to both by our Saviour and the Apostle Paul, but he never prophesied of any of those matters which constitute the bulk of the Scripture prophecies—such as the kingdom of the Messiah, the rewards of the obedient or the punishment of the wicked. He was very unsuccessful in early life, and he committed a crime which brought great trouble on himself, and which is severely condemned in both the Old and New Testaments, yet he appears to have been after his repentance a successful man, and his descendants are at this day very numerous.

KEY. Gen. 2 : 24; Matt. 19 : 5; Eph. 5 : 31.
23

XV.

A place which, at the time we first hear of it, appears to have been quite wild and uninhabited, became afterwards very much frequented, and was favorably known even beyond the land of Palestine. Our Saviour was more than once at the place, and spoke an impressive prophecy concerning it.

KEY. Gen. 22 : 2-14; 2 Chron 3 : 1 and 9 : 1-6; Acts 8 : 27.

A CLASSIFIED CATALOGUE

OF THE PUBLICATIONS OF

REV. A. SIMS

FOR

Christian Life, Work and Study

"We would recommend the books and tracts published by Rev. A. Sims."—Report on Publications, Susquehanna Conference, 1886.

SALVATION BOOK AND TRACT REPOSITORY:

REV. A. SIMS, Publisher,

OTTERVILLE. ONT   CANADA.

Bible Salvation and Popular Religion Contrasted.

Third Edition. 14th thousand. Revised and enlarged. Cloth covers, 50c. Paper covers, 30c.

This book aims to show the great difference between true and false religion. It is heart-searching. God is owning it in the conversion of sinners both in and out of Zion, and in the sanctification of hungry souls.

CONTENTS:

PART I.—POPULAR RELIGION.
1. The State of the Church.
2. Spurious Conversions.
3. Spurious Holiness.
4. Compromising Preachers.
5. Backsliders.
6. Church Entertainments.
7. Pride in the Church.
8. Rented Pews.
9. Sabbath Desecration.
10. Secret Societies.
11. Fashionable Suicides.
12. Coveteousness.
13. Dancing and Skating Rinks.
14. The Church Walking with the World.

PART II.—BIBLE SALVATION.
1. The Nature and Necessity of Repentance.
2. Marks of a Justified State.
3. The Nature of Entire Holiness.
4. Living Without Sin.
5. Can We be Made Entirely Holy in this Life?
6. How to Obtain Holiness.
7. Entire Holiness not Received at Conversion.
8. Results of Entire Holiness.
9. Heart-Searching Questions.
10. Bible Teaching on Dress.
11. Prohibition a Bible Doctrine.
12. Choice of Companions and Marriage.

It is radical, plain, and thorough, and cannot fail to benefit its readers—just the book needed to waken up a formal professor of religion, and enable him to see his condition before God.—**Michigan Holiness Record.**

This is a book that I would like every professing Christian to read and digest. It would do a blessed work among the churches.—**Pacific Herald of Holiness.**

We most heartily commend the book to our people to read, to lend, to sell, to give away.—**Rev. J. Travis.**

The book has been very useful in the past, and is likely to be so in the future.—**Montreal Witness.**

This is a sound, practical, useful book, neatly printed. We cordially commend it to all our readers.—**Free Methodist.**

Has an awakening power about it that attends the reading of not many books ; it enlightens the sinner, and shows up the great sin of worldly conformity in the churches. One copy of this book will do more good in a community in the way of arousing people to action than almost any other book published. Thirty cents invested in it, for the purpose of loaning it to others, will carry the plain, unvarnished truth to the homes and hearts of many families in twelve months' time. How much money are you willing to invest in the Lord's cause in this way?—Gospel Flame.

The topics are handled in a masterly and telling manner, style terse and incisive, particularly attractive to those who are in love with the whole truth, and must be read to be fully appreciated. We heartily commend the work as worthy of careful reading, having been personally profited and fired to new zeal while reading its intensely interesting and practical themes.—The Wesleyan.

MORE TESTIMONIALS.

A brother minister writes us: "Your book has been instrumental in saving a soul on my circuit."

Another brother, referring to this book, says : "It confirmed my convictions that I had no heart religion, and only a head theory. I was honest, but deceived."

I believe your book came in answer to prayer. I have professed sanctification, not in hypocrisy, but in ignorance. I made a profession of religion several years before I received the witness. When I did receive the witness I called it sanctification. When your book came into my hand, which states so clearly the experience of justification and sanctification, I saw clearly I had not been entirely sanctified.—H. H. Harpham.

Helps to Bible Study, with Practical Notes on the Books of Scripture.

Or how to Read, Search, and Study the Word of God, so as to secure an ever-increasing interest in the same, a stronger faith, deeper spirituality, and greater usefulness.

We have prepared a new and much enlarged edition of this work. Much valuable matter has been added, including two new chapters, and the contents made much more comprehensive. Cloth covers, beautifully and strongly bound. Price $1.00.

CONTENTS OF NEW EDITION.

Chap. I. DIFFERENT METHODS OF BIBLE STUDY.—Giving the experience and advice of the most devoted and successful Bible students of the day.

Chap. 2. RULES OF INTERPRETATION.—These rules are plain, yet thorough and comprehensive. They show how to interpret parables, prophecy, and the Scriptures generally, so as to arrive at the truth.

Chap. 3. INTERPRETATION OF BIBLE TYPES AND SYMBOLS.—This chapter shows the meaning of the peculiar symbols of color, size, number, and substance, etc. This part is, of itself, well worth the price of the book.

Chap. 4. HELPS TO THE INTERPRETATION OF SCRIPTURE.—The earnest student of God's Word will find much practical and yet comprehensive help in this chapter.

Chap. 5. THE EXAMPLES OF SCRIPTURE.—Perhaps this will be found by a large class of Christian workers more instructive and spiritual than any other portion of this work, at least we have worked hard to make it so.

Chap. 6. ANALYSIS OF THE BOOKS OF THE BIBLE.—Full of practical thoughts and suggestions. The cream of many valuable works on Bible Study is contained in this chapter—the largest in the whole book.

Chap. 7. MISCELLANEOUS HELPS.—All Christian workers should have this book, and especially those who wish for some Bible helps written from the standpoint of holiness—nonconformity to the world. It is adapted to all who are thirsting for a deeper acquaintance with the Word of God.

☞ Agents wanted in every town, city and country, to sell our Publications. Liberal terms for cash. Write for particulars. Catalogue free.

Shining Lights.

This is a new work, giving sketches of eminent saints, of different ages, nations and churches, illustrating the wondrous power of divine grace. The deep experiences and triumphant deaths which are here briefly sketched will afford the reader a rich feast for his soul. Price, beautifully bound in cloth, 75c. Paper, 35c.

WHAT IS SAID ABOUT THE BOOK.

Rev. P. Doddridge says: "My own heart has been so much edified and animated by what I have read in the memoirs of persons who have been eminent for wisdom and piety, that I cannot but wish the treasure may be more increased."

The Rev. John Lancaster says: "The benefit to be derived from a serious perusal of such writings are peculiarly interesting. The unfold to us the secrets of other hearts, and thus qualify us to commune more profitably with our own; they increase our stock of facts with regard to the human mind, and powerfully promote our advancement in one of the most useful branches of knowledge—the knowledge of man: they enable us to trace the sublime march of an immortal and redeemed spirit through the intricacies and dangers of this land of peril to the kingdom of our heavenly Father; they evince the efficacy of grace; they publish the triumphs of faith, the pleasures of devotion, the truth of the promises, the faithfulness of God; they especially tend to elevate our hopes, give a higher and better tone to our feelings, and with a sweet constraining influence stimulate to high and laudable endeavors.

"By the pious records which eminent Christians have left behind they set forth the power of divine grace, in first subjecting their own hearts, and then in leading them forward from joys of conquest to the possession of an eternal crown. They beckon to posterity to follow them as they followed Christ. By publishing their errors they warn of danger; by telling of their conflicts they summon still conflicting champions to gird on the whole armor of God; by recording the trophies they have won they unfurl the banners of the Cross, and proclaim as with shouts of triumph certain victory to all who continue faithful unto death."

> "We gather up with pious care,
> What happy saints have left behind;
> Their writings in our memory bear,
> Their sayings on our faithful mind.
> Their works which traced them to the skies,
> As patterns to ourselves we take;
> And dearly love and highly prize
> The mantle for the wearer's sake."
> —*C. Wesley.*

"The record of the lives of the pious and devoted Christians set forth the power of divine grace so clearly and beautifully as to impress the heart of the reader more forcibly than ever that the Christian life is the noblest of lives. We commend this book to our readers, as we believe it will prove to be a blessing to many."—**The True Believer.**

"It is well arranged, and gives a fair estimate of the person's life and work. For busy people, and the young, the book will supply a demand and do good. It should have a wide circulation."—**The Highway.**

"The sketches are brief, but are pithy, and tell clearly of the grace from on high with which these disciples were blessed. The book is a good one, and the only objection to it is that there are not more than the twenty-one sketches referred to."—**Montreal Witness.**

"A most excellent book. Every family should have it. It is excellent for the older children in Sunday-schools."—**The Vanguard.**

"This work will be found interesting and encouraging to all who will read it. We take pleasure in recommending it to our readers, feeling assured that it will accomplish good in every home where it is read."—**Church Advocate and Highway of Holiness.**

"Another work from the pen of this indefatigable writer of religious tracts and literature. There is always a freshness about everything from friend Sims' pen; and this feature marks in a large measure the present volume. The book is eminently practical as a reference work of religious literature, and is assuredly inspiring and helpful to a higher life to all who will read it."—**Canada Citizen.**

"Certainly calculated to benefit all who read it. . . . . . Many worldly professors sneer at the idea of reading religious biographies; but, in all ages, those who have desired to be really holy have loved to read the lives of the truly pious of former ages. The LIFE OF HENRY MARTIN has, no doubt, given many missionaries to foreign lands; and no doubt the reading of this book will do much to make the rising generation really devoted to God's service. In compiling this little book Brother Sims has started a wave of influence which will, in its widening circle, touch many hearts."—**Free Methodist.**

"My soul melted under your sketches of William Clowes, C. G. Finney and Billy Bray."—**Rev. L. L. Pickett.**

The Secret Instructions of the Jesuits. Published by an ex-Romanist. Price 50c.

This work is a translation from the Latin of the "Secret Instructions of the Jesuit Society." Its revelations are startling, showing to what depths of deceit the Jesuit priest and all connected with this Order of "Spies" and "Traitors" will descend to accomplish their unholy aims. It is printed in the original Latin with the English translation parallel, thus doing away with the anticipated charge of forgery by those who set a premium on murder and treason.

A history of the Order of Jesuits and their expulsion from every Catholic country is given; also, the reason why the Public Schools must go.

Why Priests Should Wed. Price $1.25; Manilla covers, 50c.

This book, so praised and cursed, is at last unbound and free. Every Protestant should support it. Every father and mother should know its contents. It is brimful of startling facts. A book written to save women and girls. Every Catholic should read it. Hundreds have read it and have been converted. It is called "THE MOST FASCINATING BOOK OF THE AGE."

"Why Priests Should Wed" has been spoken of as a suppressed book; and yet more than 200,000 copies have been printed and sold.

Handbook of Freemasonry. By E. RONAYNE, Past Master of Keystone Lodge, No. 639, Chicago. New Revised Edition. Enlarged to 275 pages, well illustrated. Flexible cloth, 50c.

This work gives the correct or "standard" work and ritual of Masonry; the proper position of each officer in the lodge-room, order of opening and closing the lodge, dress of candidate, ceremony of initiation, the correct method of conferring the three degrees of "Ancient Craft Masonry"—Entered Apprentice, Fellow Craft and Master Mason; the proper manner of conducting the business of the lodge, and giving the signs, grips, passwords, etc., all of which are accurately illustrated with engravings. The oaths, obligations and lectures are quoted *verbatim*, and can be relied upon as correct. In short, it is a complete and accurate lodge manual. The high standing of Mr. Ronayne in the fraternity, his popularity and success as a teacher and lecturer in the lodge, together with the testimony of high Masonic authority, leaves no doubt of the accuracy of this work. The price is so low that it is within the reach of all.

The Holy Day; or, Remember the Sabbath. By Rev. L. L. Pickett. 61 pp. Price 10c.

A short treatise on the practical observance of the Day of the Lord. A pamphlet which deals in pointed logic and language with the evils of Sunday trains and travelling, both from the standpoint of the traveller and the corporation which forces its employees to desecrate the Sabbath. This little book hurls solid shot at Sunday street-cars and livery teams, Sunday mails and voluminous trashy newspapers. It treats the subject from the positive, negative, and, indeed, all sides of the question. Wherever read it must do good.

"It is the very book which all who have any respect for the Sabbath or fear of punishment for its desecration ought to read. Mr. Pickett writes in a plain, forcible, colloquial style; quotes the laws requiring and regulating Sabbath keeping from the Bible, and supports all his arguments, *pro* and *con*, from the same source, so that if any dislike his book, it is only an evidence that their carnal minds are at enmity with God's holy Book. It is not a tedious book to read, and the wonder is that Mr. Pickett could condense so much valuable information in so small a volume. He takes a wide range; goes over the whole ground; takes in the railroad syndicates, with all their Sabbath breaking, including that of their employees; Sabbath street-car and livery teams; Sunday mails and newspapers; Sunday travelling for worldly purposes or pleasure, etc. In a word, he exposes Sabbath breaking wherever he finds it—in individuals, families, in the churches, in communities, corporations, among commercial men, or elsewhere. And all who admit the authority of the Bible must feel the force of his arguments."—**J. G. Jones, in New Orleans Advocate.**

Seventh-Day Adventism Renounced, after an experience of 28 years, by a prominent minister and writer of that faith—Rev. D. M. Canright. 413 pages, 5½ × 8 inches, bound in fine cloth, with portrait of the author. Second edition, enlarged and improved. Price $1.50; in paper covers, without portrait, 60c.

Introduction by Rev. Dr. Nelson; doctrines and methods of the Adventists; my experience; a yoke of bondage; history and mistakes of Adventists; objections to the system; the two-horned beast; the three messages; mark of the beast; the sanctuary; Mrs. White's visions; why we keep Sunday; did the Pope change the Sabbath? the Sabbath in both Testaments; the Jewish Sabbath abolished; Sabbatarian failures; the law in all its phases; the two covenants; Christ's law; all their prominent texts from Genesis 2: 1-3 to Rev. 22: 14 (42 in all) examined; the question of immortality discussed, etc.

"Seventh-Day Adventism Renounced" is a book which every minister should have. The errors of Adventism are being felt more or less in every community; in many sadly. This book furnishes, ready prepared, just the facts and arguments with which to meet it. It will save a minister many days of research and labor in preparing to answer it. It gives him just the quotations from scores of authors which he needs.

We quote from the **Bible Banner** the reasons of Mr. Canright for leaving the Seventh-Day Adventists:—

"I gave up the observance of the seventh day because I became fully convinced that the evidence was not sufficient to justify its observance, and that the blessing of God did not go with the keeping of it Like thousands of others, when I embraced the seventh-day Sabbath I thought the argument was all on one side, so plain that one hour's reading ought to settle it, so clear that no man could reject the Sabbath and be honest. I felt willing to meet the world in its defence. The only marvel to me was that everybody did not see and embrace it.

"But after keeping it twenty-eight years; after having persuaded more than a thousand others to keep it; after having read my Bible through, verse by verse, more than twenty times; after having scrutinized, to the very best of my ability, every text, line and word in the whole Bible having the remotest bearing upon the Sabbath question; after having looked up all these, both in the original and in many translations; after having searched in lexicons, concordances, commentaries and dictionaries; after having read armfuls of books on both sides of the question; after having read every line in all the early church fathers upon this point; after having written several works in favor of the seventh day, which were satisfactory to my brethren; after having debated the question for more than a dozen times; after seeing the fruits of keeping it, and after weighing all the evidence in the fear of God and of the judgment, I am fully settled in my own mind and conscience that the evidence is against the keeping of the seventh day."

The book is having a large circulation.

Sowing the Gospel, and What Came of It.

An interesting and encouraging narrative, showing what can be done by one Christian to save souls from death. Price 5c. each.

PACKET G.—THE CHRISTIAN WORKERS' SERIES.

An assortment of small books and tracts for the encouragement and edification of all who would win souls. 50c. per packet.

How Every Christian May Win Souls. 10c.

This little book points out certain practical means within the reach of every child of God, in the use of which he may become gloriously successful in winning souls to Christ. Pointed and pithy. Contains some striking facts, incidents and illustrations. Is designed to stir up Christians everywhere to zeal in this holy calling. Every worker should secure a copy.

"It is calculated to do much good—rousing to zeal dull and inactive Christians."—Miss E. A. Sterling.

"That little book has done me so much good."—Mrs. E. A. Free.

"It is not only full of sound advice and encouragement, but a real inspiration to work for Jesus."—Mary L. Hopkins.

Self-Deception: Its Nature, Evils and Remedy.
15c.

"I find it a great blessing to my own heart, and I know it will be of great service to me in my ministerial labors, for I find that this little booklet goes to the very bottom of the subject, searching out the sandy foundation of every deceived professor. Every possible effort should be put forth for its universal distribution among the members of our various Churches. Every minister of the Gospel should read it, that he might the better be able to undeceive those who are deceived. May God bless it to the good of thousands—yea, millions of souls."—Rev. J. P. Kester.

One minister bought one hundred copies of this book for circulation among his congregation.

Thanksgiving Ann. 3c. each; 20c. per doz.

This is a most thrilling and powerful narrative on the subject of systematic giving. Don't fail to purchase a copy or a dozen.

The Revival Needed, and How to Promote It.
5c. each; 50c. per doz.

Full of facts and powerful truths. Should be circulated by the hundred previous to holding special meetings.

Living Without Sin. 8 pages; 15c. per doz.; $1 per 100.
This is a new tract, which takes up all those portions of Scripture—including the seventh chapter of Romans—which are usually held as teaching the impossibility of living without sin. It gives the opinions of learned Calvinistic and Arminian divines, including such eminent men as Pres. Edwards, Prof. Stuart, C. G. Finney, John Wesley, and Dr. Adam Clarke. The subject is thoroughly discussed, and yet brought into a brief compass.

The Open Door; or, An Account of the Origin, Character and Progress of THE SOUL-WINNERS' BAND; the efforts of which are intended to reach every part of the habitable globe, and to give abundant scope for usefulness to every Christian, irrespective of his denomination, circumstances, or place of abode. 3c. each; 20c. per doz.

☞ Any of the books in above series can be had separately, if desired, but we would recommend every one to purchase the entire assortment.

Salvation Tract Envelopes. 25 for 12c.; 40c. per 100
Sold only in assorted packets.
Printed with striking and useful mottoes, verses of Scripture, short pointed truths, and attractive illustrations. They are well adapted to do good. There are twenty-five varieties, which will enable the purchaser to adapt his envelope to almost every class of people. We recommend you to use these envelopes because:

1. They scatter the truth where it otherwise would not reach, and in a novel manner, which arrests the attention of all classes of people. They are read and re-read while passing through the mails. We estimate that a thousand of them preach to at least four thousand readers. 2. An envelope with a tract printed on it costs no more for postage than if it was plain. Thus postmen are made to turn tract distributors free of postage. 3. These envelopes have done, and are still doing, an excellent work. You have to buy envelopes, why not purchase these?

To use with our tract envelopes, we have published a new series of **Motto Note Paper.**

Sold only in assorted packets of not less than 50 single sheets, post-paid, 20c.; or 50 single sheets and 50 tract envelopes, post-paid, 40c. The mottoes mainly consist of striking verses of Scripture containing weighty truths. These are printed in tasty type on single loose sheets of ruled note paper of good quality. These mottoes will, doubtless, be exhibited to friends, and thus many persons will read these Salvation truths.

TRACTS IN PACKETS.

"These tracts go to the quick. Help to scatter them far and wide. Would like to get a million pages of them before the people the ensuing year."—Gospel Flame.

"Those who like to spread the truth and believe in attacking personal sin and the vices too common among professing Christians will very likely be glad to use his tracts."—Banner of Love.

"I think your tracts are more modern, and meet a present need, better than any I have ever seen."—Rev. H. D. F. Gaffin.

Packet A.—Awakening and Alarming Series. 25c. per Packet.

The Loss of the Soul.
A Vision of Hell.
Christianity and Infidelity Contrasted.
The Judgment Day.
The Nature and Necessity of Repentance.

Packet B.—Prohibition and Tobacco Series. 25c. per Packet.

Prohibition a Bible Doctrine.
The Saloon-Keeper and the Devil.
Does the Tobacco Habit Glorify God?
The Tobacco Habit: Its Sin and Cure.
Tobacco-using Parents injure their Offspring.
The Song of the Decanter.

Packet C.—Reform Series. 25c. per Packet.

The Evils of Corsets.
Secret Societies.
Bible Teaching on Dress.
Sabbath Desecration.
War *versus* Arbitration.
The Evils of Dancing and Skating Rinks.

Packet D.—False Religion Series. 25c. per Packet.

The State of the Church.
Spurious Conversions.
Compromising Preachers.
Church Entertainments.
Marks of a Backslidden State.
The Church Walking with the World.

Packet E.—True Religion Series. 25c. per Packet.

The Revival Needed.
Marks of a Justified State.
Living Without Sin.
A Plain Guide to Entire Holiness.
The Way to Heaven.

Packet F.—Leaflet Series. 15c. per Packet.

An assortment of pointed, short, red-hot truths on vital themes, suitable for enclosure in letters and for general distribution. Sold only in assorted packets.

Packet G.—Christian Workers' Series. 50c. Per Packet.

An assortment of small books and tracts for the encouragement and edification of all who would win souls.

☞ A sample packet, containing specimens of all our tracts and leaflets advertised in this catalogue, will be sent for 50 cents.

☞ Always carry a packet of assorted tracts with you, and when you see an opportunity to do good, look over your list, and select the tract most suitable for the person you meet.

☞ For practical advice as to the best methods of tract distribution, read Chap. 3 of *How Every Christian May Win Souls*. 10c.

NEW TRACTS.

ZIGZAGGERY · · · · · · 2 pages, 25c. per 100.
QUENCH NOT THE SPIRIT · · · 2 " 25c. "
HOT SHOT FOR PROHIBITION CAMPAIGN, 4 " 50c. "
COVETOUSNESS · · · · · 4 " 50c. "
BACK NUMBERS OF GOSPEL TRUTH · 4 " 50c. "

RECOMMENDATIONS.

"Your tracts suit me better than any I know of. You seem to be especially called to that work. Send them out. Flood the whole world with these pointed missiles of God's truth."—**Rev. W. S. Sansom.**

"I gave your tract on THE EVILS OF CORSETS to a sister, and the results are glorious. She at once saw light had come and she must walk in it. From that one tract six of our sisters have been led to lay them (corsets) off."—**J. S. Guy** (March, 1887).

"I wish we had a thousand of your tracts on THE EV LS OF COR-SETS. Several women have laid off their corsets through the influence of these tracts."—**Rev. A. H. Norrington** (Feb. 15, 1889).

"GOSPEL TRUTH,"

is a monthly 4-page tract paper, published and paid for the same as any other paper. Size of page the same as this one. *Payment invariably in advance.* The rates are as follows:—

15 copies per month for one year,	$0 75
20 " " "	1 00
30 " " "	1 50
60 " " "	2 75
100 " " "	5 00

No subscription will be received for less than 15 copies.

The advantages of this tract paper over the plan of buying tracts are these:

1. It is much cheaper: 15 copies per month for one year contain 720 pages, and cost only 75c. and no postage. The same number of pages in ordinary tracts would cost 82c. and postage besides. And the larger the number of copies subscribed for, the greater will be the saving effected.

2. It affords a much greater variety of subjects for the same amount of money than in tracts. Each issue contains a different subject or subjects, so that subscribers will be able to reach all classes of people.

The topics are on True and Spurious Religion, Repentance, Justification, Conversion, Holiness, Backsliding, Worldliness, Prohibition, Tobacco and Salvation—in short, such truths as are adapted to both saint and sinner. Specimen copies 10c.

☞ If you do not want the papers yourself, then pay the subscription for some needy worker, and have them sent to his address

Please make remittance by registered letter or money order, tc

REV. A. SIMS,
OTTERVILLE, ONT.

www.ingramcontent.com/pod-product-compliance
Lightning Source LLC
Chambersburg PA
CBHW020232240426

43672CB00006B/495